T0301489

Fiscal Reforms in the Least Developed Countries

About UNCTAD

The United Nations Conference on Trade and Development (UNCTAD) is the principal organ of the General Assembly in the field of trade and development. It was established as a permanent intergovernmental body in 1964 in Geneva as a result of the first session of the Conference, with a view to accelerating economic growth and development, particularly that of the developing countries. UNCTAD discharges its mandate through: policy analysis; intergovernmental deliberations, consensus-building and negotiations; monitoring, implementation and follow-up; and technical cooperation. These functions are interrelated and call for constant cross-fertilization between the relevant activities. UNCTAD members aim to achieve steady sustained growth in all countries and to accelerate the development of developing countries, so that all people can enjoy economic and social well-being.

UNCTAD is composed of 188 member States. Many intergovernmental and non-governmental organizations participate in its work as observers. The UNCTAD secretariat forms part of the United Nations Secretariat. With a staff of about 480 and located at Geneva, the Secretariat is headed by a Secretary-General, currently Rubens Ricupero (Brazil). UNCTAD's annual operational budget is approximately $55 million drawn from the United Nations regular budget. Technical cooperation activities, which have developed as a result of UNCTAD's sectoral expertise financed from extrabudgetary resources, amounted to approximately $22 million in 1995.

The most recent Conference, UNCTAD IX, was held in Midrand (Johannesburg), South Africa from 27 April to 11 May 1996. The theme of the Conference was 'Promoting growth and development in a liberalizing and globalizing world economy'.

The Conference, which brought together over 2000 senior officials from 134 countries (including five Heads of State and Government and sixty-two Ministers, and Heads of the main international institutions), adopted the Midrand Declaration, submitted by the President, Alec Erwin, Minister of Trade and Industry of South Africa.

UNCTAD IX agreed on a major reform of the organization in order to focus its work 'on a new priority trade and development issues of central importance on which it can make a substantial impact' on people's lives in developing countries, in particular the least developed among them (LDCs).

The Declaration gives a strong political boost to international cooperation for development and to UNCTAD as the focal point within the United Nations for the integrated treatment of development and inter-related issues in the areas of trade, finance, technology, investment and sustainable development. The Declaration calls for greater partnership between developed c ountries, developing countries and the least developed countries. It also emphasizes the benefit of involving the civil society in the partnership for development.

Fiscal Reforms in the Least Developed Countries

Edited by

Chandra Kant Patel

United Nations Conference on Trade and Development, Switzerland

Edward Elgar

Cheltenham, UK • Brookfield, US

© United Nations 1997

All rights reserved. No part of this publication may be reproduced, stored in a retrieval system or transmitted in any form or by any means, electronic, mechanical or photocopying, recording, or otherwise without the prior permission of the publisher.

Published by
Edward Elgar Publishing Limited
8 Lansdown Place
Cheltenham
Glos GL50 2HU
UK

Edward Elgar Publishing Company
Old Post Road
Brookfield
Vermont 05036
US

A catalogue record for this book
is available from the British Library

Library of Congress Cataloguing in Publication Data
Fiscal reforms in the least developed countries / edited by Chandra K.
   Patel.
      Includes bibliographical references.
      1. Fiscal policy—Developing countries. 2. Economic stabili-
   zation—Developing countries. 3. Structural adjustment (Economic
   policy)—Developing countries. I. Patel, Chandra K., 1941–   .
   HJ1620.F574   1996
   336.09172'6—dc20   96–18298
                                                                CIP

ISBN 1 85898 513 7

Printed and bound in Great Britain by
Biddles Limited, Guildford and King's Lynn

Contents

Tables

Explanatory notes to the tables

Two dots (..) indicate that the data are not available, or are not separately reported.

One dot (.) indicates that the data are not applicable.

A dash (–) indicates that the amount is nil or negligible.

Details and percentages do not necessarily add up to totals, because of rounding.

The term 'dollar' ($) refers to United States dollars, unless otherwise stated.

Contributors

Priya Basu, Asian Development Bank, Philippines

Martin Brownbridge, University of Sussex, UK, and United Nations Conference on Trade and Development, Switzerland

David P. Coady, Department of Economics, University College London, UK

Norman Gemmell, CREDIT, Department of Economics, University of Nottingham, UK

David Greenaway, CREDIT, Department of Economics, University of Nottingham, UK

Chris Milner, CREDIT and University of Loughborough, UK

Oliver Morrissey, CREDIT, Department of Economics, University of Nottingham, UK

Chandra Kant Patel, United Nations Conference on Trade and Development, Switzerland

Susan Toh, United Nations Conference on Trade and Development, Switzerland

Abbreviations

ACP	African, Caribbean and Pacific (Group of States)
AfDB	African Development Bank
ADMARC	Agricultural Development and Marketing Corporation
ADP	Annual Development Programme
ASAC	Agricultural sector adjustment credit
BOP	Balance of payments
CFA	Communauté financière africaine
CMEA	Council for Mutual Economic Assistance
DAC	Development Assistance Committee (of OECD)
DMECs	Developed market-economy countries
ECA	Economic Commission for Africa
ECAFE	Economic Commission for Asia and the Far East
EDDRP	Entrepreneurship development and drought recovery programme
EEC	European Economic Community
EC	European Community (or Communities)
EPZ	Export processing zone
ERP	Economic Recovery Programme
ESAF	Enhanced Structural Adjustment Facility
ESCAP	Economic and Social Commission for Asia and the Pacific (formerly ECAFE)
ETS	Economic time series (UNCTAD Data Base)
FAO	Food and Agriculture Organization of the United Nations
FDI	Foreign direct investment
FY	Fiscal year
GDP	Gross domestic product
GNP	Gross national product
GSP	Generalized system of preferences
GSTP	Global System of Trade Preferences among Developing Countries
IDA	International Development Association
IFAD	International Fund for Agricultural Development
ILO	International Labour Organisation
IMF	International Monetary Fund
ITPAC	Industry and trade policy adjustment credit
LDCs	Least Developed Countries

MFA	Multi-Fibre Arrangement
NGO	Non-governmental organization
ODA	Official development assistance
OECD	Organisation for Economic Co-operation and Development
OGL	Open general licence
PFPs	Policy framework paper(s)
PSD	Programme for Sustained Development
SAL	Structural Adjustment Loan
SAP	Structural Adjustment Programme
SEP	Social expenditure programme
SITC	Standard International Trade Classification
STABEX	Stabilization of exports
UNCTAD	United Nations Conference on Trade and Development
UNDP	United Nations Development Programme
UNEP	United Nations Environment Programme
VAT	Value-added tax

Foreword

Fiscal reform is now widely understood to be crucial for the success of macro-economic stabilization and growth-oriented structural adjustment policies. In the early 1980s, governments in many of the Least Developed Countries (LDCs) found themselves facing unsustainable fiscal deficits, the response to which inevitably involved difficult cutbacks in public expenditure with adverse social and economic consequences. In order to both enhance revenue mobilization (and so limit the extent of required expenditure cutbacks) and to promote greater efficiency in terms of resource allocation, many LDCs began to implement wide-ranging tax policy reforms later in the decade. A central feature of tax reform was the emphasis on the re-orientation of the tax base from an over-reliance on trade taxes towards a broader domestic consumption base. Governments in LDCs have also recognized the need to complement changes to the structure of taxation with administrative reforms to enhance the efficiency of tax collection and of public administration in general.

In order to better understand the issues involved in the design and implementation of fiscal reforms, the United Nations Conference on Trade and Development (UNCTAD) secretariat initiated case studies on the process of fiscal reforms in a selected number of LDCs. The purpose of these studies is to provide a wider understanding and appreciation of the efforts LDCs are undertaking and to share these experiences with a wider group of countries.

The work undertaken is reflected in the papers that follow. These studies have benefited from the comments of a number of other institutions, notably the International Monetary Fund, the World Bank and the Regional Commissions of the United Nations. The country work was undertaken jointly by UNCTAD and Professor David Greenaway of the University of Nottingham and his colleagues.

Financial support for the project was provided by the Netherlands Government through a Trust Fund (Fiscal Policy Reforms in the Least Developed Countries, INT/91/A20), financed by them and executed by the UNCTAD secretariat.

I wish to extend our sincere appreciation to the Netherlands authorities for their generous financial support in carrying out this work. My appreciation also extends to United Nations Development Programme (UNDP) offices in many countries for facilitating the work of the UNCTAD secretariat and the consultants engaged in this work.

Rubens Ricupero
Secretary-General of UNCTAD

1. Overview

Chandra Kant Patel, Susan Toh
and Martin Brownbridge

---

1 INTRODUCTION

This chapter presents an introductory overview of the nature and experience of fiscal reforms implemented in the LDCs over the last decade.[1] It also summarizes some of the salient findings of the subsequent five chapters of this volume, the first of which analyses the theoretical principles guiding the design and reform of fiscal systems while the following chapters consist of empirical studies of four LDCs (Bangladesh, Malawi, The Gambia and the United Republic of Tanzania) which undertook reform programmes beginning in the 1980s. It is organized as follows.

Section 2 provides an outline of the reasons behind fiscal reform in LDCs. It examines the economic and fiscal context in which LDCs embarked on programmes of policy reform and also discusses the main characteristics of LDC tax systems which have given rise to the impetus for reform. Section 3 explores the nature of fiscal reform in LDCs. It notes the economic principles underlying fiscal reform in general and changes to the tax structure in particular, the objectives of tax reform and the specific policy measures most commonly enacted by LDC governments. In Section 4 the experience of public expenditure restraint in LDCs is briefly outlined. Cuts in capital expenditures appear to have borne the major share of the burden of fiscal adjustment in the first half of the 1980s.

The experience of fiscal reform in the four case studies covered in subsequent chapters of this volume is summarized in Section 5. The section begins by noting the magnitude of fiscal imbalances in these countries during the early 1980s, and then outlines the nature of tax and expenditure reforms undertaken and some of the results arising from these reforms. The subsequent sections summarise some of the lessons which may be learnt from the experience so far of fiscal reform in LDCs. Section 6 discusses the administrative constraints on fiscal reform. Factors which influence the sustainability of fiscal reform in LDCs are considered in Section 7. These include the scope of reforms, the speed with which they are implemented, the sequencing of fiscal reforms and other elements of adjustment programmes, and government commitment to, and involvement in, the design of the reforms. Finally Section 8 notes some of the areas in which fiscal reforms need to be strengthened and extended if their objectives are to be fully realized.

2   ECONOMIC AND FISCAL CONTEXT OF REFORMS IN LDCS

Fiscal performance had deteriorated in most LDCs in the period prior to the implementation of programmes of economic reform. This deterioration was characterized by persistent fiscal deficits, which in many countries had reached unsustainably high levels by the early 1980s. High fiscal deficits were in part due to exogenous factors such as worsening terms of trade and drought. They also reflected domestic constraints on resource mobilization – typical of countries in an early stage of development – which obliged governments to seek external financing of their budgetary expenditures, combined with the expansion of public expenditures during the 1970s to provide employment, social services and industrial and infrastructural investment.

Fiscal deficits in many LDCs were associated with balance of payments deficits, the latter reflecting a number of factors including the often poor performance of exports, the adverse impact of external shocks and the expansionary effects on domestic demand of the fiscal deficits themselves. In some LDCs the impact of expansionary fiscal policies on the real exchange rate damaged the competitiveness of the export sector, especially when fiscal deficits were financed through domestic credit creation. Moreover both fiscal and external deficits were exacerbated by the need to service the external public debt accumulated during the 1970s to finance public expenditure increases. In turn severe external deficits often proved to be the major constraint, via the reduced availability of imports, on sustainable output growth in LDCs.

Significantly, the emergence of large fiscal deficits during the early 1980s coincided with the tightening of access to external finance, and an increase in its cost, in the wake of the debt crisis and the intensification of global competition for scarce official development assistance (ODA) resources. Alternative domestic sources of borrowing, other than central bank credit creation with its attendant inflationary implications, was limited by the lack of well-developed financial markets. Governments of LDCs were consequently obliged to embark on fiscal reform with the objective of eliminating or reducing fiscal and external deficits while at the same time enhancing domestic revenue mobilization in order to offset the fall in external finance.

Fiscal reform in most LDCs has taken place within the context of more wide-ranging programmes of macro and micro economic reform. These programmes, generally called structural adjustment programmes (SAPs), have included trade and exchange rate reforms and have been designed to address macroeconomic imbalances and enhance the efficiency of resource mobilization and allocation. The efficiency objectives of these programmes have also entailed an important fiscal element because the structure of taxation, as well as many aspects of public expenditure, influence the prices at which private agents trade and therefore the allocation of resources. Reducing tax-induced distortions has therefore been a major element of many adjustment programmes in LDCs.

All four of the LDCs featured in the case studies in this volume implemented adjustment programmes supported by the IMF and World Bank during the 1980s. These programmes included fiscal reforms, in particular public expenditure restraints and tax policy reforms. An important aspect of the analysis in these country studies is the interrelationship between fiscal reforms and the other components of adjustment programmes, in particular trade policy reform.

The structure of the tax and revenue systems prevalent in many LDCs prior to the implementation of fiscal reform programmes was characterized by a number of elements which had negative consequences for resource mobilization, allocative efficiency and the vulnerability of revenues (and thus fiscal balance) to exogenous shocks. First, tax revenues, which constitute the bulk – about 82 per cent on average – of government revenue in LDCs, tend to be lower as a proportion of GDP in these countries than in other developing countries. The second relevant feature of these tax systems has been their heavy dependence on taxes on international trade, which on average account for about 40 per cent of tax revenues.[2] This not only has negative implications for the long-term international competitiveness of these economies but also renders tax revenue vulnerable to fluctuations in international commodity prices and in the volume of imports.

Third, with the exception of some Asian LDCs such as Bangladesh, the share of sales and excise taxes in total revenue and GDP in LDCs throughout the 1980s was relatively small, in spite of the relatively high legal rates levied on some commodities. As is noted below, efficiency considerations suggest that tax structures should emphasize raising revenue from final consumption expenditures (i.e. from sales and related taxes). The low level of taxes accruing from these sources was owing to a combination of factors including inefficient administration and enforcement and the existence of numerous categories of exemptions. Value-added at the retail and wholesale level has usually been tax exempt as have most services as well as many different categories of goods. Legal exemptions have probably been compounded in many countries by tax evasion. Consequently, sales taxes have in most countries essentially been confined to imports and certain domestically produced manufactured products. In practice, therefore, the sales tax is equivalent mainly to an import tax.[3]

Moreover, because sales taxes have often been levied at the production, rather than the consumption stage, they have resembled turnover taxes. In practice taxes of this nature have often led to tax pyramiding (or cascading taxes) with the attendant distortions and inefficiencies in resource allocation which this creates.[4]

Direct taxes (mainly comprising individual and corporate taxes on income, profits and capital) do not in general provide a major source of government income in LDCs, contributing on average only 25–30 per cent of tax revenues. Many practical difficulties – for example, poor accounting standards, low literacy levels, the prevalence and wide dispersal of activities in the informal sector and/or in small establishments – inhibit the effective administration and collection of such taxes. Agricultural incomes, fringe benefits and, in some countries, wages in the public sector, are usually tax exempt. The collection of taxes on wealth, land and property is also difficult to administer. As a consequence personal and corporate taxes are levied on a small tax base representing only a fraction of the whole economy. Nominal rates are usually high, although exemptions of various types are often available which lead to substantial inequities in the tax regime, distort production and investment decisions and encourage tax evasion.

As a result of these features the tax structure in LDCs has been characterized by *inelasticity* (or unresponsiveness to economic growth because of the narrow tax base). It is also *complex* in terms of administration and tax compliance while at the same time being *inefficient* as the taxes not only raise little revenue, but also have distortionary effects on production, expenditure and investment decisions. Moreover, the tax structure is often *inequitable*; individuals and businesses in similar circumstances are not treated alike and the system tends to favour the strongest (politically and economically), with the wherewithal to evade taxes.[5]

3   THE NATURE OF FISCAL REFORM IN LDCS

As part of the stabilization and adjustment programmes referred to above, most LDCs have implemented major tax and expenditure reforms over the past several years. Because the initial priorities of governments facing serious economic crises often emphasized the restoration of macroeconomic stability, which necessitated reducing fiscal deficits to more sustainable levels, the short- to medium-term objectives of fiscal policy focused on cutting public expenditures and raising revenues. As the programmes have progressed reforms aimed at the longer term efficiency objectives have been introduced, consisting in particular of changes to the structure of taxation, in order to remedy some of the deficiencies in the tax systems noted in Section 2 above. In addition fiscal reforms have more recently begun to address the need to improve administrative efficiency in tax and revenue collection and the management and control of public expenditures. Fiscal reforms in a number of LDCs have also encompassed the restructuring and/or privatization of public enterprises with the aim of increasing efficiency and reducing losses and the attendant budgetary subsidies and transfers from central governments.

The economic theory underlying fiscal reform in developing countries is discussed by Coady in Chapter 2 of this volume. Coady notes that theory can provide a number of valuable insights into the design of optimal fiscal systems and the reform of existing systems. He argues that an optimal fiscal system should incorporate efficiency (i.e. minimize distortions) and equity (distributional) considerations, although in practice some aspects of the fiscal system will inevitably involve a trade-off between these objectives. The design of the revenue side of the fiscal system should not be undertaken separately from that of the expenditure side, in particular because the extent to which distributional objectives can be addressed via government expenditures allows greater scope for orienting tax policy towards minimizing distortions.

In terms of tax policy, economic theory suggests that indirect taxes should be levied on final consumption (rather than on production inputs) with the equity/efficiency trade-off determining optimal rates for specific goods and services and that the taxation of imports should in general correspond with the taxation of domestically produced goods so as to minimize trade distortions. Economic theory also indicates that, although uniform indirect taxation is unlikely to be optimal, large dispersions in tax rates on different commodities are likely to be distortionary. Similar arguments apply to the taxation of assets and factor incomes.

Coady argues that a theory of reform, which takes account of the interactions between the different distortions in the economy, can provide useful guidelines as to an appropriate sequence of reform measures for LDC governments wishing to undertake gradual or piecemeal fiscal reforms. Coady also notes the administrative deficiencies which characterize the fiscal systems in many LDCs and the adverse implications this has for efficient revenue collection. Consequently he stresses the importance of undertaking administrative reforms and argues that the implementation of such reforms might be crucial in determining the scope for reforming the structure of the tax system.

Many of the economic principles discussed by Coady have formed the basis of fiscal reform programmes undertaken in LDCs and, in particular, the changes to the structure of the tax system. The changes to the tax system most commonly undertaken have focused on a number of specific objectives. These include the broadening and diversifying of the tax base in order to expand revenues, to enhance the stability of the tax base (so as to reduce fluctuations in tax revenues) and to reduce the distortionary effects arising from concentrating taxation on a narrow base, such as imports. In addition, attention has been directed towards the need to eliminate the disincentive effects of onerous levels of taxation (such as those which had been levied on certain agricultural export commodities in some LDCs) and to reduce the allocative inefficiencies induced by the distortionary differential taxation of different assets, goods and sectors of the economy. Related to this has been a desire to improve incentives so as to augment and diversify private sector activity, promote competition in domestic markets and discourage inefficient, high cost domestic production. The design of tax reforms in many LDCs has also tried to ensure that reforms are not regressive in order to protect the poorest and most vulnerable groups from the tax net.

The tax policy changes enacted in pursuit of revenue enhancement and diversification objectives have, in the main, emphasized the reduction of the traditional dependence on narrowly based international trade taxes in favour of more broadly based consumption (or modified value-added) taxes. Specifically, such reforms have involved the gradual phasing out or rationalization of export and import tariffs (in conjunction with trade liberalization measures such as removing quantitative restrictions on imports), and of sales and excise taxes and their replacement by a 'turnover' or value-added tax (VAT). Tariff rationalization has generally encompassed a lowering of the average nominal tariff rates together with a reduction in tariff dispersion (i.e. the divergence between tariff rates levied on different goods). In addition some LDCs have undertaken steps to eliminate the numerous tariff exemptions which had been made available to various categories of importers.

Alongside the efficiency gains of raising revenue from consumption as opposed to import or production based taxes, the principal benefits of the VAT lie in its potentially broad tax base, its relatively high tax elasticity and buoyancy[6] and its ability to raise revenues without distortionary cascading effects.[7] It is also argued that VAT encourages proper record keeping by traders and that as this practice spreads the tax base will broaden and revenues increase.

Many of the hypothesized advantages of VAT introduction have however yet to be fully realized because, although notionally based on sales, VAT in most LDCs is in practice typically levied at the manufacturing and import stages and not at the wholesale and retail stages. Moreover a range of goods such as utilities, services and basic consumption items are normally exempt from the tax base for various reasons including administrative difficulties involved in tax collection and equity concerns, while luxuries – whether domestically produced or imported – are subject to various rates of supplementary duties. There are plans, however, in many countries to gradually extend the VAT base to include a wider range of goods and services.

Direct taxes on both personal incomes and corporate profits have also been subject to reform in LDCs. In general governments have endeavoured to reduce nominal marginal tax rates, to broaden the tax base by including categories of income (such as the profits earned by public enterprises) which had previously been outside the tax net and to remove or reduce the various exemptions.

Reforms of this nature have had a number of objectives including the promotion of efficiency through reducing the disincentives accruing from high marginal tax rates and the distortions arising from the differential tax treatment of competing assets and sectors, encouraging tax compliance (by reducing incentives and opportunities to evade tax) and facilitating administrative efficiency. To mitigate the potentially adverse effects on the poor of widening the direct tax base some countries have raised tax thresholds applicable to taxes on personal income, urban property and agricultural land.

In sum, revenue enhancement, economic efficiency, horizontal equity and simplicity constitute the broad policy orientations of recent tax reforms in LDCs. While the overall direction and nature of reforms are remarkably similar in most countries undertaking them, the actual procedures, sequencing and timing, and indeed the actual outcome of reforms on government revenues, has varied considerably. Several LDCs, including those in our case studies, initially undertook somewhat ad hoc and piecemeal tax reforms, such as increasing the rates of already existing taxes (alongside cutbacks in expenditure) in response to the growing fiscal deficits in the early 1980s before embarking on more fundamental reforms of the type described above in the second half of the decade.

4 EXPENDITURE RESTRAINT IN LDCS

Governments in a number of adjusting LDCs succeeded in reducing fiscal imbalances during the 1980s. However, although modest revenue increases were attained in some LDCs, the major contribution to deficit reduction in many countries was made by cuts in public expenditure, especially during the first half of the 1980s. Although the experience of LDCs varied, it is apparent that capital budgets suffered substantial reductions in many LDCs while cutbacks in recurrent expenditures were generally less severe.

Recurrent budgets have proved more difficult to cut than capital budgets for several reasons. First, interest payments on public debt, which are non-discretionary in nature, have increased in many LDCs during the 1980s, with the share of interest payments in total expenditures rising in most countries which recorded rising recurrent expenditures.[8] Second, socio-political pressures to keep public sector workers on the payroll limited the extent to which governments could reduce their wage bills. Moreover, cutting public employment levels often entails substantial budgetary outlays on severance pay, retraining, and so on. Third, continued recourse to the recurrent budget has been made by transfers and subsidies, in particular to loss making state-owned enterprises. With a few exceptions, those LDCs which did manage to achieve significant reductions in the recurrent budget did so by sharply reducing outlays on the maintenance of public facilities and on purchases of goods and services.

Cuts in capital expenditures in some countries were necessitated by reduced aid and external capital inflows, on which governments have relied for a large part of the financing of capital projects. Linked to this were bureaucratic and administrative delays in the recipient countries, shortfalls in government counterpart funding of the local financing costs (of capital projects) and delays in releasing counterpart funds from commodity aid. Capital expenditures by public enterprises declined sharply as a result of the financial problems experienced in this sector and because of a reduction in capital transfers and lending by central governments which had in the past provided a major source of finance for public enterprise investment.[9] Given the more market oriented economic strategy adopted by most LDCs, an expansion of private investment would, it was hoped, replace public enterprise capital in some of the sectors of the economy producing marketable goods.

The magnitude and composition of the public expenditure reductions implemented by LDCs are clearly causes of concern. There is scope in most countries for reducing non (or less) productive aspects of public expenditure such as an overly large bureaucracy, military spending, prestige capital projects, poorly targeted subsidies and inefficient public enterprises. However it appears that expenditure cutbacks have also affected areas of the budget such as infrastructural investment and maintenance, and social services, which are likely to be far more valuable in terms of the provision of public goods needed to complement private sector production and to enhance public welfare.

In a number of LDCs which undertook programmes of fiscal retrenchment in the 1980s, the provision of social services such as education and health has suffered owing to a lack of funds to purchase essential supplies and maintain equipment.[10] The vulnerability of social expenditures to cuts during periods of public expenditure restraint has been an issue of particular concern in LDCs, given their already very low level of human capacity development. More recently, with increasing global recognition of the need to remedy the negative social consequences of adjustment, many LDCs have adopted special measures to protect and promote human development. These have included greater emphasis within overall budgets on primary education, and on rural and primary health care. Attempts have been made to decentralize social service provision in order to mobilize local resources, as in the United Republic of Tanzania, and a number of other LDCs have levied 'user charges' to allow cost recovery as a means of safeguarding health and education expenditures.

The sharp cutbacks in capital expenditures also have potentially serious implications for development over the long term.[11] Clearly there is a danger, if capital budgets remain excessively compressed, that the quality of social overhead capital will deteriorate and that this will have adverse consequences for productivity in other sectors of the economy. Moreover an expansion and upgrading of the existing public capital stock, at least in terms of infrastructure, may be required to complement the desired increases in private sector investment, especially in the export sectors, which is one of the primary objectives of the reform programmes being undertaken in LDCs.

5 THE EXPERIENCE OF FISCAL REFORMS IN BANGLADESH, MALAWI, THE GAMBIA AND THE UNITED REPUBLIC OF TANZANIA

This section provides a summary of the main conclusions of the four country case studies of fiscal reforms included in this volume. The countries are Bangladesh, Malawi, The Gambia and the United Republic of Tanzania. Each of these countries faced serious macroeconomic difficulties during the 1980s, which included the growth of unsustainable fiscal deficits, as a consequence of which both tax and expenditure reforms were undertaken, a process which remains ongoing. The magnitude of fiscal imbalances in these four LDCs is indicated by the fact that the overall fiscal deficit in The Gambia stood at 14 per cent of GDP in 1980/81, while that of the United Republic of Tanzania was 16 per cent in 1981/2. The deficit in Malawi in 1981/2 was 12 per cent while in Bangladesh in 1983 it stood at 11 per cent of GDP.

5.1 Bangladesh

Bangladesh has undertaken a major economic reform programme since the mid-1980s, although many of the most radical elements have only been introduced since 1989. The fiscal components of the reforms included the rationalization and liberalization of nominal tariff rates and the introduction of VAT. The VAT has been set at a uniform rate, although certain basic items are exempt and a range of luxuries are subject to additional excise duties. Reforms to direct taxes have also been implemented, including a reduction of the highest marginal rates. Measures to strengthen tax administration and collection were also given high priority in the government's agenda for fiscal reform.

Expenditure reforms initially focused on reductions in the capital budget but since the late 1980s the emphasis has changed to include retrenchment of public employees, a reduction in subsidies and privatization.

Fiscal performance improved in the post-1990 period as a result of these reforms, along with the expansion and diversification of the revenue base. The share of revenues in GDP rose from 9.3 per cent in fiscal year (FY) 1989/90 to 10.9 per cent in FY 1991/2. Total expenditures during the same period fell from 17.1 per cent to 15.5 per cent of GDP, with the budget deficit falling from 7.7 per cent of GDP to 4.6 per cent.

Having now completed the stabilization phase of its fiscal reform programme, a number of challenges confront further progress in Bangladesh.

Notable among these are administrative and informational bottlenecks which, in combination with the prevalence of highly dispersed, unrecorded, informal activities pose formidable problems for tax collection and enforcement. In addition, problems may arise from the donors' reluctance to support some aspects of the reforms, for example, the funding of compensation packages to cushion the impact of public sector retrenchment programmes, which can potentially undermine progress.

5.2 Malawi

Malawi faced severe economic difficulties at the start of the 1980s mainly resulting from adverse external shocks including a sharp fall in the terms of trade. In 1981 the Government began a series of adjustment programmes supported by financial assistance from the IMF and World Bank. The initial emphasis was on reducing macroeconomic imbalances; as such, fiscal policy in the first half of the 1980s focused on raising tax rates, including those of import taxes, and steep cutbacks in public investment.

More fundamental fiscal reforms were begun in 1987 following a second round of negative external shocks. These included tax reforms, the objective of which was to enhance revenue generation, efficiency, equity and ease of administration. The broad thrust of reforms aimed to shift the base for indirect taxation from production to consumption. The surtax (a sales tax) on commodity transactions was converted to a VAT-type system and its coverage extended from the manufacturing sector to wholesalers and retailers. Distortionary export duties were eliminated and excise and duty rates were applied on an ad valorem basis. These reforms had the effect of de-emphasizing the revenue function of trade taxes in favour of the new surtax. As a consequence, the contribution of taxes on goods and services to GDP increased after 1987, more than offsetting the fall in international trade taxes.

In the area of direct taxes, the reforms sought to remove inter-sectoral biases and inter-asset biases in the business income tax. The system of investment allowances was unified and simplified, parastatals (public enterprises) became liable for taxation in 1987 and a system of advance payment of corporate tax was introduced in 1988. The corporate tax and the marginal rate of individual income tax were reduced to encourage compliance.

The reforms bolstered revenues but only temporarily: the ratio of indirect taxes to GDP rose from 6.4 per cent in 1986/7 to 7.7 per cent in 1989/90, while that of total taxes to GDP rose from 17.8 per cent to 19.2 per cent. Combined with continued restraint on public expenditures, the increased revenues led to a sharp reduction in the overall budget deficit from 11.5 per cent of GDP in 1986/7 to 2.1 per cent in 1989/90. However the declining trend in both tax and overall revenues over the three years since 1989/90 exposed major administrative limitations which have reduced the effectiveness of the reforms. Major con-

straints include understaffing and inadequate levels of the requisite skills resulting from uncompetitive public sector salaries and a lack of training. In addition
the constant rotation of qualified senior civil servants between different departments and/or ministries is also a serious problem. Sustaining further reforms
will therefore require urgent attention to building up human skills and the
necessary administrative capacity. Moreover the reforms in direct taxes may
have reduced revenue mobilization from this source; taxes on personal income
declined owing mainly to reductions in the top marginal rate of income tax in
1989/90.

5.3 The Gambia

As in Malawi, The Gambia experienced severe balance of payments and fiscal
deficits following the external shocks of the 1970s and, beginning in the mid-
1980s, undertook major economic reforms supported by conditional finance
from the international financial institutions. The fiscal components of these
reforms included substantial reductions in public expenditure and the privatization of parastatals. Although capital expenditure declined as a proportion of
GDP in the first half of the 1980s, the major burden of expenditure reductions
was borne by recurrent expenditure cutbacks owing in part to a 20 per cent fall
in public employment.

The main objective of the tax reforms was the promotion of efficiency, and
the most important elements of the reforms consisted of the staged introduction
of a VAT-like system of commodity taxation (the National Sales Tax), the
rationalization of excise and import duties and the removal of export taxes.
Corporate tax rates were also reduced while measures were undertaken to
broaden the tax base. Meanwhile efforts were made to improve administrative
efficiency and tax collection in order to enhance revenues.

The tax reforms were associated with only very modest increases in government revenue as a percentage of GDP. Nevertheless, given the steep cutbacks in
recurrent expenditures, the overall fiscal deficit recorded a substantial improvement, falling to around 1 per cent of GDP at the start of the 1990s. In addition to
the success in reducing the deficit, fiscal reforms have led to a limited diversification of the tax base away from the pre-reform dependence on trade taxes. On
the expenditure side, the burden of providing financial support to loss-making
parastatals has been reduced with privatization. The efforts to tackle administrative deficiencies have brought some benefits although more progress is required
in this area.

5.4 United Republic of Tanzania

The United Republic of Tanzania suffered a very severe economic crisis in the
early 1980s characterised by large fiscal deficits, acute shortages of foreign

exchange and declines in output. In the first half of the decade the Government implemented an adjustment programme without support from the IMF and World Bank but in 1986 it eventually reached agreement with these institutions on a comprehensive reform package known as the Economic Recovery Programme (ERP). Fundamental tax reform began in 1988, with the rationalization of tariffs, followed in 1989 by a broadening of the tax base for sales and excise taxes. Further rationalization of tariffs, sales, income and corporate taxes was implemented in 1992 and the eligibility for tax exemptions was reduced. A presidential commission established to examine the fiscal system has recommended the introduction of a VAT system. Tax revenues as a percentage of GDP recorded a modest increase during the ERP (from 20 per cent in 1984/5 to 23 per cent in 1989/90) but this was mainly owing to the effect of devaluation on tariff revenue rather than to the tax reforms per se.

Steep cuts in government expenditure, which included both capital projects and public services, had been implemented in the first half of the 1980s, and this brought about some reduction in the overall deficit from the very high levels prevailing at the start of the decade. By 1985/6 development expenditures in relation to GDP were half the 1980/81 level, a fall exacerbated by reduced external concessional finance. Government expenditures experienced a limited recovery during the ERP, although this was mainly due to higher interest payments, and this resulted in a widening of the overall budget deficit. Nevertheless the government was able to reduce its domestic borrowing as a result of increased external financing.

6   ADMINISTRATIVE CONSTRAINTS TO FISCAL REFORM

One of the most pertinent findings of our four country studies is that the effective implementation of many of the fiscal reforms, and reforms to the tax structure in particular, has been impeded by administrative constraints, especially deficiencies in the quality, training and level of staffing. Until recently, administrative reforms had been relatively neglected although they are now receiving more attention. A number of problems which appear to be fairly typical of the administrative systems in many LDCs were highlighted by the case studies.

First, there are very serious staffing constraints in many LDCs. Many departments, particularly in field offices and at the local level, are severely understaffed. This problem has been exacerbated in some countries because the deterioration in public sector salaries has made it difficult to attract qualified personnel, particularly at the middle and junior levels. Second, staff training and development has been neglected. This is especially serious in view of the fact that substantial training is required to familiarize staff with the major changes enacted to the structure of the tax systems, such as the introduction of VATs. Third, working conditions in many departments, in particular the lack of equipment and congestion in offices, hamper administrative efficiency. One of the major consequences of administrative weaknesses in many LDCs is the failure to curtail tax evasion, partly because staffing levels and training are insufficient to support the type of detailed monitoring and inspection of records which is required if tax evasion is to be reduced. Fourth, the effectiveness of the more senior civil servants, who are generally well trained and committed, has sometimes been impaired by frequent rotations between ministries or departments.

Administrative constraints have also caused problems on the expenditure side of the fiscal system. These problems include leakages and inefficient targeting of public expenditures, poor planning and inadequate coordination of the budget. In some countries, such as Malawi, responsibility for the recurrent budget, on the one hand, and the development budget, on the other, is vested in two different ministries, with little coordination between them. Moreover, the absence of long-term planning of budgets creates inefficiencies and often results in overspending and a mismatch between recurrent and development expenditures, as well as in imbalances within each budget. The rate of return to public investment has been reduced in many LDCs because, while funds have been allocated to complete the construction of development projects (often from external donors), insufficient attention has been paid to ensure that the long-term recurrent funding of these projects is adequate for their efficient operation and maintenance.

7   THE SUSTAINABILITY OF FISCAL REFORM

The sustainability of tax reforms will be affected by *their sequencing and timing*. The experience of LDCs suggests that pervasive and broadly based reforms are more likely to endure than those that are narrowly based. It also suggests that in order to be successful reforms need not be sweeping; although some radical departures are necessary, many changes can be achieved simply through modifying existing systems of revenue generation and expenditure. Also, rapid implementation of reforms appears to be more conducive to sustainability than phased programmes, although much depends on national circumstances. Countries such as the United Republic of Tanzania and The Gambia had longer periods of tax reform, whereas Bangladesh and Malawi carried out major changes in one go, over a short period of time. In Bangladesh, for instance, given the pervasiveness of controls prior to adjustment and the influence of well-entrenched interest groups, rapid implementation of a broadly-based programme was undoubtedly more appropriate than a gradualist piecemeal strategy. Experience of LDCs in sequencing suggests that trade and fiscal reforms must precede the liberalization of factor markets and the capital account. As regards fiscal reform, the evidence of administrative weaknesses noted above suggests that comprehensive administrative reforms must precede, or at least accompany, any major overhaul of the structure of taxes and expenditure.

Political and social considerations crucially bear on the *credibility and sustainability* of reforms. Almost all fiscal reforms produce winners and losers. It is almost always more difficult to introduce reforms in highly controlled regimes, such as existed in pre-reform Bangladesh, where large influential interest groups have secured, individually or collectively, property rights to the rents derived from import protection or have managed to secure 'special treatment' with respect to certain taxes. The reform process in a country such as The Gambia, on the other hand, was much smoother because there were no such major interest groups.

A second and related factor influencing the success of reforms centres on where the initiative for reform has come from. As mentioned above, many aspects of fiscal reform tend to be painful. In a number of LDCs, politicians therefore do not want to be directly associated with the reforms, and the burden of implementing them falls on the bureaucracy, which is unwilling to introduce changes for ideological reasons as well as because of its vested interests. Commitment from the top is as necessary if reform is to succeed as is the ownership of the proposals by the political and civil service elite. Such commitment often depends on whether the reforms represent an indigenous effort (as in The Gambia) or whether the package has been virtually forced on the country by international financial agencies.

Finally, public awareness of reform proposals is crucial in improving compliance, and in ensuring the acceptability of the reforms.

8   SCOPE AND DIRECTIONS FOR FUTURE POLICY ACTION

The outcome of fiscal reforms that have been undertaken clearly indicates that many of the gains achieved are fragile. So far, reforms have focused on the relatively 'easy' stages. For example, while VAT has been introduced, it is confined to manufacturers and importers, leaving out services (including wholesaling and retailing), and in general small firms. As long as the tax base remains overly dependent upon imports, there will be continued vulnerability of tax revenues to changes in the balance of payments in most LDCs. The removal of export taxes on primary commodities as in The Gambia, has nevertheless removed one source of revenue volatility. There is clearly a need to broaden the VAT base and in particular to include as many services as possible under the

VAT net; some governments have indeed recently extended VAT to certain utilities and services. In the medium term, it will be necessary to shift the imposition of VAT from the manufacturing/import stage to the wholesale/retail stage, although the wide prevalence of informal sector activities poses a formidable challenge to this task.

The extent of tariff reform which has been achieved in LDCs such as Bangladesh and The United Republic of Tanzania has been considerable and this has reduced distortions in general and the anti-export bias in particular. Nevertheless average nominal rates remain relatively high in most LDCs, and the dispersion of rates, although much reduced through the concertina approach to tariff reform, is still quite large.

The next stage to fiscal reform may well prove to be much more difficult to implement both politically and administratively. This will involve applying tariff cuts that effectively expose local products to greater competition; reducing employment levels in the public sector; raising efficiency levels in public services and improving the utilization of aid, especially in respect of investment projects. Connected with the problems of reforming expenditure and revenue systems is the important issue of improving administrative efficiency. Enforcement, implementation and minimizing tax evasion are three areas of immediate concern. Administrative constraints have highlighted the crucial need for *human capacity building* and personnel training to impart tax-related skills at all levels – from managers down to tax collectors – to enhance understanding of the intricacies involved in the newly introduced VAT-type taxes. Training is also required in auditing, budget planning, expenditure monitoring and control, and computing skills. Technical assistance from lending agencies and donor governments could be very helpful. In some countries, raising the number of staff and their quality will require more attractive compensation packages, better working conditions, and adequate facilities and equipment.

Also desirable are enhanced information flows on taxpayers, both individuals and firms, which could be achieved through computerization. At present, many LDCs rely on a combination of manual and computerized information flows. Progress in computerization of the VAT system has been generally slow in many countries; sometimes computer equipment has become obsolete even before the commencement of staff training in the use of the equipment. It is also well worth investing resources to secure better dissemination of information to taxpayers to improve their understanding of new taxes introduced.

The reform of the budgeting and expenditure control system is also under way in many countries. There is an urgent need to improve coordination of recurrent and development budgets, and of central government and local government budgets. This calls for improvements in accounting, flash reporting, better information flows, and computerization. Governments should strengthen the role of the rolling three-year public sector investment programmes in expenditure planning.

Priorities and programmes for recurrent and development spending should also be reviewed periodically. In this context, efforts towards more efficient and effective social sector spending need to be continued. As regards the development budget, stricter control and monitoring of contracts involving the purchase of equipment and the hiring of labour, so as to minimize rent-seeking, would release considerable resources in many LDCs. Project selection and approval also merit greater care.

Reforms of the tax structure and public expenditure need, moreover, to be coordinated with other macroeconomic and sectoral reforms. A prerequisite for the success of supply side reforms, including those tax reforms which are designed to minimize distortions so as to raise efficiency in resource allocation, will be maintenance of macroeconomic stability. Moreover the sustainability of reform is likely to depend upon the restoration of more rapid rates of economic growth.

Finally, since the reforms appear to have 'worked' in most LDCs in the sense of enhancing fiscal performance, governments may feel more committed to them, which in turn may help maintain the momentum of reform. Longer term success depends on the momentum being maintained which will depend on the supply side response of the private sector to the reforms. It is this response which not only ensures growth but also broadens the tax base to provide greater tax buoyancy.

NOTES

1. The impetus for such reforms in LDCs was discussed extensively in a previous UNCTAD publication. See UNCTAD (1992).
2. In some countries the ratio was much higher. For example, in the late 1970s/early 1980s, it was as high as 60–70 per cent in Gambia. See the case study in this volume.
3. See Tanzi (1987).
4. Cascading arises because, at each stage of the production and distribution channel, it is the price inclusive of tax at the previous stage which is taxed. Optimum tax theory favours consumption taxes over production taxes because they do not distort choices between inputs and factors and do not have cascading effects or encourage vertical integration as is the tendency for some production taxes. Consumption taxes are therefore considered the most desirable means of raising revenue through commodity transactions, as they do not affect the efficiency of domestic production (see Coady, Chapter 2 of this volume).
5. See Khalilzadeh-Shirazi and Shah (1991, p. xvi).
6. The elasticity of a tax refers to the amount by which revenue derived from that tax changes in response to a change in its tax base. Buoyancy refers to the amount by which tax revenue changes as a result of both changes in its base and changes in the structure of the tax.
7. For a detailed discussion of the subject see UNCTAD (1992), p. 44.
8. The cost of servicing debt has been increased in many LDCs undertaking adjustment programmes by exchange rate devaluation, which raises the domestic currency costs of servicing external debt, and by domestic financial market liberalization which usually raises nominal interest rates (Nashashibi et al., 1992 p. 23–4).
9. See Nashashibi et al. (1992, pp. 10–14).

10. See Pinstrup-Anderson et al. (1987).
11. It is not possible, however, to assess the actual outcomes of capital expenditure cuts on countries in the absence of more detailed knowledge of the effects of such factors as capacity utilization, the quality of investment forgone and the response of private sector investment to reduced public sector investment.

REFERENCES

Easterly, William and Klaus Schmidt-Hebbel (1993), 'Fiscal Deficits and Macroeconomic Performance in Developing Countries', *World Bank Research Observer*, vol. 8, no. 2.

Khalilzadeh-Shirazi, Javad and Anwar Shah (1991), 'Introduction and Overview', in Khalilzadeh-Shirazi, Javad and Anwar Shah (eds), *Tax Policy in Developing Countries* (Washington DC: World Bank).

Nashashibi, Karim, Sanjeev Gupta, Claire Luiksila, Henri Lorie and Walter Mahler (1992), *The Fiscal Dimensions of Adjustment in Low-Income Countries*, Occasional Paper 95 (Washington DC: International Monetary Fund).

Pinstrup-Anderson, P., M. Jaramillo and F. Stewart (1987), 'The Impact of Current Expenditure', in Cornia, G.A., R. Jolly and F. Stewart (eds), *Adjustment with a Human Face* (Oxford: Clarendon Press).

Sahn, David E. (1992), 'Public Expenditures in Sub-Saharan Africa During a Period of Economic Reforms', *World Development*, vol. 20, no. 5.

Shalizi, Zmarak and Lyn Squire (1988), *Tax Policy in Sub-Saharan Africa* (Washington DC: World Bank).

Tanzi, Vito (1987), 'Quantitative Characteristics of Tax Systems', in Newbury, D. and N. Stern (eds), *The Theory of Taxation for Developing Countries* (Oxford: Oxford University Press).

World Bank (1991), *Lessons of Tax Reform* (Washington DC: World Bank).

UNCTAD (1992), *The Least Developed Countries 1991 Report* (New York: United Nations).

2. Fiscal Reform in Developing Countries

David P. Coady

1 INTRODUCTION

The central objective of this paper is to show how economic theory can contribute to the analysis of fiscal policy and help policy makers and tax analysts determine the appropriate design of fiscal systems. We will suggest that economic theory has a lot to offer in this respect. Optimal tax theory has identified important features which one should attempt to incorporate into fiscal systems. In this respect it provides the tax analyst with a model towards which it is desirable to move in the long term. It helps to highlight the fact that taxation has both efficiency and equity implications and that both of these should be considered when identifying the appropriate system. The problem of tax reform is therefore presented in terms of raising sufficient government revenue as efficiently and equitably as possible while also taking account of the administrative capability of the government.

At any point in time it is highly unlikely that the fiscal system in place in any country is consistent with all of the features of an optimal system. We will show that this is particularly so in developing countries, where fiscal systems have been built up in an ad hoc manner in response to various internal and external pressures and reflect a host of historical, social, political and economic factors. The question is one of fiscal reform defined as identifying the changes in the present system which will raise revenue in a more efficient and equitable manner and thus increase welfare. Reforms should not only reflect the present administrative capacity of the government but also how this is expected to evolve over time. Indeed, the reform of the administrative system itself should be part of the whole reform package. Neither should the reforms lose sight of the long-term 'model' mentioned above. Obviously, the optimal fiscal design is one for which it is not possible to identify any improvements.

In our discussion of fiscal policy we will emphasize that the appropriate design of reforms will depend crucially on a number of factors which can vary significantly across countries. These include the degree of monetization, the extent and nature of market transactions, the extent of formal and informal activity, the education level of the population and its ability to keep accounts, the capabilities of the government administration system, the extent of poverty and the nature of policy instruments available to tackle it, the enforcement mechanisms available and the nature of the legal system, the presence and strength of vested interests and the degree of political stability. In some sense this reflects the real challenge to the tax analyst: to find the appropriate set of tax bases and rates which raise sufficient revenue given the constraints of the administrative system. We will also suggest that welfare improvements can be made by redirecting revenue among the various tax handles already in operation.

Throughout we will emphasize that the revenue and expenditure sides of fiscal reform should not be analysed separately. There are three main reasons for analysing both sides simultaneously within the same framework. Firstly, the appropriate level of expenditure should reflect both the administrative and efficiency costs of raising revenue as well as the social benefits arising from the expenditures themselves. The optimal level of government expenditure is the level at which the marginal social cost of raising extra revenue is equal to the marginal social value of extra expenditures. Therefore, the nature of policy instruments available to the government for directing expenditures towards useful ends, whether they be for investment or for social protection, will be an important factor in determining the amount of revenue which should be raised. This aspect of fiscal reform is obviously intimately connected with arguments concerning the appropriate role for and extent of government intervention in developing countries. Secondly, many forms of expenditures (e.g. subsidies) are analytically similar to taxes in that they also distort prices. Thirdly, the appropriate structure of taxation depends on the policy instruments available on the expenditure side. For example, if certain expenditures are very efficient at transferring income to the less well off, the revenue side of the budget can focus more on raising revenue efficiently with less concern for the trade-off with equity. The extreme (but probably uninteresting) case is where optional lump-sum expenditures are available and tax and pricing policies should focus on efficiency alone. However, in general one should remember that most policy instruments have both efficiency and equity impacts and these should be compared when deciding on the appropriate fiscal design.

One must also be aware that when trying to locate welfare improving reforms in tax and pricing policies one should not focus on particular tax tools in isolation. The welfare implications of changing any particular tax or price is sensitive to the level and nature of other taxes in the system as well as the policy instruments that are available. For example, increasing a tax on a good with a low tax can be welfare improving if it leads to a substitution of expenditure towards highly taxed substitutes. Such issues can be particularly important for agricultural pricing policies, given the high level of distortions involved and the magnitude of cross-price effects. Also, if producer prices are distorted so that producer and shadow prices are not proportional, taxes can take on a corrective as well as a revenue raising function.

Although the fiscal reform policy described here is often part of the stabilization and adjustment programmes of major lending institutions – fiscal reforms are usually included under the 'structural adjustment' objectives which focus on the reform of institutions and prices so that both are conducive to efficient resource allocation – the process itself and its desirability is relevant even when internal and external disequilibria (high unemployment, accelerating inflation, fiscal deficits and balance of payments deficits) are not major problems. The need for fiscal reform can derive solely from the desire to raise present revenue levels in a more efficient and equitable manner. One should also recognize that domestic resource mobilization is but one of the ways of financing expenditures; alternatives are foreign borrowing and printing money. However, recent experiences have underlined that such methods of financing usually result in severe internal and external disequilibria and are not sustainable in the longer term. Therefore, an efficient and equitable domestic resource mobilization mechanism appears to provide the only viable long-run method of financing government expenditures. That this is the case is further reinforced by the present high levels of interest rates and difficulties in securing foreign borrowing.

Before setting out the format of the paper we should highlight two important points. Firstly, the approach to fiscal analysis adopted here mirrors that of the modern public finance literature where one specifies objectives in terms of social welfare and revenue requirements, identifies available policy instruments and employs them in such a way as to raise the appropriate revenue in a way that minimizes the associated welfare losses. We believe that this is a useful and practical way to proceed. However, this is not the only way and others have focused on different criteria which would determine the way in which governments should intervene in the economy. Some have taken the extreme view that any form of government intervention violates individual liberties and rights and should therefore be kept to the bare minimum (see, for example, Nozick, 1974, and Hayek, 1960). Others have suggested that the ability of the government to intervene successfully is so restricted that the sole guiding principles should be the need for a simple and clear set of rules which can be easily understood by all citizens and an administrative structure which is transparent and efficient (see, for example, Buchanan, 1966). More recently some have focused on the tendency of initially 'functional' bureaucracies to develop into entities in their own right with objectives which can differ from those of the government (and nation) and even frustrate the achievement of the latter. It is argued that leviathan 'bureaucracies' develop enormous fiscal appetites for their own sake and that these need to be controlled. Also, interest groups emerge from within and outside the bureaucracy and allocate substantial resources to capturing rents which are associated with various government policies – in particular the use of quantity controls. These views are reflected somewhat in recent trends which try to determine how and when different aspects of government involvement should be 'privatized' (see, for example, Brennan and Buchanan, 1980 and 1985, and Krueger, 1990).

It is our belief that, while some of these alternative approaches can contribute usefully to discussion concerning the design of fiscal policy, they are less useful when discussing piecemeal or gradual fiscal reform. The main focus of this paper is on the latter. Also, our emphasis on normative analysis is not meant to suggest that the positive theory of taxation has nothing to offer. On the contrary, the positive side of the analysis is crucial and is often the more difficult part of the analysis. The evaluation of any reform requires us to follow through all of the general equilibrium (i.e. direct and indirect) impacts of the reform in terms of changing prices and incomes and so on, a process which obviously involves numerous assumptions concerning the objectives of consumers and producers and how they interact. Positive theory focuses on these issues. However the calculations required in practice involve an enormous amount of painstaking work, although simple but insightful models can make our task substantially easier. The search for models which identify robust but simple rules for calculating shadow prices stems from such objectives. Once the positive side of the analysis is complete, one must evaluate all the changes brought about by the reform using our criteria of efficiency and equity. The latter criterion always involves value judgements whether or not they are made explicit.

The layout of this paper is as follows. Section 2 charts the contribution of economic theory to the analysis of tax design and reform, arguing that very useful insights can be gleaned. We set out the basic underlying principles for tax design. We discuss the importance of agriculture in developing countries, its organization and the implications for fiscal policy. The role and scope for public-sector pricing is also examined. In practice fiscal systems are often very inefficient and inequitable and can be reformed only gradually. We show how the theory of tax reform can suggest guidelines for reform policy. In Section 3 we describe the design of fiscal systems in practice in many developing countries and highlight the central features of the fiscal reform packages implemented during the 1980s. Lessons are drawn from these experiences for future tax reforms. Section 4 emphasizes the important role of social expenditure policy and its implications for tax design and reform. A summary and conclusions are presented in Section 5.

2   THE CONTRIBUTION OF ECONOMIC THEORY

In this section we show that the standard theoretical models offer very useful insights regarding the appropriate design of a tax and transfer system and help us to focus on their efficiency and equity implications. However, some of their assumptions make them less applicable in developing countries which are constrained by the nature of available policy instruments. They also tell us very little about how we should move towards the appropriate design from a situation characterized by multiple distortions, some of which cannot be eliminated immediately. In this respect the theory of the second best warns us to be wary since the removal of one or more distortions while others remain in place is not necessarily welfare enhancing. We argue that the theory of reform can be used to identify welfare-improving reforms in such situations and argue that a reform approach is especially useful for policy advice. We look at the appropriate tax and pricing policies in agriculture given its importance in LDCs. Finally we examine in more detail the implications for public sector pricing.

2.1 Standard Tax Models

Although the general principles underlying optimal (marginal cost) pricing and lump-sum transfers were recognized in the late 19th century (see, for example, Wicksell, 1896), the first attempt at formalizing the efficiency implications of distortionary pricing was Ramsey (1927). Later papers by Samuelson (1951) and Boiteux (1956) revived interest in the subject. Ramsey (1927) used, as his point of departure, the two basic theorems of welfare economics, namely: (i) if all markets exist and there are no externalities then a competitive equilibrium is Pareto efficient, and (ii) if we further assume that production and preferences are convex and that revenue can be raised and distributed in a lump-sum manner, then any Pareto efficient allocation can be decentralized as a competitive equilibrium. These theorems, if valid, indicate that the only role for commodity (indirect) taxation is in correcting for externalities, that is, the standard Pigovian corrective taxes. Ramsey considered the problem of raising government revenue when lump-sum taxes were not available so that indirect taxation was necessary. His analysis showed that 'the obvious solution that there should be no differentiation is entirely erroneous' (Ramsey, 1927, p. 47) and that the optimal set of indirect taxes are such that taxes should be higher on goods with lower (compensated) price elasticities of demand implying equi-proportionate reduction in these demands.

Diamond (1975) extended the Ramsey model to the many-person case so as to introduce income distribution considerations and showed that, ceteris paribus, goods which account for a higher proportion of the budgets of more deserving (poor) households should have relatively lower taxes. Since, in practice, these goods are often necessities with low demand elasticities there is often a trade-off or conflict between efficiency and distributional considerations when setting indirect taxes.

Much of the literature in the 1950s and 1960s, in particular that concerning developing countries, was occupied with analysing the consequences of tariff and other trade distortions which had accumulated along with import-substituting industrialization (ISI) policies and had resulted in a high and unwieldy level of (effective) taxation. The main approach which involved the ranking of such distortions showed that the first best policy entailed the targeting of interventions directly on the existing distortions or externalities. Therefore, much of the debate centred around the question of when departures from free trade were optimal and the case for infant-industry protection (see, for example, Chenery, 1961; Bhagwati, 1964 and 1968; and Johnson, 1965). The three main arguments against free trade were: (i) monopoly power in export markets making optimal export taxes desirable; (ii) the belief that manufacturing industries generated substantial positive externalities which could not be internalized by firms and which therefore justified the use of 'first-best' *permanent* Pigovian subsidies, and (iii) the 'infant industry' argument that learning-by-doing or economies of scale led to dynamic productivity gains so that initially unprofitable industries would eventually become profitable and therefore *temporary* subsidies were desirable given imperfections in capital markets and inappropriate institutional structures.

However, it was also recognized that hindering free trade, especially through the use of quantitative restrictions (QRs), may remove an important stimulus for technological innovations and productivity growth and often lead to monopolistic structures resulting in both allocative and export inefficiencies. The additional distortion of consumption decisions inherent in import tariffs meant that they should be accepted only as 'second-best' substitutes for production subsidies, say for reasons of public finance and the difficulty or time-scale of institutional reforms.

Backed up by effective protection studies (see Balassa et al., 1971), it was also argued that exporting industries should be compensated for such tariffs through export subsidies which presumably would be much higher for manufactured exports to allow for the above externalities. Because of the difficulty in identifying differing external effects within manufacturing, a uniform level of (effective) protection was desirable (note that this does not necessarily make uniform nominal tariffs desirable). We return to the approaches suggested for the reform of existing tariff structures later. Note also that discussion of desirable departures from free trade was not concerned with issues of public finance or with constraints on revenue-raising policy instruments as was Ramsey (1927). However, it was recognized that taxation for revenue purposes should focus on final consumer goods and that intermediate taxation was only desirable when other (output) tax instruments were restricted (see Little, Scitovsky and Scott, 1970, p. 331 – henceforth LSS). This intuition anticipated the literature which was to evolve in the 1970s.

The literature on optimal indirect taxation greatly expanded in the 1970s after the publication of Diamond and Mirrlees (1971). They showed that production efficiency was desirable under very general circumstances, namely when markets were perfectly competitive, the production sector exhibited constant returns to scale, and production and preferences were convex. The requirement for production efficiency tells us that all producers (public and private) should face the same prices (and thus marginal rates of transformation in production) and there should not be any taxation of intermediate goods.

A crucial assumption of this model is that total final consumption can be taxed. The assumptions also mean that the analysis can be formulated as if producer prices (which are proportionate to shadow prices) are fixed so that taxes are totally shifted on to the consumer. Circumstances under which production efficiency may not be desirable, and the optimal nature of departures thereof, were discussed by Stiglitz and Dasgupta (1971) and involved using input taxes as proxies for output taxation when the latter was not feasible.

So far we have focused only on commodity taxation to the exclusion of income taxation. This reflects the fact that the (small) number of general results from theoretical models did not bear much resemblance to actual practice and were very sensitive to model structure (see Mirrlees, 1971, and Stern, 1984 and 1987). This is less of a constraint when analysing tax policy in developing countries since, in general, they do not raise much revenue from income taxes, a situation which is likely to prevail for some time. Efficiency considerations suggest that income from all sources should be included in the income tax base to avoid distorting individuals' allocation of time between various income-generating activities. As we will see later, policy prescriptions have therefore focused on such issues as broadening the tax base, including fringe benefits, removing loopholes, simplifying the rate structure and collection system, and reducing marginal tax rates. Since the only role for corporate taxation in the theory is as a way of taxing pure profits or collecting income taxes at source, the literature has emphasized the need to integrate the corporate and personal income taxation systems and to ensure neutrality as regards competing investments and sources of finance.

Theory has provided some useful insights into the interaction between direct and indirect taxation. Atkinson (1977) examined the interaction between direct (income) and indirect taxation and showed that uniform indirect taxation was optimal when there is an optimal poll subsidy discriminating across individuals who differ only in their wage rate and have identical preferences. In this case the optimal poll subsidy essentially takes care of income distribution and is financed by indirect tax revenue. Deaton (1979 and 1981) identified the crucial assumptions for optimality of uniform indirect taxation as individuals having both identical (constant) marginal propensities to consume and minimum (subsistence) requirements across goods, and weak separability between goods and labour so that the marginal rates of substitution between goods were independent of leisure and consumption. Deaton and Stern (1986) extended this result to the case where minimum requirements differed according to household characteristics and where there is an optimal system of family grants that depend on household structure.

Since the restrictions on preferences and the availability of instruments necessary for uniform indirect taxation to be optimal are very strict, one might assume that it is not in general desirable. Moreover, it would be hard to argue that the necessary optimal transfers (i.e. poll subsidies and family grants) are feasible especially in developing countries. The models also highlight the fact that tax and expenditure policies need to be analysed together since the optimal design of indirect taxes depends sensitively on the availability of other direct tax/transfer instruments. In developing countries such instruments are generally not available, although subsidized rations, allocated across families according to household structure, are common. In general, the more powerful the direct distributional instruments that are available the greater the argument for uniform indirect taxation.

To summarize, optimum tax theory helps us to identify certain basic principles which should be followed when designing tax and transfer systems:

- Where possible, lump-sum taxes and transfers, or close approximations, should be used to raise revenue and transfer resources. Examples include land taxes and subsidized rations linked to the demographic structure of households.
- Indirect taxation should focus on final consumption (e.g. a VAT) and relative rates should be determined by the trade-off between efficiency and equity. For example, ceteris paribus, goods with relatively high price elasticities of demand should have relatively low tax rates. From an equity viewpoint, goods which figure prominently in the budgets of low-income households should have low tax rates.
- Taxation of intermediate goods is not desirable unless it is difficult to tax the final goods which use these intermediates as inputs or there are strong distributional reasons for doing so.
- Public sector prices should be set according to the same principles as indirect taxes, e.g. marginal (social) cost for intermediate goods, with an additional element of tax for final goods.
- The conditions necessary for uniform indirect taxation to be optimal are very stringent, i.e. a powerful system of income distributional instruments which are set optimally, and the general presumption is therefore that (at least) some degree of differentiation is desirable.
- The taxation of trade should also be consistent with the above underlying principles: taxes on the import of final goods at the same rate as for the corresponding domestically produced goods, taxation of intermediate imports only when the taxation of final consumption is difficult, and

tariffs for infant-industry protection only when more direct instruments (e.g. subsidies) are not feasible.
• The taxation of certain goods on externality grounds is also desirable, for example, the taxation of road usage and energy, tobacco and alcohol consumption.

From the above we can see that optimum tax theory gives some very useful guidance on the design of the overall tax and transfer system. It highlights inter alia the central role of final goods taxation for raising revenue, the conditions under which final goods taxation is desirable, and the importance of taking into account the ability and flexibility of the expenditure side of the budget for improving income distribution. It also tells us to be wary of certain reform arguments which are commonly used, in particular the arguments for uniform final goods taxation and for the removal of subsidized rations. Although there may be important arguments for such policies on the grounds of administrative feasibility or the existence of widespread corruption, the disadvantages should also be recognized. The trade-off between equity and efficiency often found in practice when choosing tax rates suggests that there may be very strong efficiency gains arising from the design of expenditure (and other) programmes which help to alleviate the extent of, and vulnerability to, poverty and redistribute income or assets more equitably. Again, these efficiency gains should be set against the costs of such schemes.

The standard models have two important shortcomings. Firstly, for developing countries where a large proportion of the population rely directly on agriculture as their main source of income, the assumptions above are unrealistic. For example, it is widely accepted that taxation of profits from agricultural production is very difficult so that the assumption of 100 per cent (or optimal) profits taxation would be hard to accept. Also, since most farm households consume from their own produce before marketing their surplus, it is not possible to tax all consumption goods. However, if there are no agricultural profit taxes, one can treat the (non-market) agricultural sector along with the consumer sector with inputs taxed or subsidized at the optimal rates (see Diamond and Mirrlees, 1971). In this case production efficiency is desirable only in the remaining 'limited' production sector, and the relevant elasticities in the tax rules relate to marketed surplus or net trade rather than total consumption (assuming that the Diamond–Mirrlees assumptions apply to this sector).

Secondly, more often than not the tax and transfer systems in place in many developing countries bear little resemblance to those suggested by optimal tax models, even when we think in terms of a second-best optimum situation. A risk-averse government with politically sensitive expenditures to finance will be understandably wary of policies which require a major redesign of the existing system. However, it will probably be more receptive to 'welfare-improving' policy recommendations which involve small or gradual movements away from the status quo even when these are presented within a framework which involves a longer term redesign of the existing system. It is therefore helpful to have a theory of tax (or price) reform and we return to this issue below.

We have focused here on indirect taxation policy. However, the principles highlighted above also apply directly to pricing policy since we can interpret the differences between output prices and (marginal) costs as a tax. Many important industries, for example, electricity, gas, transport and fertilizers, are often in the public sector or under strict government control. The pricing of their outputs is therefore also under the control of government and should be guided by the principles outlined above. In the rest of the paper we use the terms 'indirect tax policy' and 'pricing policy' interchangeably. Before discussing what theory has to say about the transition from existing fiscal systems in developing countries we first discuss the importance of agriculture and its organization and the implications for fiscal policy.

2.2 The Importance of Agriculture

It is instructive to consider why we should give particular consideration to the agricultural sector and not just see it as one production sector among many. A common feature in developing countries is that agriculture accounts for both a large proportion of total output (25–50 per cent) and of total employment (50–75 per cent) in the economy. Therefore, agricultural policies can affect the incomes of a substantial number of households and this in turn can have implications for goods and factor markets throughout the economy.

In the 1950s agriculture was perceived by many as a declining sector which should provide food, labour and finance for a growing industrial sector. Although this 'extractive' approach towards agriculture was challenged in the 1960s (see, for example, Johnston and Mellor, 1961) – with greater emphasis being placed on agriculture as a source of increasing food supplies, essential foreign exchange earnings, and of expansion of demand for industrial outputs – it still appears to have dominated the development strategies followed in many developing countries (see, for example, Government of India, 1956).

The view of agriculture as a resource reservoir has been reflected in the taxation and pricing policies formulated by governments. Since agriculture accounts for such a high proportion of total incomes in developing countries it must be included in the tax base if sufficient revenue is to be raised to finance growing government expenditures. However, the presentation of the question as one of agricultural versus industrial taxation is not very fruitful and ignores the diversity in patterns of production, consumption and income, access to resources and technology and social rates of return within each sector. When deciding on appropriate tax and pricing policies the government must take account of this diversity of characteristics within each sector and the different constraints on policy instruments since both of these determine the efficiency and distributional implications of taxes.

Economic theory tells us that where possible revenue should be raised and distributed using 'lump-sum' instruments or with as 'little distortion' as possible. It is for this reason that land taxation is often seen as an attractive way of taxing rural households. In principle land provides a relatively easy base to measure since it has a fixed location and owners have an incentive to register property rights. These factors should ensure that administration costs are low relative to potential revenue, at least compared with other taxes. Land taxation may be seen as attractive from both efficiency and equity viewpoints since it is in inelastic supply and is unequally distributed. One could argue that land taxation based on land quality might deter investments to improve land quality and output and thus have adverse efficiency effects. But it may be possible to base valuations for land tax on such exogenous characteristics as rainfall, soil quality or access to a canal network. However, in spite of these apparent economic advantages and although historically important (see Ahmad and Stern, 1991, Chapter 8, for a discussion of India and Pakistan) land taxes presently raise very little revenue in most developing countries and attempts to impose them have been strenuously opposed, possibly reflecting the visibility of such taxes and the political influence wielded by those with large landholdings. It should also be noted that complete reliance on land taxes to the exclusion of output taxes may not be desirable when output and incomes are uncertain and complete insurance markets do not exist (see Hoff, 1991).

The inability or unwillingness of governments in developing countries to use 'lump-sum' or more direct policy instruments to raise and redistribute revenue has meant that they have had to rely predominantly on more indirect methods by manipulating the prices facing consumers and producers. Economists have therefore focused on minimizing the excess burden and distributive impact associated with 'distorted' prices. Unfortunately, the question has often been presented as a choice between agricultural and industrial taxation. Proponents of a greater reliance on agricultural taxation have pointed to the low price elasticity of aggregate supply in this sector. Some empirical studies do support such claims (see, for example, Binswanger et al., 1985) when concerned with aggregate agricultural output. However, empirical studies also show that individual elasticities can be quite high (see Askari and Cummings, 1976, and Timmer et al., 1983) and the relevant net trade elasticities are even higher (see Coady, 1992). One can also argue that although the direct effect of the taxation of agricultural output (more precisely, marketed surplus) is to decrease the income of relatively wealthy farmers the indirect effects on labour markets may imply a fall in the incomes of rural labourers whose standard of living may already be quite low. Obviously the conclusions we come to in relation to all of these arguments will ultimately depend on empirical analysis (as well as the theoretical structuring of the problem).

2.3 Public Sector Pricing

The standard rule for efficient pricing of a good produced by the public sector is price equal to marginal cost of production (i.e. P=MC). The assumptions necessary for such a rule to be optimal are that: (i) revenue can be raised and distributed using lump-sum transfers, (ii) the rest of the economy is competitive, and (iii) there are no externalities. If there are production or consumption externalities associated with the good then the optimum policy involves the use of the standard Pigovian taxes or subsidies. If lump-sum transfer instruments are not available then public-sector prices should take account of the need to raise and redistribute revenues using distortionary policy instruments. The appropriate tax, defined as (P−MC), will then depend on elasticities of demand (for efficiency) and the pattern of consumption across households (for equity). If the good in question is also an intermediate good and if production efficiency is desirable then purchases by other industries should be exempt. The potential for price discrimination that is often available means that such goods can be very useful ways for raising revenue efficiently and equitably.

If other markets are imperfect or contain certain unremovable pricing distortions then this should be allowed for when setting public-sector prices. The extent of deviation from marginal-cost pricing then depends on how the markets interact. For example, if the public-sector good is a substitute for another good which is priced above its marginal cost of production (i.e. it is taxed) then, ceteris paribus, the public sector good should also have its P>MC. Two other reasons for deviating from marginal-cost pricing are: (i) the presence of excess demand can mean that the efficient price is greater than marginal cost, and (ii) the long-term survival or investment prospects for an industry may depend on its ability to raise revenue through higher prices, reflecting the fragile budgetary conditions of some governments.

It is common in both developed and developing countries for governments to either regulate or directly control industries which exhibit external economies. Industries with external economies in production, for example utilities, exhibit decreasing marginal costs and are thus prone to monopoly control. Additionally, marginal-cost (efficient) pricing would lead to losses so that the private sector would be unwilling to invest if restricted to such pricing policies. The joint-product nature of some of these industries, for example, electricity consumption at different times of the day or by different consumers, also means that some degree of discriminatory pricing is often possible. Similarly, where sectors are thought to have externalities in consumption (e.g. health, education and water) where the utility of one person is positively affected by the consumption of the good or service of another, welfare is maximized by setting prices below the marginal cost of production. Private agents would therefore be unwilling to provide or consume the optimal level of each good or service.

For some sectors exhibiting economies of scale potential or actual competition from imports provides adequate control of their monopoly power. However, in spite of this it is common to find such sectors (e.g. coal, oil and
fertilizers) in the public sector. The reasons for this include the high transport
costs of coal which limits the degree of competition provided by imports, and
volatile prices for oil and fertilizers which creates uncertainties for consumers
and producers thus reducing consumption and production. The strategic importance of some of these products also makes public control attractive (e.g. timely
and reliable supplies of fertilisers are important for agriculture). For these
reasons profits are often either guaranteed to private producers or the industry is
placed wholly in the public sector with government revenues bearing the
uncertainty. Consumer prices are also often controlled.

It is important to understand that the objective of marginal-cost pricing is to
inform users of the extra cost incurred by the producer in providing an extra unit
of output. For example, a higher peak-time price reflects the fact that older
equipment has to be used at high levels of demand. This encourages users to
switch demand away from peak hours. One should therefore ensure that users
understand the pricing system so as to base demand decisions on prices which
reflect marginal costs. For this reason, and also because elaborate metering is
often too costly for all but the largest of consumers, the pricing system may have
to be simpler than the cost structure that it represents. Neither should one
neglect the implementation side of the process. An inefficient metering, billing
and collection system can often mean that very little revenue is raised in spite of
high prices. However, even if it is difficult to ensure that consumers face prices
reflecting marginal costs (e.g. because metering costs are too high) the very act
of disaggregating costs can have benefits by providing feedback into project
design and improving operational performance.

2.4 The Theory of Reform

As part of their efforts to industrialize through import-substituting industrialization (ISI) in the 1950s and 1960s many governments in developing countries
maintained overvalued exchange rates combined with high import tariffs or
quotas which protected import-substituting manufacturing. The absence of
offsetting subsidies for manufacturing exports meant that these were effectively
taxed. In contrast, agricultural imports were often subsidized and agricultural
exports taxed. The resulting system of taxes was made more complex and
unwieldy by ad hoc measures taken in response to budgetary and BOP crises.
Administrative and political constraints in mobilizing resources meant that
governments resorted to manipulating the prices of agricultural inputs and
outputs in order to tax farmers. These interventions included: (i) the imposition
of export taxes, (ii) the procurement of agricultural outputs at prices below

world prices, (iii) the subsidization or taxation of agricultural imports, (iv) price support to farmers, (v) subsidized agricultural inputs, and (vi) taxes on final consumer goods consumed by rural households.

One consequence of the above policies was that the system of indirect taxes and price controls bore little resemblance in practice to that suggested by the theory outlined earlier. Risk-averse governments who require revenue to finance politically sensitive expenditures are understandably wary of undertaking major reforms but are likely to be more open to implementing a series of gradual or piecemeal reforms. Therefore, a theory of reform is necessary. The theory of the second best indicated that in the presence of a set of 'unremovable' distortions in the economy it may not be welfare improving to remove another set of distortions (Lipsey and Lancaster, 1956–7). As a consequence the identification of possible welfare-improving reforms requires consideration of the interactions between the various distortions in the economy.

In the late 1960s and early 1970s the economics profession began to address the need to consider the problems encountered by governments when moving from a complex system of taxes, subsidies and controls, which had been built up in an ad hoc manner over many years, to a system where relative prices more closely reflect relative social values and the revenue and expenditure requirements of governments (see, for example, LSS, 1970, and Balassa, 1971). The sequence of steps in the reform process included (see LSS, Chapters 9 and 10):

(a) Replacing quantitative restrictions on imports with equivalent tariffs so that domestic prices did not change and the government captured the associated economic rents as revenue. Where some sectors would be undesirably adversely affected or where balance of payments difficulties would emerge, quotas could be removed more gradually, but the process should be put in place at the initial stages of the reform. Other quantitative controls (e.g. industrial licensing) which may encourage corruption and create administrative barriers to efficient resource allocation should be treated similarly.

(b) A once and for all real devaluation which is considered consistent with balance of payments equilibrium in the post-reform state, accompanied by compensating changes in import tariffs and export taxes to ensure that domestic prices for tradeables did not change. These taxes should then be reduced gradually according to an announced schedule in order to facilitate the appropriate redirection of investment.

(c) The desirable post-reform situation is one which allows for Pigovian taxes/ subsidies to correct for externalities (e.g. subsidies to labour in manufacturing), export taxes on goods where the country has monopoly power in international trade, taxes on final consumption, and input taxes where output taxes are not feasible.

(d) To ensure efficient resource allocation in such a decentralized system a variety of institutional or infrastructural changes may be necessary in order

to facilitate the movement of factors in response to the new prices which
correctly reflect relative social costs and benefits.

(e) It was recognized that budget deficits needed to be controlled in order to
avoid inflation which would otherwise undermine the objectives of reforming the price structure. This meant careful monitoring of revenue and
expenditure policies to ensure that the former was raised as efficiently as
possible (with appropriate regard for distributional consequences) and the
latter was not squandered on socially unprofitable investments or programmes.

The need to allow for the presence of distortions elsewhere in the system
when evaluating reforms was highlighted in the mid-1980s. Ahmad and Stern
(1984) emphasized the key role for shadow prices in an analysis of fiscal reform
when producer prices were distorted, and showed how marginal tax reform
analysis could be used in structuring such a discussion, in identifying welfare-
improving reforms in the existing structure and/or the most appropriate ways of
raising extra revenue. Later applied work (e.g. Newbery and Stern, 1987, and
Ahmad and Stern, 1991) re-emphasized the contribution that marginal reform
analysis could make to policy making. The flexibility of such analyses and their
plausible data requirements are but two attractive features. Another important
feature was the emphasis on the 'corrective' role for taxes in the presence of
other distortions, which is consistent with the theory of the second best.

Whilst not particularly focusing on fiscal reforms in the context of inflationary economies, LSS did recognize the difficulties such an environment would
create (see LSS, pp. 76–9, 327–9 and 373). Inflation combined with controlled
prices (i.e. public sector prices, interest rates and exchange rates) itself distorts
relative prices thus undermining the objectives of fiscal reform. Consequently
LSS saw macroeconomic stabilization policies as a pre-requisite for a successful fiscal reform programme in an inflationary environment, while fiscal reforms generally did form part of the stabilization packages advocated from the
mid-1970s in response to higher oil prices and the consequent balance of
payments (BOP) and inflationary problems of oil importing countries (see
Dornbusch, 1982).

In both the 'traditional' and monetarist approaches to stabilization, BOP and
internal disequilibria were viewed as having a common origin in budget deficits
financed by domestic credit creation. The reforms advocated to restore equilibrium included both a real devaluation to encourage expenditure switching away
from tradeables (and an increase in the production of tradeables) and fiscal
reforms to raise revenue and/or reduce expenditures and therefore cut budget
deficits. The fiscal reform process advocated in LSS incorporates this
stabilization process but also highlights the need for both sequencing and the
appropriate reforms of the pricing and institutional structures. The latter elements became the central focus of the structural reforms of the mid 1980s (see

Ferreira, 1991) which in combination with stabilization policies have formed the major policy components of structural adjustment programmes (SAPs).

The structural reforms have entailed policy changes which aim at ensuring that resources are allocated and used more efficiently. They include the reform of the price structure, institutional reform, training, trade liberalization, privatization and improving the operation of markets. The reallocation of existing public expenditures is often included as part of structural adjustment, e.g. increasing investment expenditures on infrastructure and human capital and reducing 'wasteful' public-sector subsidies. Obviously then, fiscal reform in the broad sense, that is, reforming the way revenue is collected and allocated between various expenditures, is a crucial part of structural adjustment. Fiscal reforms have therefore played a dual role in SAPs; firstly as a key component of the strategy to improve domestic resource mobilization necessitated by the reduced availability and higher cost of external finance and secondly as part of the strategy to enhance the efficiency of resource allocation in both the public sector, and via the reduction of distortions, in the private sector.

3 FISCAL POLICY – PRACTICE AND REFORM

In this section we first describe the structure of fiscal systems in developing countries, identify the most important sources of revenue and show that the status quo often bears little resemblance to the appropriate structure indicated by theory. We then give a brief description of the nature of fiscal reform attempts in the 1980s. Experiences with these reforms suggest a number of areas where reform may prove most fruitful and help to identify a number of pitfalls that can occur. We emphasize that reform of the administration system and the tax system should be undertaken simultaneously, with the former having strong implications for the feasibility of the latter. We also underline the fact that the role of the revenue-raising instruments will be determined to a large extent by the range of policy instruments that are available for redistributing income and wealth (or assets). For a more detailed description of existing fiscal systems and of previous reform attempts see Burgess and Stern, 1993, and references therein.

3.1 Fiscal Policy in Practice

The level of government revenue and the manner in which it is raised varies across countries as a result of a combination of historical, social, political and economic factors. A number of variables such as export ratios, literacy rates, urbanization, and the monetization and openness of economies are all correlated with the level and structure of taxation (see, for example, Musgrave, 1969; Tait et al., 1979; and Tanzi, 1981 and 1987).

Musgrave (1959 and 1969) argues that as economies develop the number of market transactions increase and the government administration system becomes more efficient and sophisticated. This enables a widening of the tax base, in the sense of a greater availability of feasible tax instruments, and a more effective coverage of existing bases. The combined effect is a reduction in evasion and greater diversity in sources of revenue (see also Gillis, 1989). One therefore sees an increased emphasis on domestic taxes on goods and services and, as production and employment become more formalized and administrative and accounting procedures more widespread, the taxation of individual incomes and levying of social security contributions become more important. Also, the pressure to provide social services increases with urbanization, and subsidization of these services has led to increasing claims on government expenditures necessitating larger government revenues.

In general total tax revenue and the level of direct taxation both increase with national income with a consequent decline in the importance of indirect taxation in total government revenue. On average developing countries collect 15–20 per cent of GDP as tax revenue compared to around 30 per cent in developed countries. Whereas developed countries rely mainly on direct taxation (20 per cent of GDP and 64 per cent of total tax revenue), developing countries rely more heavily on indirect taxation (10 per cent of GDP and 60 per cent of total tax revenue).[1] Among developing countries there is a greater reliance on trade taxes, this reliance being negatively correlated with income levels. Although import taxes are on average more important, the poorest countries often rely heavily on export taxes on primary commodities, especially in Sub-Saharan Africa. High levels of direct taxation in developing countries often reflect a heavy dependence on corporate taxes levied on private companies responsible for the extraction, processing and export of natural resources (e.g. Botswana, Congo, Gabon and Venezuela). Such taxes are also administratively easy to collect. Where personal income tax has raised substantial revenues the base has often been confined mainly to employees of the public sector or foreign corporations with the concomitant problems which are associated with small bases and high marginal tax rates.

Governments often nationalize certain activities (e.g. resource extraction, processing and export or agricultural marketing boards) with profits accruing as non-tax revenue. This is commonly seen as an effective way of taxing either producers or users of the commodity. However, the nationalization of industries or the procurement of commodities by marketing boards can reflect objectives other than revenue raising, for example, the stabilization of producer prices, the operation of agricultural extension programmes, the development and maintenance of rural infrastructure, ensuring food security and quality, and the coordination of export activities (see Abbott, 1987). Countries which rely heavily on the taxation of single commodities often encounter problems arising from the instability of commodity prices and hence revenue. Since the revenue raised from the government control of certain activities depends closely on the pricing policies followed, and since public-sector pricing policies and indirect tax policies are analytically identical, we can include this form of revenue under indirect tax revenue with the consequent increase in the importance of this source for developing countries.

The low level of income taxation in developing countries reflects the importance of sectors where information gathering is extremely difficult because of the large number of small-scale income generating activities (e.g. in agriculture, small firms or the informal sector) where literacy is very low, record keeping is very poor or non-existent, and administrative systems are often weak (see e.g. Musgrave, 1969, and Goode, 1984). This limits the scope for direct taxation thus requiring other tax instruments. For example, given the difficulties involved in obtaining information on and measuring income in agriculture, governments have resorted to manipulating prices or procuring outputs sometimes with large efficiency losses. Since agriculture accounts for such a high proportion of national income in developing countries it cannot be excluded from the revenue base (regardless of the difficulties involved) if adequate revenue is to be raised. The task then is to raise the required revenue as efficiently and equitably as possible.

3.2 Fiscal Reform in Practice

The 1980s saw a number of attempts at fiscal reform in developing countries, for example, Columbia, Indonesia, Jamaica, Korea, Malawi, Mexico, Sri Lanka and Turkey (see Burgess and Stern, 1993, for a summary). There were a number of factors which led to these reforms. The system of taxation had developed in an ad hoc manner over time in response to increasing government expenditures and internal and external shocks. There was an over-reliance on particular taxes and narrow bases. Excise taxes were levied on a small range of commodities with inelastic demand (e.g. alcohol, tobacco, petroleum, beverages and sugar). Trade taxes were viewed as convenient tax handles by poor countries with small domestic manufacturing bases and weak administrative systems. Import taxes, which also provided protection consistent with the ISI policies popular at the time, became the single most important source of revenue. Quantity restrictions (e.g. import quotas and industrial licensing) were pervasive and gave rise to corruption and limited the ability of the fiscal system to respond to shocks. The income tax base was narrow and the extent of evasion reflected the large number of loop-holes along with complicated and unclear laws. The net result was a system which was inefficient, inequitable, beset with complications and anomalies and unable to cope with rising expenditure requirements or external shocks.

An increased emphasis on outward rather than inward oriented industrialization policies meant that large and variable import duties and quotas were no longer seen as compatible with growth and were recognized as being biased against exports (see Balassa, 1971 and 1983). In many cases import restrictions led to monopoly rents and an inefficient manufacturing industry. The pressure for reform was further exacerbated by the oil price shocks of the mid and late 1970s, to which the initial response was a large international transfer of funds (especially from oil-rich states) to developing countries, but the hike in real interest rates and the squeeze on foreign borrowing in the early 1980s forced countries to search for internal solutions to their BOP disequilibria and rising budget deficits. Fiscal reform became inevitable and was seen as such by major international institutions such as the World Bank and the IMF who made structural adjustment a pre-requisite for receiving loans.

Fiscal reforms have focused on three areas: the direct and indirect tax systems and the administrative system. For the most part, reform of the direct tax system concentrated on broadening the income tax base by including fringe benefits, reducing exemptions and removing loopholes. At the same time marginal rates were usually decreased, while greater effort was put into simplifying and clarifying the relevant tax laws and improving enforcement and collection procedures. The integration of personal and corporate income taxes was given greater priority. Although these reforms did not usually result in increased revenues they did generally lead to a decrease in evasion and a more equitable distribution of the burden – it is widely believed that loopholes and exemptions benefited mostly the rich who could easily reclassify incomes so as to lower their tax burdens. The future revenue potential of the direct tax system has also been enhanced.

Reform of the indirect tax system has been central to most of the fiscal reform packages. The main emphasis has been on a switch from trade taxes to a broader tax base. This is in line with trade liberalization policies and enhances efficiency. However the redirection of taxes towards domestic products and final consumption (domestically produced and imported) is often limited by a relatively small domestic manufacturing industry and weak administrative system.

According to Cnossen (1991, p. 1) the successful introduction and operation of VAT systems has been 'the most significant event in the evolution of tax structure in the latter half of this century'. A number of developing countries have implemented a VAT system, or variants of it, and achieved impressive success in terms of revenue raised, even in the short term. Many other developing countries have created 'sales tax rings' where 'members' are rebated input taxes – those outside or unregistered are not however entitled to such rebates. Such rings are often a prelude to the adoption of a full VAT system (see Tait, 1988). The advantages of a VAT system are: equal tax rates can be imposed on both imported and domestically produced goods and services; the inclusion of services broadens the base; it eliminates input taxation, thus avoiding the production inefficiency associated with it and the concomitant cascading effects; exports can have a zero rate with input taxes rebated, thus removing any bias against exporting firms; it contains in-built administrative checks which help reduce evasion and encourages firms to improve administration with consequent knock-on advantages in terms of improved management practices.

However the operation of a VAT system does impose administrative demands, both for the government and the private sector. For instance, all firms must keep records of VAT paid on inputs and balance these against VAT payable on their outputs in order to evaluate, and provide proof of, the net amount payable to the revenue authorities. This involves a basic degree of education and literacy on the part of the population. But these disadvantages have often been exaggerated and many countries with relatively unsophisticated administrative systems have implemented VAT systems successfully in terms of the numbers of firms covered and revenue raised. It can also be the case that the audit trail involved in the collection of VAT provides information which may be very useful in improving the measurement and collection of other taxes.

Although indirect taxation is limited in its effect on income redistribution, concern thereof can be incorporated in the form of administratively viable differentiation. For example, one could have a standard VAT rate (say 10–15%) with exemptions for food and higher rates for luxuries. If this is combined with excises on certain goods (e.g. alcohol, tobacco and petroleum products) which may be price inelastic and involve consumption externalities then such a system encourages production and consumption efficiency, incorporates distributional concerns, raises substantial revenue which increases in line with GNP (i.e. is 'buoyant'), and is administratively implementable (see Ahmad and Stern, 1991). If such a system could be coupled with an effective income support mechanism then much will have been achieved.

The reforms of the administrative system have shown that much revenue can be raised, even within existing systems, by investing in improved administrative practices and enhancing the skills of personnel and management. Much can be achieved by improving the conditions under which tax officials operate, for example, clarifying the legal system, giving officials the necessary manpower and authority to implement taxation, and ensuring that administrative constraints are recognized when selecting tax bases and setting rates. Appropriate incentives can be introduced to encourage efficiency and reduce corruption. Badly conceived tax structures with small bases, extensive exemptions, loopholes and low pay can create severe difficulties for and demoralize tax personnel leading to inefficient operations and corruption. However, along with such infrastructural investments should go the appropriate controls. Staff should be monitored for performance, measures to detect inefficiencies and corruption should be introduced and the powers to dismiss errant staff increased. An example of what can be achieved is provided by the experience of Ghana which in the latter half of the 1980s introduced substantial reforms in the tax administration including bonuses for reaching revenue targets, the recruitment of qualified accountants and improved powers for dismissing errant staff. The result of these and other reforms was that revenue increased by 7–8 per cent of GDP in just over three years.

Changes in administrative structures are also desirable. For example, combining the collection of all taxes under one authority (and even under one roof) can have substantial rewards through coordination of information gathering, assessment and enforcement. In developing countries the collection and processing of information on tax bases to enable assessment is often particularly difficult. Agricultural income taxes are often impossible to collect in a cost-effective, reliable and efficient manner with the consequent need to rely more on price controls. In some cases (e.g. with the self-employed and small businesses) self-assessment may be a more appropriate way to proceed, although the desirability or ability to shift the burden of assessment onto private agents depends crucially on the level of education and literacy of the population and the prevalence of an adequate standard of book-keeping.

Since all the above factors will change over time so too will the nature of the fiscal system which can be feasibly implemented. The early adoption of certain policies (e.g. investments in the administration infrastructure) and policy instruments (e.g. VAT and social protection systems) may enhance this process and such reforms should be evaluated in the light of the consequent efficiency gains resulting from a more efficient tax collection mechanism. The success of VAT in many instances has taught us that pessimism can be unwarranted and may reflect a complacent administration system (see Tait, 1988). Vested interests, whether they be administrators who fear change or have illegally benefited from inefficient practices, or private agents who have managed to avoid or evade tax under the present system, will always oppose reforms under many banners.

It is also important to view the fiscal system from the viewpoint of the taxpayer. Evasion in developing countries is rife and as there are numerous ways that individuals and firms evade tax much of the intended tax base escapes the tax net. Individuals under-report incomes, and information and measurement problems can make this hard to detect. Often the rich are in a better position to reclassify or under-report incomes so that any progression in the system may be illusory. The higher tax rates imposed on a smaller base often cause great discomfort and cultivate an adversarial relationship between taxpayers and administrators, which in turn perpetuates evasion.

Failure to collect taxes also sends the wrong signals to taxpayers, often making it difficult to redress the situation without creating undesirable distress – tax amnesties are a popular response to this problem but must be combined with a public perception that rules will subsequently be strictly enforced with no further amnesties. With indirect taxation, under-invoicing and smuggling of imports and exports are the main problem (see Pitt, 1981, and Alano, 1984). The pervasiveness of smuggling and so on is usually closely associated with high tax rates (relative to the cost of smuggling) so that lowering these rates can often reduce evasion substantially and even increase revenues.

A number of indirect measures can be adopted in the fight against evasion. The incorporation of administrative constraints into the decision as to which tax bases and instruments to choose ensures that collection is feasible. Proper monitoring of how public funds are allocated can allay public fears that their tax contributions are being squandered or flow directly into the pockets of corrupt officials. 'Earmarking' a portion of the revenue collected for certain 'local' expenditures can be useful to this end. Simplifying collection and assessment procedures diminishes the burden on taxpayers and administrators alike, and broader bases ensure that everybody pays their 'fair share'. The extent of evasion in developing countries means that it needs to be tackled on all fronts if it is to be reduced to any noticeable extent.

The design and/or reform of any fiscal system must not be undertaken in a political vacuum. To do so will increase the chances of failure, and diminishes the future status of tax advisers as well as the prospects for future reform. Interest groups are likely to try to block reforms or demand sweeping concessions in order to protect their incomes and privileges. Very often it is the rich who are most effective at such activities and, unlike the poor who are less coordinated, they are often a very influential political lobbying force (see Gillis, 1989). The absence of significant wealth and property taxation is often explained in this way. Wealth is usually concentrated in the hands of a few and therefore its taxation on distributional grounds is attractive. Very often it is the ease with which such wealth (eg. 'immobile' or property wealth) can be targeted directly which ensures fierce opposition to such tax handles (see Ascher, 1989; Bates, 1989; Bird and Oldman, 1964; Wald, 1959). The case of land taxation (with land concentrated in the hands of a relatively small number of politically influential landlords) is a case in point: it is a very attractive source of revenue from both efficiency and equity perspectives but its significance has diminished over time. However, certain types of wealth are difficult to observe, measure and assess for tax. Financial capital is often very mobile (domestically and internationally) and is easy to conceal or reclassify so as to make use of loopholes or lower marginal rates. Often the removal of such loopholes and the widening of the base combined with lower tax rates results in greater compliance and reduces collection costs.

In general the mobility of capital can severely limit the effectiveness with which it can be taxed without large efficiency losses. Therefore, the scope for revenues from the taxation of interest income or corporate income is restricted. But problems such as capital flight can arise for many other reasons, for example, interest rate differentials, expected devaluations when exchange rates are overvalued, and high inflation or debt arising from excessive budget deficits. So sensible macroeconomic policy is crucial in preventing capital flight (see Buiter, 1990; Pastor, 1990). In the present climate of high real interest rates and constraints on foreign borrowing, reform packages should bear in mind the consequences for investment and growth when determining the appropriate level of capital taxation. Revenue objectives need to be set against the desire to attract foreign direct investment and finance. One type of response to such issues has been to set up tax-free investment zones and/or provide tax holidays while others emphasize the need to rely on indirect taxes which do not discourage investments (see Shah and Toye, 1979; Gersovitz, 1987).

Another issue that needs to be considered when designing or reforming tax systems in large or federal economies concerns revenue sharing and autonomy over fiscal instruments (see World Bank, 1988, for discussion). There are a number of arguments for the decentralization of decision making to provinces or states so that they have more autonomy over the amount of revenue collected, how it is collected and how it is allocated over various expenditures. Firstly, lower tiers of government may have more information on the feasibility of using various policy instruments and on the 'appropriate' tax bases. This can reduce the collection costs of tax revenue. Secondly, incentives to evade taxes may be reduced if taxpayers see the benefits brought about through their financing of 'local' expenditures. Such 'earmarking' of expenditures is common in practice, even in more centrally run systems. Thirdly, where regions are responsible for public-sector pricing they are less likely to argue for low user charges, and for many publicly provided services this is often desirable from both efficiency and equity viewpoints.

However, it is important to recognize that decentralization of fiscal decision making also has disadvantages. Firstly, the mobility of goods, services and factors suggests that tax policies need to be set nationally to minimize efficiency costs. Secondly, the high fixed capital costs of certain infrastructural investments may mean that, in some regions at least, such investments benefit from central funding. Thirdly, decentralization may create vested interests whose objectives differ fundamentally from the 'national welfare'. Fourthly, macroeconomic policy needs to be controlled at the national level and this requires control over the size and financing of regional budget deficits. Fifthly, the information arguments for decentralization are reduced when effective information transfer mechanisms between centre and region exist. It may be that flexibility is the key issue.

A judgement on the desirability and extent of decentralization should therefore identify and balance the pros and cons carefully. Where decentralization is thought desirable one should ensure that the rules of operation are as clear and simple as possible, that cooperation between the various administrations in terms of exchange of information and harmonization of fiscal policies is maximized, and that all parties are given adequate incentives to facilitate the achievement of national objectives. One should also ensure that regions are responsive to reforms initiated from the centre – this has been an important issue, even a stumbling block, for fiscal reform in India.

4 FISCAL REFORM AND SOCIAL EXPENDITURES

Throughout our discussion of theoretical models we emphasized that the appropriate fiscal design depended sensitively on the nature of policy instruments which were available to redistribute income. For this and other reasons the revenue and the expenditure sides of the budget need to be analysed simultaneously. In this section we take a brief look at expenditures, concentrating on what we call social expenditures. We define the purpose of these expenditures as raising and maintaining the standard of living of the less well-off groups in society. For a more detailed discussion of the objectives of social expenditures, the role of government, and some of the issues discussed below see Ahmad et al. (1991), Burgess et al. (1992), Burgess and Stern (1991), Drèze and Sen (1989) and Stern (1991).

There are obviously many ways of helping underprivileged groups in society. We can, for instance, distinguish between 'income support' and 'direct provisioning', where the former concentrates on increasing the purchasing power of the underprivileged (e.g. food subsidies or employment schemes) and the latter involves the direct intervention of the state in providing basic necessities (e.g. food, health care, sanitation and education) thus bypassing private markets. Both methods require some form of targeting or selection mechanism whether it be administrative selection (e.g. food rations targeted according to family composition and/or income), market selection (e.g. universal subsidies), or self-selection (e.g. public work schemes with low wages used as a screening device). Whatever targeting mechanism or indicator is used it should be easily observable, correlated with the problems we are trying to solve, and should not have indirect consequences which frustrate the objectives of the expenditure. For example, it is widely accepted that the use of income levels or 'poverty lines' as a selection mechanism is seriously flawed because of the difficulties in observing incomes accurately, especially in rural areas. Moreover there are other determinants of welfare besides income and these are often not strongly correlated with income. We may also wish to focus separately on issues such as health, sanitation and nutrition which, because of high fixed costs or production and consumption externalities, will not be provided by the market or will be provided or consumed at sub-optimal levels.

It is likely that the appropriate social expenditure programme (SEP) will consist of a combination of both income support and direct provisioning together with various targeting mechanisms. The best combination will depend on a number of factors including administrative capacity, and how the schemes interact with each other and with existing individual and group-support mechanisms, and so on. These and other factors will determine the costs and benefits of the various schemes.

As with all programmes, projects and reforms, SEPs should be subjected to the rigours of social cost-benefit analysis – we need to identify the direct and indirect impacts and value them accordingly. This is sometimes referred to as cost-effectiveness (see, for example, World Bank, 1986b). It must additionally be remembered that there are costs associated with the raising of public revenue to finance SEPs – efficiency costs resulting from the misallocation of resources and the administrative costs of collection. Therefore, the optimal level of social expenditure will depend both on the cost-effectiveness of the schemes which make up the SEP and the cost of raising finance. In general, the less effective government schemes are in alleviating deprivation the lower the desirable level of social expenditure.

Universal schemes have the direct advantage that they attract wide public support for their retention when expenditures are being cut and when more targeted programmes may be more vulnerable, and many argue that they are in general a most cost-effective approach. However experience has indicated that different schemes work best in different circumstances.

A view widely held is that well-targeted direct provisioning schemes (e.g. for sanitation, nutrition, health, education, literacy and training) have two crucial features which make them more desirable. Firstly, they minimize the expenditure required by eliminating the leakage of subsidies to non-targeted groups. This is particularly relevant in revenue constrained economies with limited (and distortionary) tax handles. Secondly, they often involve investment in human capital which enhances the long-run growth potential of the economy. Public works schemes with in-built self-selection through low wages also score well on this count. Moreover the services involved are often those characterized by consumption and production externalities. However, the institutional framework necessary for the effective implementation of these schemes may not be in place and the necessary institutional reforms may be expensive and take some time to carry out. It may therefore be the case that the existing schemes, be they universal or targeted, are the most effective in the short run and should not be eliminated until more cost-effective schemes can be put in place (see Ribe et al., 1990).

The above discussion highlights the fact that the 'appropriate' SEP will vary across countries and that this programme should change over time as conditions and constraints change. This has an obvious implication for reform analysis: the appropriate reforms will depend on the initial point, the environment in which one is operating and the way and speed at which the environment is expected to change.

Although the above framework for analysing social expenditure reform (and fiscal reform on the whole) is valid in all circumstances, in practice reforms have generally been implemented as part of SAPs undertaken within the context of (often severe) macroeconomic disequilibria. To emphasize the implications which this has for social expenditures and objectives it is useful to briefly recall the nature of SAPs.

SAPs have generally entailed a package of expenditure switching (e.g. devaluation), expenditure reducing (e.g. fiscal and monetary restraint) and supply side (e.g. trade liberalization and agricultural price reform) policies. These policy reforms have implications for income distribution and poverty; devaluation, for example, benefits net producers of tradeables at the expense of net consumers while fiscal restraint may lead to cutbacks in food subsidies and other social expenditures and increased user charges for social services and utilities. It has been argued that both the rural and urban poor have suffered welfare losses as a result of SAPs (see Glewwe and de Tray, 1988, and Bourguignon and Morrison, 1992, for discussion).

Concerns with poverty and deprivation were downgraded in the first half of the 1980s but research at UNICEF which called for 'adjustment with a human face' helped to return the issue of social protection to centre stage (see Cornia, Jolly and Stewart, 1987). This was further reinforced by Demery and Addison (1987) who argued that careful monitoring of social expenditures was required. The renewed importance attached to alleviating poverty resulted in the 1991 World Development Report (World Bank, 1991) being devoted to the issue of poverty and its alleviation.

The above highlights the importance of reallocating and probably increasing social expenditures as part of structural adjustment. The content of the SEP should reflect the issues discussed earlier in this section. For example, if the infrastructural and institutional base for targeting social expenditures towards nutrition, health, education, training, and so on is not adequate and takes time to reform, then in the short run it may be desirable to retain universal subsidies and subsidized food rations, as well as instituting public works programmes. In the words of Ribe et al. (1990, p. 10): 'What is crucial is that subsidies that are effective in reaching the poor should not be reduced or eliminated unless and until alternative means of reaching the poor are in place'. This may involve keeping agricultural prices below world prices. In an analysis of agricultural price reforms in Pakistan, Coady (1992) argues that although low procurement prices have very large efficiency losses they also have very attractive distributional effects – the former reflects the high price elasticity of marketed wheat surpluses while the latter reflects the fact that small farmers and landless labourers are net consumers of wheat. The desirability of these policies in certain situations highlights the fact that what are the 'right prices' depends sensitively on taxes and distortions elsewhere in the economy and the nature of policy instruments available to the government to redistribute income and for social protection.

Some countries, for example Indonesia and Chile, have managed to maintain social expenditures while successfully implementing stabilization policies. The use of labour-intensive infrastructural programmes have also been common, for example the Emergency Social Fund (ESF) scheme in Bolivia and Programme of Actions to Mitigate the Social Costs of Adjustment (PAMSCAD) scheme in Ghana (see World Bank, 1991). One must not, however, overestimate what can be achieved by reallocating expenditures within a fixed social expenditure budget. The importance of reforming the fiscal system as a whole to enable extra revenue to be raised in an efficient manner must not be lost sight of, especially since the demand for social expenditures is likely to increase during periods of structural adjustment.

5   SUMMARY AND CONCLUSIONS

In this paper we have argued that economic theory has provided useful insights into what constitutes a 'desirable' or 'appropriate' fiscal system. The modern theory of public finance has focused on the implications of fiscal policy for efficiency and equity and set the question of what is 'desirable' or 'appropriate' in these terms. Using optimal taxation theory, we have identified certain basic principles which should be used to guide the design of fiscal systems. These focus on the importance of lump-sum transfers, the role of taxation of final consumption, the stringent requirements for uniform indirect taxation to be optimal, the importance of realizing that most feasible policy instruments have consequences for both efficiency and equity, the need to consider the range of policy instruments that are available and how they interact, and the implications for both trade policy and public-sector pricing.

Throughout we have emphasized that the appropriate fiscal policy will depend on what is administratively feasible to implement. We have argued that difficulties in measuring incomes, in particular agricultural incomes, often necessitated more indirect methods of raising revenue. Attention was drawn to the importance of agriculture in developing countries and the consequent implications for fiscal policy given the need to use more distortionary revenue-raising instruments. We also discussed some additional issues which need to be addressed when setting public-sector prices. As with other instruments, constraints on the ability to raise revenue in this manner were important, but we argued that the actual process of disaggregating costs could have important feedbacks into project design and operational performance. The need for adequate resources to ensure that the implementation of pricing policies and the collection of revenue were effective was underlined. We also suggested that the design of public-sector pricing often provided the potential to raise substantial revenue efficiently and equitably.

Our discussion of the theory of reform showed that many of the recommendations made in the early 1970s concerning fiscal reform found their way into the stabilization and structural adjustment packages of the 1980s. The literature in the early 1970s focused on the need for institutional reform as well as reform in the structure of taxation and expenditure. The role of sequencing was emphasized as was the importance of removing quantitative controls as soon as possible. Budgetary and political constraints were incorporated through the gradual or piecemeal approach to reform. Control of inflationary pressures was seen as necessary before fiscal reform could proceed and for prices to play their intended role in allocating resources efficiently. We also argued that while fiscal reform is a crucial element in any stabilization package it is also important in its own right, even in the absence of BOP and internal disequilibria.

The description of the existing fiscal systems and recent reform attempts in developing countries indicated that reform was both necessary and possible. We showed that useful lessons can be drawn from recent reform experiences. We emphasized that reform of the administrative system and the structure of taxation should be undertaken simultaneously, and that the former determined in many ways the scope for the latter.

Throughout we have emphasized that the revenue and expenditure sides of the budget have to be considered together. The availability of policy instruments which are efficient at redistributing income strongly influences the role for the revenue-raising side of the budget. The more powerful the former the more taxation should focus on efficiency. We argued however that the speed at which reforms of the social expenditure programmes could be implemented might be constrained by institutional, infrastructural and financial factors. This has implications for the desirability of retaining existing social expenditures in the short run. Also, evaluation of the cost-effectiveness of social expenditure programmes should allow for the efficiency gains from releasing other tax instruments to focus more on efficiency when raising revenue – this is a consequence of the strong trade-off between efficiency and equity often found in practice.

All in all, theory and evidence do suggest that much can be done to improve the way in which revenue is raised and allocated in developing countries. While there are constraints on the speed at which such reforms can be implemented one should not be over-pessimistic. Experience has shown that much can be done in a short time if the political will exists. But common sense is required and the fiscal analyst should be aware of administrative and political constraints that will inevitably impinge on the reform process. Fiscal reform should therefore be viewed as a medium- to long-run objective, and both the content of reform packages and the speed at which they can be implemented will vary according to the country under consideration. A substantial part of any tax analyst's work will involve understanding the environment in which the fiscal system must operate and on how this environment will (or can be) changed over time. This is not an easy task but can be a rewarding one.

NOTE

1.   See Burgess and Stern (1993, Tables 1 and 2).

REFERENCES

Abbott, J.C. (1987), *Agricultural Marketing Enterprises for the Developing World* (Cambridge: Cambridge University Press).

Ahmad, S.E., J.P. Drèze, J. Hills and A.K. Sen (eds) (1991), *Social Security in Developing Countries* (Oxford: Clarendon Press).

Ahmad, S.E. and N.H. Stern (1984), 'The Theory of Reform and Indian Indirect Taxes, *Journal of Public Economics*, 25, pp. 259–95.

Ahmad, S.E. and N.H. Stern (1987), *Alternative Sources of Government Revenue: Illustrations from India, 1979–80*, in David M.G. Newbery and Nicholas H. Stern (eds) (1987).

Ahmad, S.E. and N.H. Stern (1989), *Taxation for Developing Countries*, in H. Chenery and T.N. Srinivasan (eds) (1989).

Ahmad, S.E. and N.H. Stern (1991), *The Theory and Practice of Tax Reform in Developing Countries* (Cambridge: Cambridge University Press).

Alano, B.P. Jr (1984), 'Import Smuggling in the Philippines: An Economic Analysis', *Journal of Philippine Development*, 11, pp. 157–90.

Anand, S. and R. Kanbur (1990), 'Public Policy and Basic Needs Provision: Intervention and Achievement in Sri Lanka', in Drèze and Sen (eds), *The Political Economy of Hunger* (Oxford: Clarendon Press) (New York: Oxford University Press).

Ascher, W. (1989), 'Risk, Politics and Tax Reform: Lessons from some Latin American Experiences' in M. Gillis (ed.) (1989).

Askari, H. and J.T. Cummings (1976), *Agricultural Supply Response: A Survey of Econometric Evidence* (New York: Praeger).

Atkinson, A.B. (1977), 'Optimal Taxation and the Direct Versus Indirect Tax Controversy', *Canadian Journal of Economics*, vol. 10, no. 4 (Nov.), pp. 590–606.

Atkinson, A.B. (1987), 'James M. Buchanan's Contributions to Economics', *The Scandinavian Journal of Economics*, 89, pp. 5–15.

Atkinson, A.B. (1989), *Poverty and Social Security* (London: Harvester Wheatsheaf).

Atkinson, A.B. and J.E. Stiglitz (1980), *Lectures on Public Economics* (New York: McGraw-Hill).

Bailey, M.J. (1956), 'The Welfare Costs of Inflationary Finance', *Journal of Political Economy*, 64, pp. 93–100.

Balassa, B. (1982), *Development Strategies in Semi-Industrial Countries* (Johns Hopkins University Press for World Bank).

Balassa, B. (1983), 'Policy Responses to External Shocks in Sub-Saharan African Countries', *Journal of Policy Modeling*, vol. 5, pp. 75–105.

Balassa, B. (1989), 'Outward Orientation', in H. Chenery and T.N. Srivinasan (eds) (1989).

Balassa, B. et al. (1971), *The Structure of Protection in Developing Countries* (Baltimore: Johns Hopkins University Press).

Bates, R.H. (1989), 'A Political Scientist Looks at Tax Reform', in M. Gillis (ed.) (1989).

Best, M.H. (1976), 'Political Power and Tax Revenues in Central America', *Journal of Development Economics*, 3 (Mar.), pp. 49–82.

Bhagwati, J.N. (1964), 'The Pure Theory of International Trade: A Survey', *Economic Journal*, 74, pp. 1–84.

Bhagwati, J.N. (1968), 'On the Equivalence of Tariffs and Quotas', in R.E. Baldwin et al. (eds), *Trade, Growth and the Balance of Payments: Essays in Honour of Gottfreid Harberler* (Amsterdam: North Holland).

Bhagwati, J.N. (1987), 'Directly-Unproductive-Profit-Seeking Activities', in J. Eatwell, M. Milgate and P. Newman (eds), *The New Palgrave* (London: Macmillan).

Binswanger, H., Y. Mundlak, Maw-cheng Ying and A. Bowers (1985), Working Paper 1985/3, World Bank, Commodity Studies and Project Division.

Bird, R.M. and O. Oldman (eds) (1964), *Readings on Taxation in Developing Countries* (Baltimore: Johns Hopkins University Press).

Bird, R.M. (1989), 'The Administrative Dimension of Tax Reform in Developing Countries', in M. Gillis (ed.) (1989).

Bird, R.M. and O. Oldman (eds) (1990), *Taxation in Developing Countries* (Baltimore: Johns Hopkins University Press).

Boiteux, M. (1956), 'Sur la gestion des monopoles publics astreints à l'equilibre budgétaire', *Revue d'Économie Politique* (66) 1, jan.–fev., pp. 43–74.

Boiteux, M. (1971), 'On the Management of Public Monopolies subject to Budgetary Constraints', *Journal of Economic Theory*, vol. 3, no. 3 (Sept.), pp. 219–40. Translation of 1956 *Econometrica* article.

Bourguignon, F. and C. Morrisson (1992), *Adjustment and Equity in Developing Countries: A New Approach* (Paris: OECD Development Centre).

Brennan, G. and J.M. Buchanan (1980), *The Power to Tax* (New York: Cambridge University Press).

Brennan, G. and J.M. Buchanan (1985), *The Reason of Rules* (Cambridge: Cambridge University Press).

Buchanan, J.M. (1966), 'Externality in Tax Response', *South Economic Journal*, 33(1) (July), pp. 35–42.

Buiter, W.H. (1990), *Principles of Budgetary and Financial Policy* (London: Harvester Wheatsheaf).

Burgess, R.S.L. and N.H. Stern (1991), *Social Security in Developing Countries: What, Why, Who and How?*, in S.E. Ahmad, J. P. Drèze, J. Hills and A.K. Sen (eds) (1991).

Burgess, R.S.L. and N.H. Stern (1993), 'Taxation and Development', *Journal of Economic Literature*.

Burgess, R.S.L. et al. (1992), 'Social Protection and Structural Adjustment', STICERD, London School of Economics (mimeo).

Chenery, H.B. (1961), 'Comparative Advantage and Development Policy', *American Economic Review*, 51, pp. 18–51.

Chenery, H.B. and T.N. Srinivasan (eds) (1989), *Handbook of Development Economics* (Amsterdam: North Holland).

Cnossen, S. (1991), 'Design of the Value Added Tax: Lessons from Experience', in Javad Khalizadeh-Shirazi and Anwar Shah (eds) (1991).

Coady, D.P. (1992), 'Agricultural Pricing Policies in Developing Countries: The Case of Pakistan 1960–88', PhD submitted to University of London (London School of Economics), Feb. 1992.

Cornia, G., R. Jolly and F. Stewart (1987), *Adjustment with a Human Face: Protecting the Vulnerable and Promoting Growth* (Oxford: Clarendon Press).

Deaton, A.S. (1979), 'Optimally Uniform Commodity Taxes', *Economic Letters*, vol. 2, no. 4, pp. 357–61.

Deaton, A.S. (1981), 'Optimal Taxes and the Structure of Preferences', *Econometrica*, vol. 49, no. 5 (Sept.), pp. 1245–60.

Deaton, A.S. and Nicholas H. Stern (1986), 'Optimally Uniform Commodity Taxes, Taste Differences and Lump-Sum Grants', *Economics Letters*, 20, pp. 263–6.

Demery, L. and T. Addison (1987), *The Alleviation of Poverty Under Structural Adjustment* (Washington DC: The World Bank).

Diamond, P.A. (1975), 'A Many-Person Ramsey Tax Rule', *Journal of Public Economics*, vol. 4, no. 4 (Nov.), pp. 335–42.

Diamond, P.A. and J.A. Mirrlees (1971), 'Optimal Taxation and Public Production: Part 1 – Production Efficiency, and Part 2 – Tax Rules', *American Economic Review*, vol. 61, pp. 8–27 (Mar.) and pp. 261–78 (June).

Dornbusch, R. (1982), 'Stabilisation Policies in Developing Countries: What Have We Learned?', *World Development*, vol. 10, no. 9.

Drèze, J.P. and H. Gazdar (1991), 'Hunger and Poverty in Iraq', *World Development*, 20(7) (July 1992), pp. 921–45.

Drèze, J.P. and A.K. Sen (1989), *Hunger and Public Action* (Oxford: Clarendon Press).

Ferreira, F. (1991), 'The World Bank and the Study of Stabilisation and Structural Adjustment in LDCs', STICERD, London School of Economics, mimeo.

Gersovitz, M. (1987), 'The Effects of Domestic Taxes on Foreign Private Investment', D.M.G. Newbery and N.H. Stern (eds) (1987).

Gillis, M. (ed) (1989), *Tax Reform in Developing Countries* (Durham: Duke University Press).

Glewwe, P. and de Tray (1988), 'The Poor During Adjustment: A Case Study of Côte d'Ivoire', *LSMS Working Paper*, no. 47 (Washington DC: World Bank).

Goode, R. (1984), *Government Finance in Developing Countries* (Washington DC: The Brookings Institution).

Government of India (1956), *Second Five-Year Plan, 1956–61*, Planning Commission.

Hayek (1960), *The Constitution of Liberty* (Chicago: University of Chicago Press).

Hoff, K. (1989), 'Land Taxes, Output Taxes and Sharecropping: Was Henry George Right?', World Bank Conference on Agricultural Development Policies and the Theory of Rural Organisation, Washington DC, June.

Hoff, K. (1991), 'Introduction: Agricultural Taxation and Land Rights System', *World Bank Economic Review*, 5(1) (January), pp. 85–91.

Johnson, B.F. and R. Mellor (1961), 'The Role of Agriculture in Economic Development', *American Economic Review*, 51, pp. 566–93.

Johnson, H.G. (1965), 'Optimal Tariff Intervention in the Presence of Domestic Distortions', in R.E. Baldwin et al., *Trade Growth and the Balance of Payments: Essays in Honour of Gottfried Haberler* (Amsterdam: North Holland Publishing).

Johnson, O. and J. Salop (1980), 'Distributional Aspects of Stabilisation Programmes in Developing Countries', *IMF Staff Papers*, 27 (Mar.) (Washington DC: IMF).

Khalizadeh-Shirazi, Javad and Anwar Shah (eds) (1991), *Tax Policy in Developing Countries* (Washington DC: World Bank).

Krueger, A.O. (1974), 'The Political Economy of the Rent-Seeking Society', *American Economic Review*, 64, pp. 291–303.

Krueger, A.O. (1990), 'Government Failures in Development', *Journal of Economic Perspectives*, 4, pp. 9–24.

Lipsey, R. and K. Lancaster (1956-7), 'The General Theory of the Second Best', *Review of Economic Studies*, vol. 24, no. 63, pp. 11–32.

Little, I.M.D., T. Scitovsky and M.F.G. Scott (1970), *Industry and Trade in Some Developing Countries* (London: Oxford University Press).

Mirrlees, J.A. (1971), 'An Exploration in the Theory of Optimum Income Taxation', *Review of Economic Studies*, vol. 68, no. 114 (Apr.), pp. 175–208.

Musgrave, R.A. (1959), *The Theory of Public Finance* (New York: McGraw-Hill).

Musgrave, R.A. (1969), *Fiscal Systems* (New Haven, CT: Yale University Press).

Newbery, D.M.G. and N.H. Stern (eds) (1987), *The Theory of Taxation for Developing Countries* (New York: Oxford University Press).

Nozick, R. (1974), *Anarchy, State and Utopia* (New York: Basic Books).

Pastor, M. (1990), 'Capital Flight from Latin America', in *World Development*, vol. 18, no. 1.

Pitt, M.M. (1981), 'Smuggling and Price Disparity', *Journal of International Economics*, 11 (Nov.), pp. 447–58.

Ramsey, F.P. (1927), 'A Contribution to the Theory of Taxation', *Economic Journal*, vol. 37, no. 1 (Mar.), pp. 47–61.

Ribe, H., S. Carvalho, R. Liebenthal, P. Nicholas and E. Zuckerman (1990), 'How Structural Adjustment Programmes Can Help the Poor: The World Bank's Experience', *World Bank Discussion Paper* no. 71, Washington DC.

Samuelson P.A. (1951), 'The Theory of Optimal Taxation', Memorandum to the US Treasury. Published in *Journal of Public Economics*, vol. 30, no. 2 (July 1986), pp. 137–44.

Shah, S. and J. Toye (1979), 'Tax Policy in Sub-Saharan Africa', *Policy and Research Series*, no. 2 (Washington DC: World Bank).

Stern, N.H. (1984), 'Optimal Taxation and Tax Policy', *International Monetary Fund Staff Papers*, vol. 31, no. 2 (June), pp. 339–78.

Stern, N.H. (1987), 'The Theory of Optimal Commodity and Income Taxation: An Introduction', Chapter 2 in Newbery and Stern (eds) (1987).

Stern, N.H. (1989), 'The Economics of Development: A Survey', *Economic Journal*, vol. 99, pp. 597–685.

Stern, N.H. (1991), 'Public Policy and the Economics of Development', *European Economic Review*, 35, pp. 241–71.

Stiglitz, J.E. and P.S. Dasgupta (1971), 'Differential Taxation, Public Goods, and Economic Efficiency', *Review of Economic Studies*, vol. 38(2), no. 114 (Apr.), pp. 151–74.

Tait, A.A. (1988), *Value Added Tax: International Practice and Problems* (Washington DC: IMF).

Tait, A.A., Wilfrid L.M. Graetz and Barry V. Eichengreen (1979), 'International Comparisons of Taxation for Selected Developing Countries, 1972–76', *IMF Staff Papers*, 26.

Tanzi, V. (1977), 'Inflation Lags in Collection, and the Value of Real Tax Revenue', *IMF Staff Papers*, 24.

Tanzi, V. (1981), 'Taxation in Sub-Saharan Africa: A Statistical Evaluation', *IMF Occasional Paper*, 8, pp. 43–73.

Tanzi, V. (1987), 'A Review of Major Tax Policy Missions in Developing Countries', in H. van de Kar and B. Wolfe (eds), *The Relevance of Public Finance for Policy Making*, pp. 225–36 (Detriot: Wayne University Press).

Tanzi, V. (1990), *Fiscal Policy in Open Developing Economies* (Washington DC: IMF).

Tanzi, V. (1991), *Public Finance in Developing Countries* (Aldershot: Edward Elgar).

Timmer, C.P., W.P. Falcon and S.R. Pearson (1983), *Food Policy Analysis* (Baltimore: Johns Hopkins University Press).

Wald, H.P. (1959), *Taxation of Agricultural Land in Underdeveloped Economies* (Cambridge, MA: Harvard University Press).

Wicksell, K. (1896), *Finanzheoretische Utersuchungen nebst Darstellung und Kritik des Steuerwesens Schwedens* (Jena: Verlag von Gustav Fischer).

World Bank (1981), *World Development Report 1981* (New York: Oxford University Press).

World Bank (1986a), *World Development Report 1986* (New York: Oxford University Press).

World Bank (1986b), *Poverty and Hunger* (Washington DC: The World Bank).

World Bank (1988), *World Development Report 1988* (New York: Oxford University Press).

World Bank (1989), *World Development Report 1989* (New York: Oxford University Press).

World Bank (1991), *Lessons of Tax Reform* (Washington DC: World Bank).

3. Trade Policy Reforms and the Government Budget Constraint in Bangladesh

Priya Basu and David Greenaway

1 INTRODUCTION

Whether judged by reference to nominal GDP per capita, or a range of human resource indicators, Bangladesh is one of the least developed countries (LDCs). It is also one of the most populous, with a population of 110 million, and is more densely populated than either India or China. Thus, the economy is relatively well endowed with labour but relatively poorly endowed with both natural resources and capital; the latter being a function of historically low savings and investment ratios. Until recently exports were dominated by traditional exportables and imports by foodstuffs and intermediates. Trade and industrial policies were geared to sustaining a strongly inward oriented trade regime. The relatively high tariffs associated with this trade regime accounted for around 40 per cent of public finances.

Over the last eight years, Bangladesh has embarked upon a major reform programme aimed at macroeconomic stabilization, industrial restructuring and a reorientation of trade policy. Reforms have included inter alia changes in the composition of government expenditure, restructuring of direct and indirect taxes, changes in industrial incentives and financial sector reforms. The major donor agencies, in particular the IMF and World Bank, have been closely involved in the design and implementation of the reforms, commitment to which has unlocked conditional finance from both agencies.

The process of reform and restructuring which began in 1985 is far from complete, many of the most radical reforms are of fairly recent origin (such as the introduction of the VAT and the launch of a public sector retrenchment programme). Notwithstanding this, the programme is sufficiently well advanced and its characteristics are sufficiently clearly defined to warrant an assessment. This paper focuses on the fiscal dimension, rather than on the impact of reforms on industrial incentives or economic growth. The rationale for this focus is partly the fact that some of the reforms are explicitly designed to be fiscal augmenting and partly because broader assessments of adjustment lending strongly suggest that slippage from commitment is related to fiscal depletion (Greenaway and Milner, 1991). The relationship between fiscal constraints and policy reform in the LDCs is especially important given their typically heavy dependence on indirect taxes in general and trade taxes in particular.

The remainder of the paper is organized as follows: in Section 2 we map out the features of the reform programme with particular reference to context, timing and sequencing. Section 3 evaluates the impact of the reforms on government revenue and expenditure. Section 4 assesses the longer term viability of the reforms and draws some lessons for other reforming LDCs from the Bangladesh experience. Section 5 concludes.

2   POLICY REFORMS IN BANGLADESH: CONTEXT, TIMING AND SEQUENCING

Policy reforms of one form or another have been underway in Bangladesh since 1985, with the most radical reforms being implemented over the last two years (1991–3). Reforms have resulted in changes to trade and industrial policy, changes in government taxation and expenditure policies, changes in investment policy and changes in monetary and exchange rate policies. The background to reform has been well documented elsewhere (for example World Bank, 1989 and 1990; GATT, 1992) and does not require detailed analysis here. Suffice to note that between independence in 1971 and the initiation of reforms, the government had followed a strongly inward oriented trade strategy which relied heavily on extensive import controls, relatively high tariffs, direct control over large areas of economic activity and pervasive direction of investment. Low savings and investment ratios, relatively low growth rates and macroeconomic imbalances characterized pre-reform economic performance. Combined with relatively high population growth, this resulted in declining GDP per capita and poor performance on the key human development indicators. This performance was poor in absolute terms and relative to other LDCs.

Table 3.1 outlines the major reforms initiated since the mid-1980s. The key international donor agencies, in particular the IMF and World Bank, have been closely involved in pressing for reform and beyond that in programme design. Leverage to this end has operated through the provision of conditional finance: standby and Structural Adjustment Facility (SAF) credits in the case of the IMF, SECAL credits in the case of the World Bank. Details of the timing and levels of these credits are set out in Table 3.2. Without this input from the donor agencies, in particular the World Bank, many of the reforms set out in Table 3.1 may not have been undertaken.

Table 3.1   Policy Reforms in Bangladesh

Policy focus	Timing	Measures
Trade policy	1985–93	Streamlining of import procedures
		Rationalization of the number of tariff rates
		Reduction in the number of QRs
		Tariff liberalization
		Tariff exemptions for exporters
		Minimum export prices for jute
		Elimination of export duties
		Export subsidies
		Introduction of special supplementary duty
Fiscal policy:	1991–93	Introduction of VAT
Revenue		Replacement of some tariffs with specific excise duty
		Phase–out of sales tax
		Introduction of turnover tax
		Reform of income tax
		Reform of corporation tax
Fiscal policy:	1991–93	Privatization of state enterprises
Expenditure		Public sector retrenchment
		Public enterprise reform
		Reduction of subsidies
Investment	1989–93	Reorientation of the Board Investment
policy		Simplification of approved procedures
		Fiscal incentives to MNEs
		Non-fiscal incentives to MNEs
Exchange rate	1989–93	Elimination of multiple exchange and monetary rates
policy		Revision of foreign exchange allocation resources
		Progression to market determined interest rates
		Relaxation of credit controls

*Table 3.2 Arrangements in Support of Structural Adjustment
             (Millions of SDRs)*

IMF Arrangements Standby/extended SAF/ESAF		World Bank Loans and Credits Struct. Adjust. Sector and Other (non) adjusmt IDA		Purpose
July 1979– July 1980	85.0	June 1987	147.8	Industrial Policy Reforms
Dec. 1980– Dec. 1983	800.0*	Apr. 1989	137.0	Energy Sector
Dec. 1983– Mar. 1985	68.4	Oct. 1989	1.8	Energy Sector
Dec. 1985– June 1987	180.0	June 1990	132.7	Financial Sector
Feb. 1987– Feb. 1990	201.3	Nov. 1990	2.5	Financial Sector
Aug. 1990– Aug. 1992	345.0	Nov. 1991	2.2	Financial Sector
		May 1992	109.3	Public Resource Management

Note: * SDR 580m not purchased.

2.1   Content of Policy Reforms

Trade and industrial policy
Prior to the reform period, trade policy was both highly interventionist and restrictive. Nominal tariff protection ranged from zero to 350 per cent, with an unweighted average of over 100 per cent. Moreover the tariff structure was escalated, yielding even higher effective tariffs. Despite the high nominal rates the collection rate (i.e. total revenue divided by total value of imports) was under 30 per cent. This is partly accounted for by evasion, but also by wide-spread exemptions. Tariff revenue was also pre-empted by the use of quantitative import controls. A positive list system was operated until 1985 when it was replaced with a negative list, specifying those items which were subject to

prohibition or restriction. In 1988 there were over 2 300 (SITC eight digit) items, amounting to 40 per cent of the total, in the negative list.

Reform of trade policy has been a central plank of the entire reform programme. Although the primary motivation for liberalization has been efficiency considerations, the impact of these reforms from a fiscal perspective was especially important because customs duties accounted for 40 per cent of government revenue. Trade policy reforms have encompassed a number of features of the trade regime and collectively have been targeted at reducing anti-export bias whilst simultaneously attempting to preserve the revenue potential of customs duties. Import prohibition and restrictions have been dramatically reduced. According to the World Bank (1993) the number of eight-digit items which remain restricted has been reduced to 584, that is, about 10 per cent of the total. Nominal tariffs have been both rationalized and liberalized, with the number of scheduled rates being reduced to eight ranging from 7.5 per cent to 100 per cent. Further rationalization is intended with a lowering of the maximum rate and, where appropriate, some increase of minimum rates, towards a target level of 45 per cent. (This is a process of rationalization widely known as the concertina approach.) As a consequence of this rationalization, average nominal tariffs and their standard deviation have fallen dramatically to 50 per cent and 32 per cent respectively in 1992, compared with 94 per cent and 59 per cent respectively, in 1988 (World Bank, 1993 p. 68). Although these are important changes, the extent of liberalization and rationalization has been qualified by the number of exemptions which apply, the scope for recourse to Statutory Restrictive Orders, and Supplementary Direct Duty, as we shall see later.

All of the above were targeted at reducing the degree of distortion associated with the tariff structure and in the process, reducing anti-export bias. In addition to changes in the import regime, there were also changes with respect to exports. Export policy is under the aegis of the Export Coordination Unit. Prior to the recent reforms access to export markets was impeded by a number of factors including registration procedures, export licences and licence fees, export duties, the widespread use of minimum prices and export quotas. Furthermore, transactions involving traditional exports had to be completed at the official exchange rate which, given its overvaluation, meant in effect that a tax was levied. A number of ingredients of the reform programme have explicitly been geared to increasing the incentive to export. Thus, the unification of the exchange rate has eliminated the implicit export tax and minimum price restrictions have been removed on all products except jute. In addition several export incentives have been introduced: the EPZ (at Chittagong) is being extended, the special bonded warehouse scheme is also being extended, as are the duty drawback schemes. Given the degree of anti-export bias which exists in the trade regime, these are limited concessions. However, they do constitute some progress and they are being implemented against the backcloth of a changing export structure – in 1985 two thirds of total merchandise exports were accounted for by traditional exports and 30 per cent by non-traditionals; by 1992 these shares were 20 per cent and 65 per cent respectively. The key exports in the growth of non-traditionals are garments and foodstuffs (especially frozen shrimps).

Fiscal policy: revenue

Fiscal policy reforms have been both extensive and radical. Direct and indirect taxes have been restructured in an attempt to simplify the tax structure, increase its transparency and improve its effectiveness. Prior to reform the key indirect (non-trade) taxes were sales tax and excise duty. The base for both was relatively narrow (being largely imports) and exemptions of various forms were quite common. These have been phased out and replaced primarily with a VAT which has been set at a uniform rate of 15 per cent. Initially, the tax is being applied at the import and manufacturing level (with exports zero rated), but not to wholesalers and retailers, and only a small number of service providers in Dhaka are subject to the tax. As a consequence the initial base is not significantly broader than its predecessors. However, the ability of producers to offset VAT on their inputs against their eventual tax liability has resulted in more comprehensive registration and therefore a higher collection rate. There are plans to extend the VAT to a broader range of services in 1993 and to the wholesale and retail sectors in 1994. The VAT is supplemented by a turnover tax of 2 per cent on small traders. The objectives of this appear to be twofold; first to raise some revenue from small businesses, and second to extend registration records as a basis for eventually broadening the VAT base. The other supplement to VAT has been the introduction of specific excise duties on a range of luxury items. For equity reasons, certain items are currently exempt from VAT. These include unprocessed agricultural goods, fish products and livestock. Supplementary duties at different rates have been introduced on luxuries, both imported and domestically produced.

These reforms are radical in nature and especially where the VAT is concerned, were introduced in the face of opposition. As we shall see in Section 3 the yield from the indirect tax base does not appear to have suffered from the reforms – indeed revenues have actually increased. There have, however, been administrative difficulties associated with their introduction which, if not addressed, may frustrate further development. This issue is addressed in Section 4.

Increased revenue collections have been generated by a number of structural and administrative reforms to income taxes. Tax rates were reduced, with a view to inducing voluntary compliance. The highest marginal rate for personal income tax rates was lowered from 45 per cent to 30 per cent and it was decided that the maximum tax would not exceed 25 per cent of income exceeding Tk. 40 000 while the tax rate on the incomes of non-company non-residents was lowered to 30 per cent. A system of rebates has been devised for small-scale and cottage industries in less developed areas, whereby these enterprises are eligible for income tax rebates on income related to increased production. Corporate income tax rates for 'publicly traded' and 'non-publicly traded' industrial companies were reduced from 45 per cent and 50 per cent respectively to 40 per cent and 45 per cent.

A number of procedural and structural simplifications have also been introduced. The new 'conventional exemption limit' has replaced the 'filing threshold system' in the case of assessments other than those of companies and non residents; the threshold income for personal income taxes is now Tk. 40 000. Investment tax credits, applied at a uniform rate of 15 per cent, have replaced deductions for investment. At the same time, measures have been introduced to broaden the tax base. The scope of the withholding tax has been extended by introducing a 0.5 per cent tax deduction on the value of exports; the scope of self-assessment has also been widened; and presumptive assessment for business and professional income with a fixed minimum tax liability has been introduced. The Government has taken steps to reduce procedural delays in framing assessments, issuing refunds, registering firms and granting tax holidays. Efforts have also been made to modernize and improve the efficiency of tax administration, enhance its accountability and transparency and reduce the discretionary powers of the tax authority.

Fiscal policy: expenditure

Paralleling attempts at broadening and deepening the tax base have been reforms directed at reducing government expenditure. These have involved three instruments: privatization of state enterprises, public sector retrenchment and a reduction in subsidies.

State control of industry prior to reform was pervasive. Following independence in 1970 the government embarked upon a massive nationalization programme which resulted in over 90 per cent of total assets in the manufacturing sector being government-held by 1973. This covered the major manufacturing industries (sugar, jute and textiles) as well as some smaller scale activities and the entire banking sector. Limited divestiture was undertaken before the recent reforms – prior to 1981 some 389 units were released from public ownership – and the pace and scale accelerated in the 1980s, but the programme left the large industrial sectors (jute and sugar) largely unscathed and these continue to be a drain on public finances.

Public sector retrenchment, that is, large-scale redundancy, is now underway. The Asian Development Bank is committed to providing a line of credit which is conditional upon retrenchment. As part of this programme, the railway services will reduce their employment from 55 000 to 40 000, with 10 000 going through voluntary redundancy. Programmes are also in place for the jute mills, textile mills, Bangladesh Road Corporation and the food distribution authority. The objective behind this two year programme is to reduce operating losses in the corporations concerned and provide the foundation for further efficiency gains in the future.

Investment policy

As noted in the introduction, Bangladesh has one of the lowest invstment ratios among developing countries. Moreover it has a poor record on foreign direct investment (FDI). One of the major objectives of trade and fiscal reforms is to create an environment which is more conducive to private sector investment, including inward investment. In addition the government has recently initiated a number of reforms directed specifically at investment promotion.

The Board of Investment has been rationalized and given a role which is geared more to the promotion of investment than its regulation. The granting of the necessary approvals to new investors, including foreign companies, has been simplified and speeded up. Like many other developing countries, Bangladesh has embraced the 'one stop shop' philosophy whereby inward investors clear the appropriate approvals quickly and in one batch. In addition a number of other fiscal and non-fiscal incentives are being introduced; tax incentives for investors in the EPZ have been extended, exchange controls relaxed and customs clearance procedures simplified. Attracting FDI is seen as important for the industrialization programme. However, Bangladesh faces serious competition from other parts of south and south-east Asia where there are not only larger stocks of manufacturing capital, but also superior infrastructural facilities. As Table 3.3 indicates, FDI levels in Bangladesh lag far behind those in other Asian countries.

*Table 3.3   Net Foreign Direct Investment in
Selected Asian Countries, 1987*

Country	Investment ($m)
Bangladesh	2
China	1 669
India	583
Pakistan	62
Sri Lanka	29
Indonesia	425
Philippines	186
Thailand	270
Malaysia	528
Korea	–143
Singapore	582
Hong Kong	282

Exchange rate and monetary policy

As with the trade regime, both foreign exchange and financial markets have been highly controlled since independence. Up until recently a system of multiple exchange rates applied. These have been gradually liberalized. In 1990 the rate structure was simplified to two rates – a shadow rate and an official rate. The former was determined by the interaction of supply and demand while the latter was kept within two per cent of the shadow rate. In 1992 the rate structure was unified which is ostensibly market determined, although the demand side of the market is influenced by the process of foreign exchange allocation and exchange controls. The objective of financial sector reforms is to create an enabling environment for private sector activity. The 1970s were characterized by financial repression and inflation. In the 1980s monetary policy was directed towards attaining positive real interest rates and since 1992 the government has embarked upon a financial sector reform programme. The key ingredients of this are: greater emphasis on the market determination of interest rates, the removal of interest rate subsidies, a strengthening of the institutional environment for commercial banks, and the introduction of new financial instruments. However the development of a stable, diversified and dynamic financial system is clearly a long-term undertaking and much remains to be accomplished.

2.2 Role of Donor Agencies and Conditionality

As we have seen in the previous sub-section, the reform process in Bangladesh has been extensive and broadly based. In the next section we evaluate the fiscal consequences of these reforms and in Section 4 we assess their medium-term prospects. Before doing this we consider the role of the donor agencies in the reform process.

Over the last decade more than 80 developing countries have engaged in reforms of a type similar to those in Bangladesh. Some of these have been implemented voluntarily, others have been policy conditioned in the sense that they would probably not have taken place without the intervention of one of the major donor agencies, especially the World Bank. What role have the donor agencies played in initiating reforms in Bangladesh? Although in the absence of a clear counterfactual it is impossible to be absolutely certain, the coincidence of timing between reforms and IMF/World Bank credits, and the explicit inclusion of so many specific recommendations in World Bank documentation makes it difficult to avoid the conclusion that the reform programme would not have been adopted without World Bank conditionality. As we can see from Table 3.2, since 1979–80 six IMF credits and seven World Bank credits or loans have been received. From the standpoint of policy reform, the most important credits are the 1990 industrial sector credit and the 1992 public sector resource management credit disbursed by the World Bank. Associated with these credits was a major drive from the World Bank intended to persuade the government to make a commitment to reform. In particular, the core reforms – VAT, direct tax changes, public sector restructuring, concertina style tariff reforms and so on – were Bank conceptions and became part of the conditionality package.

Why does this matter? In part because the provenance of any reform programme is of interest from an analytical standpoint. More important, however, it may matter to the durability of a programme. If commitment is perceived by private sector agencies to be a function of conditionality, then rational agents will expect slippage to take place once initial conditions are apparently met and will entertain doubts regarding the sustainability of the programme. If this is so then a private sector supply response may be delayed, which in turn threatens further the sustainability of the programme. Perceived 'ownership' of the programme is therefore crucial. We return to this issue in Section 4.

2.3 Summary

Although structural reforms of one type or another have been underway in Bangladesh for some years, substantive reform (and stabilization) efforts have only been implemented since the late 1980s. This timing partly reflects pressures from the economic environment, and partly reflects pressures from the donor agencies, in particular the World Bank. Reforms have been pervasive, involving changes in trade policy, fiscal policy, monetary and exchange rate policy and investment policy. Implementation has made considerable progress in several areas, in particular trade and fiscal policy, and targets for subsequent phases are in place. We turn now to the impact of these reforms on the government budget.

3   IMPACT OF REFORMS ON THE GOVERNMENT BUDGET

From the discussion in Section 2, it is clear that in broad terms two main phases in the evolution of fiscal policy since 1980 can be distinguished. The 1980s were characterized by an austere regime, largely focused on stabilizing the economy from various external shocks through 'quick-fix' measures. In contrast, the period since FY 1990/91 has been marked by the implementation of more fundamental changes in fiscal structure and administration, focusing more on longer term development objectives.

3.1 Patterns of Revenue and Expenditure in the Pre-Reform Period

The Government's main objective during this period was to reduce the fiscal imbalance, and the principal tool utilized to achieve this was restraints on development (Annual Development Programme) spending.

Expenditure under the Annual Development Programme (ADP) was cut from around 10 per cent of GDP in FY 1980/81 to 6.7 per cent by FY 1988/9 (Table 3.4). The sectors which suffered major cuts included industry and energy, their combined share of the ADP falling from 42 per cent in FY 1985/6 to 21 per cent in FY 1989/90. On the other hand, those sectors deemed as being of higher priority, namely, agriculture, water resources, human resource development and transport and communications experienced an increase in resource allocation under the ADP.

By contrast current expenditures displayed an expansionary trend, rising from 5.6 per cent of GDP in FY 1980/81 to 8.5 per cent in FY 1988/9. While expenditures on the food account (including food subsidies) were considerably reduced, current spending on pay and allowances, government administration, transport and interest payments on debt increased substantially. Government expenditures were also boosted by the need to provide subsidies and transfers to victims of the 1987 and 1988 floods.

Fiscal policy during the 1980s did not emphasize revenue enhancement, and revenue fluctuated between 8 per cent and 9.5 per cent of GDP. A small rise in the share of non-tax revenues in GDP was offset by the decline in tax revenues, the latter owing to a fall in the share of taxes levied on international trade.

Between FY 1980/81 and 1988/9, international trade taxes fell from 3.2 per cent of GDP to 2.7 per cent while sales tax on imports declined from 1.4 per cent of GDP to 0.8 per cent over the same period. Although a development surcharge was introduced on dutiable goods which was gradually increased to 6 per cent of the value of such imports, duty rates were revised with the average duty rate being lowered, and preferential treatment extended to production inputs. At the same time, the Government undertook some piecemeal changes to particular tax instruments and rates in order to raise revenues, but with limited success: the number of products covered under the excise duty schedule was expanded and rates were increased on luxury goods. These changes resulted in an increase in the share of excise duty revenues in GDP, from 1.6 per cent to 2.1 per cent, over the period FY 1980/81 and 1988/9.

The share of direct taxes in GDP also increased marginally, owing mainly to improved collection measures (Table 3.5).[1] Although the share of income taxes in total revenues rose, tax coverage remained narrow, with individual income taxes collected from only 0.5 per cent of the population, corporate taxes levied on only a limited set of businesses and with agriculture, which accounts for 40 per cent of GDP, remaining outside the tax net.

Table 3.4 Summary Data on Government Revenue, Expenditure and Budget Surplus (or deficit), 1980/81–1991/2[a] (% of GDP)

	81	83	84	85	86	87	88	89	90	91	92[e]
1. Total revenue	9.4	8.4	8.1	8.8	9.1	8.9	8.9	9.5	9.3	9.6	10.9
1.1 Tax	7.7	7.2	6.7	7.1	7.1	7.2	7.1	7.5	7.8	7.8	8.7
1.2 Non tax	1.7	1.5	1.4	1.7	2.0	1.7	1.8	2.0	1.6	1.8	2.2
2. Total expenditures	18.4	19.7	17.2	16.2	16.6	17.3	16.1	16.7	17.1	16.4	15.5
2.1 Current[b]	5.6	6.5	6.5	6.5	7.5	7.7	8.1	8.5	8.8	8.7	8.6
2.2 ADP[c]	10.1	10.2	8.5	7.5	7.8	8.6	6.4	6.7	6.4	6.2	5.7
2.3 Other capital expenditure[d] and net lending	0.7	0.8	1.0	1.1	0.9	6.9	0.7	0.9	0.7	0.6	0.6
3. Overall budget deficit	9.0	11.0	9.1	7.4	7.5	8.4	7.1	7.2	7.7	6.8	4.6

Notes:
a. Fiscal year = year ending. The FY runs from 1 July to 30 June.
b. Includes food subsidies and expenditures inc. food account.
c. Annual Development Programme includes many capital expenditures.
d. Comprise non-ADP project expenditures, the food for work programme, misc. (non-development) investment and loans, advances.
e. Based on November 1992 estimates.

Source: Ministry of Finance, World Bank and IMF estimates/data.

Table 3.5 Major Taxes, 1980/81–1991/2 (% of GDP)*

	81	83	84	85	86	87	88	89	90	91	92
1. Production, consumption and distribution taxes	6.5	6.1	5.7	5.8	5.8	5.8	5.9	5.9	6.2	6.1	6.3
1.1 Customs	3.2	3.1	2.8	2.7	2.9	2.9	2.7	2.7	2.9	2.8	3.1
1.2 Sales	1.4	1.1	1.0	1.0	1.0	1.0	0.9	0.8	0.7	1.0	0.0
1.3 Excise	1.6	1.6	1.7	1.7	1.6	1.7	2.0	2.1	2.3	2.0	1.5
1.4 VAT	.	.	.		.	.	.	.	.	.	1.8
1.5 Supplementary	0.0	0.0	0.0	0.0	0.0	0.0	0.0	0.0	0.0	0.0	0.0
2. Income taxes	0.9	1.1	0.9	0.9	0.9	1.0	1.1	1.1	1.2	1.3	1.4

Note: * Year ending for example: FY = 81 = 1980/81

Source: orld Bank 1993, NBR.

Among the different types of taxes, the single most important source of revenue continued to be customs duties, though their share in GDP declined, as noted above, as did their share in total revenue. A high dependence on these taxes as a source of revenue contributed to the relative inelasticity of the tax system in Bangladesh. The base of international trade taxes did not grow proportionately with GDP owing to a proliferation of exemptions; the ratio of dutiable imports to total imports fell from 80 per cent in 1985/6 to 70 per cent by 1988/9. In addition, the reduction in the average duty rate also contributed to the declining contribution of customs duties.

The tariff structure remained highly distortionary throughout the 1980s. Alongside quantitative restrictions on imports, most final products were pro-tected by high tariffs. Although raw materials and intermediate goods were generally subject to lower tariff rates, in some cases, effective protection was negative, the tariff rate levied on the competing final good was lower than on the raw materials or intermediate goods used in its production. These anomalies were compounded by numerous special exemptions, a large number of different rate categories and a non-transparent process of assigning rates in response to ad hoc concerns.

Although revenue performance was far from buoyant, the restraint on ADP spending resulted in an improvement in the overall budget deficit, from 9 per cent of GDP in FY 1980/81 to 7.2 per cent in FY 1988/9. The reduction helped to secure a decrease in domestic financing from 0.8 per cent of GDP to 0.1 per cent in FY 1988/9; the rest of the deficit being funded mainly by foreign aid.[2] While the fall in the deficit tended to portray a picture of fiscal prudence, the rapid expansion of current expenditures, at the expense of a sharp contraction in investment spending were features not conducive to a balanced and development-oriented fiscal policy.

In many respects, FY 1989/90 marked a watershed in Bangladesh's fiscal performance. The depressive effects of the devastating floods of 1987 and 1988, coupled with the Government's cautious fiscal management during most of the 1980s (reflected in substantial underspending by the public sector below the ceiling agreed with the IMF) resulting in large shortfalls in public invest-ment targets, contributed to a considerable economic slow-down by 1989. In the first half of FY 1989/90, the government adopted a more expansionary fiscal stance to stimulate the economy. Current expenditures increased rapidly (al-though this further limited the size of public investment programmes through induced shortfalls in the availability of domestic funds). As a result the overall budget deficit rose from 7.2 per cent of GDP in FY 1988/9 to 7.7 per cent in FY 1989/90. In response, the Government initiated a short-term stabilisation pro-gramme in March 1990. Remedial fiscal measures included controlling the rapid expansion of current expenditures, and some efforts towards mobilizing additional revenues. These were later translated into a Policy Framework Paper which was supported in early FY 1990/91 by a first year Enhanced Structural Adjustment Facility (ESAF) of the IMF.

3.2 Recent Fiscal Reforms and their Impact on Revenue, Expenditure and the Budget Balance

As we have seen, 1991 was characterized by a marked shift in government thinking, and for the first time the focus of fiscal policy shifted from short-term stabilization measures to more sustainable improvements in revenue and expenditure structure, planning and management. A substantial improvement in fiscal accounts has been achieved since FY 1990/91. The share of revenues in GDP rose from 9.3 per cent in FY 1989/90 to 10.9 per cent in FY 1991/2 while current expenditures were reduced from 8.8 per cent of GDP to 8.6 per cent over the same period. The overall budget deficit was reduced from 7.7 per cent of GDP in FY 1989/90 to 4.6 per cent in FY 1991/2.

Impact on revenue

Total revenue increased by an estimated 16 per cent between FY 1989/90 and FY 1990/91 and by a further 20 per cent between FY 1990/91 and FY 1991/2. The increase was brought about by revenues generated through the newly introduced VAT, and a sharp increase in the share of income taxes. As we have seen, the former broadened the tax base for indirect taxes, whilst the new income tax arrangements improved compliance. It is too early to say for certain whether the rise in revenues is due entirely to the reforms, or whether other factors (such as an increase in economic growth) have also contributed, but given the significant expansion in income tax collections (which have risen by 44 per cent between December 1991 and December 1992) and in the collections of indirect taxes, there is a strong presumption that the reforms have had some beneficial effects.

The increased collection of tax revenues since FY 1989/90 was also accompanied by a marked change in the structure of taxation (Table 3.7). The share of customs duties in total tax revenue has declined, reflecting a decline in imports and an adjustment/lowering of rates. The share of excise taxes has also fallen, while the VAT accounted for 23 per cent of tax revenues in FY 1991/2. The share of income and profit taxes in total tax revenue rose from 13.6 per cent in FY 1989/90 to 16.1 per cent in FY 1991/2. The performance of non-tax revenues has also picked up since FY 1989/90. As can be seen from Table 3.6, this improved performance is accounted for mainly by an increase in profits and transfers from the nationalized sector, attributable to the major reforms in public enterprises implemented in recent years.

Table 3.6 Structure of Revenues: Taxes and Non-Tax Revenues, 1980/81–1991/2* (% of total current revenue)

	81	82	83	84	85	86	87	88	89	90	91	92
1. Tax revenue	76.0	73.7	79.7	79.4	80.7	79.6	80.3	83.7	83.0	84.3	80.7	82.0
1.1 Production, consumption and distribution taxes	64.8	65.2	65.8	66.6	67.7	66.5	66.9	68.1	67.8	68.0	65.0	64.0
1.1.1 Customs duties	31.9	30.7	33.6	33.0	32.2	32.8	32.9	31.4	31.3	32.0	29.7	29.6
1.1.2 Sales tax	14.5	13.7	11.7	11.4	11.8	11.3	11.7	10.2	9.3	7.8	10.5	0.0
1.1.3 Excise duty	15.9	18.1	17.7	19.8	23.3	18.9	19.1	22.8	24.0	25.1	21.9	14.3
1.1.4 VAT	.	.	.	.	.	.	.	.	.	.	.	17.6
1.1.5 Stamp tax	2.3	2.5	2.6	2.5	3.2	3.1	3.0	3.3	2.9	2.6	2.4	2.6
1.1.6 Motor vehicle tax	0.2	0.2	0.3	0.0	0.3	0.3	0.4	0.0	0.3	0.5	0.5	0.4
1.1.7 Supplementary tax	0.0	0.0	0.0	0.0	0.0	0.0	0.0	0.0	0.0	0.0	0.0	0.2
1.2 Income taxes	9.4	10.2	11.6	10.9	11.2	11.3	11.7	12.9	12.9	12.9	13.7	13.6
1.3 Land revenue tax	1.2	1.2	0.9	1.1	1.15	1.2	1.2	1.7	1.7	1.7	..	0.9
1.4 Other taxes and duties	0.5	0.5	1.3	0.8	0.6	0.5	0.6	0.9	0.8	1.7	1.2	1.1
2. Non-tax revenue	24.0	22.9	20.3	20.5	19.3	20.4	19.7	16.3	16.9	15.7	19.3	19.5
2.1 Nationalized sector	7.9	5.6	4.6	4.0	8.1	8.9	7.4	4.2	4.4	1.1	5.6	7.4
2.2 Interest receipts	6.2	6.3	3.7	3.4	4.0	5.7	4.2	4.0	3.8	5.1	3.8	3.1
2.3 Other	9.9	11.0	11.7	6.6	7.1	5.8	8.0	7.7	11.2	8.0	9.9	8.9

Note: * Year ending, for example: FY = 81 = 1980/81.

Table 3.7   Structure of Taxes, 1989/90–1991/2 (% of total tax revenue)

	89/90	90/91	91/2
Customs duties	37.4	36.2	36.5
Sales tax	11.0	12.1	0.0
Income and profits tax	13.6	17.3	16.1
Excise duties*	28.8	26.0	17.8
VAT	0.0	0.0	23.3
Others	9.2	8.4	6.3
Total	100.0	100.0	100.0

Notes: * The decline in excise duties after FY 91 reflects the fact that some of these duties were replaced by VAT.

Source: World Bank 1993, NBR data.

Impact on expenditure

After the rapid expansion of current expenditures in the late 1980s, fiscal policy since FY 1989/90 has stressed the need to contain increases in current spending. As a consequence the share of current expenditures in GDP remained stable in the period FY 1989/90 to FY 1991/2, at around 9 per cent of GDP. This, together with increased revenues mobilised since FY 1989/90 released re-sources to finance a higher level of ADP expenditures. However, weak project implementation capacity prevented public investment from rising and the share of ADP in GDP actually declined from 6.8 per cent in FY 1989/90 to 5.7 per cent in FY 1991/2. The overall balance of expenditure allocations therefore continued to remain in favour of current spending (Table 3.8).

While analysing trends and patterns of current spending, it must be borne in mind that some elements of the current budget are non-discretionary, in particular the Government's obligations to make contractual debt service payments. The share of debt service spending in the current budget grew steadily over the period FY 1989/90 to FY 1991/2, increasing from 9.8 per cent to 14 per cent. In addition natural disasters have necessitated unforeseen current spending in the form of subsidies and transfers, with the cyclone of April 1991 and the floods during September–November 1991, contributing to an increase in subsidies and transfers during FY 1990/91. Given these circumstances, Bangladesh's ability to control overall current spending is particularly creditable.

The Government has also introduced some structural changes in expenditure prioritization (Table 3.9). Evidence suggests that the allocation of current spending across broad sectoral groups has been changed in favour of economic services, the share of which in total current spending rose from 6.8 per cent in

Table 3.8 Structure of Government Expenditure: Economic Classification, 1980/81–1991/2 (% of total)

	81	83	84	85	86	87	88	89	90	91	92[c]
1. Current[a]	41.4	44.6	44.2	46.8	47.3	44.8	56.1	54.5	58.4	58.2	59.6
1.1 Food expenditure	10.8	11.3	6.3	6.5	2.2	0.1	5.5	3.6	7.0	5.4	4.1
2. ADP[b]	53.5	51.5	49.6	46.1	47.1	46.9	39.6	40.1	37.5	37.9	36.5
3. Other capital and net lending	3.8	3.9	6.4	7.0	5.6	5.4	4.3	5.4	4.1	2.2	3.9

Notes:
a. Includes food expenditures food subsidies.
b. Mainly capital expenditure.
c. As of November 1992.

Source: Ministry of Finance, IMF, WB estimates.

Table 3.9 *Structure of Current Expenditure, 1980/81–1991/2 (% of total current)*

	81	82	83	84	85	86	87	88	89	90	91	92
General services	48.9	46.3	44.2	48.1	37.8	40.0	43.5	42.4	36.3	38.5	35.3	37.2
Social services	20.0	17.7	22.1	27.1	30.9	27.0	35.7	36.1	33.7	30.9	30.7	30.2
of which:												
Education	14.0	12.6	13.7	14.6	16.8	17.5	18.9	17.3	15.4	16.2	16.2	17.5
Health and population	5.2	4.5	4.8	5.2	5.5	3.3	7.0	6.5	5.2	5.5	5.3	5.5
Social welfare	0.8	0.7	3.7	7.3	8.6	6.1	9.9	12.3	13.1	9.2	9.2	7.3
Economic services	7.2	6.5	5.2	12.9	6.8	7.2	7.7	7.6	6.7	6.8	6.7	7.2
of which:												
Agriculture	2.0	1.7	1.9	3.2	3.7	2.8	4.4	4.1	3.8	3.8	3.4	3.8
Mfg and construction	2.3	2.0	1.4	0.2	0.3	1.9	0.5	0.5	0.4	0.4	0.4	0.4
Transport and communication	2.9	2.8	1.8	8.6	1.7	1.6	1.6	1.8	1.6	1.7	1.6	2.1
Others	0.0	0.0	0.0	1.0	1.1	1.0	1.2	1.1	0.9	0.9	0.9	0.9
Debt service	7.8	12.1	11.7	11.0	10.9	12.5	11.3	12.5	11.9	9.8	11.7	14.0
Domestic	..	..	..	..	..	..	..	..	..	..	5.7	8.0
External	..	..	..	..	..	..	..	..	..	..	6.0	6.0
Food subsidy	7.4	9.8	9.0	4.0	8.5	4.1	1.3	..	10.2	9.4	5.1	4.4
Other subsidy	8.4	7.5	7.8	2.1	0.5	..	0.5	1.4	1.3	4.6	5.4	3.1
Contingency	0.3	1.1	1.1	..	4.6	9.2	2.1	10.2	..	1.0	5.1	3.9

Source: Ministry of Finance and World Bank, 1993.

69

FY 1989/90 to 7.2 per cent in FY 1991/2, while the share allocated to general government services, social services, food and other subsidies declined.

At a more disaggregated level, expenditure allocated to education was increased from 16.2 per cent of the current budget in FY 1989/90 to 17.4 per cent in FY 1991/2 while spending on health and population planning remained constant at around 5.5 per cent of the current budget. Spending on general government services declined, from 19 per cent of the current budget in FY 1989/90 to 16.5 per cent in FY 1991/2, owing mainly to a cut in defence expenditures, although salary and wage increases boosted spending on general administration and there was also an increase in expenditures allocated to operations and maintenance.

The Government is making efforts to prioritize ADP expenditures, in order to eliminate low-yielding and locally financed projects and consequently improve the quality of development spending.

Impact on the overall budget balance

The enhanced revenue mobilization, resulting at least partly from tax reforms, combined with the control of current expenditures and the Government's inability to increase public investment spending, resulted in a sharp fall in the fiscal deficit, from 7.7 per cent of GDP in FY 1989/90 to 4.6 per cent in FY 1991/2. This decline was not fully offset by a fall in foreign inflows. The need for domestic financing thus decreased and the Government started retiring part of its debt to the domestic banking system.

3.3 Performance Relative to Objectives and Medium-Term Concerns

Table 3.10 summarizes the performance/outcomes of the fiscal reform programme against the objectives that it was intended to achieve. As far as fiscal stabilization is concerned, the Government has been largely successful, although as noted above the reduction in the overall budget deficit achieved prior to FY 1990/91 was owing mainly to cuts in spending on the ADP. Since the late 1980s fiscal reforms have encompassed broader objectives, such as tax reform, revenue mobilization, and the prioritization and expansion of development expenditures while maintaining the objective of minimizing the budget deficit.

As discussed above, progress has already been made in terms of the tax and revenue objectives but the Government continues to be faced with difficult challenges and constraints. Notable among these is the inadequate administrative capacity required to implement fully many of the reforms, resulting in significant leakages through tax evasion and non-compliance. As we shall see in Section 4, a striking example is the lack of capacity to administer fully the recently introduced VAT. In order to sustain revenue increases, the VAT will have to be extended to the wholesale and eventually to the retail stages but the

Table 3.10   Reform Objectives and Outcomes, 1980/81–1992/3

FY	Objectives	Instruments	Outcomes
80/81– 88/9	Reduce deficit and stabilize	ADP spending cut. Piecemeal tinkering with some tax rates and bases	Deficit down Investment down Current spending up Public consumption up Revenue constant Growth down
89/90	Stimulate growth	ADP spending expansion Current spending expansion	Deficit up ADP down Current spending up Fiscal distress Slow growth maintained
90/91– 92/3	Reduce and stabilize deficit	Tax reform Control current spending Stimulate ADP Prioritize ADP	Deficit down Revenues up Current spending down ADP expanding

administrative capacity to implement such changes does not exist at present. Similarly, improving the collection of direct taxes may be jeopardized by poor administration, incomplete information flows regarding taxpayers, and the lack of a proper extension/network of income tax offices throughout the country.

The fact that a significant proportion of economic activity takes place in the informal sector acts as a second major constraint to tax reform. For example, the VAT cannot be collected from activities in the informal sector, as formal book-keeping and accounting procedures are virtually non-existent, and registration would be an immense problem.

Administrative problems also affect the expenditure side of the budget. Inefficient targeting and uncoordinated budgeting of current and ADP spending has resulted in high and often ill-prioritized public spending. Reforms are now underway to strengthen project implementation, which if successful should enable the Government to effect a steady increase in ADP expenditures.

Public enterprise reforms constitute another important element in the agenda for fiscal reforms. Public enterprise losses are substantial and divert resources away from investment, operations and maintenance and other high priority activities. Reducing these losses and increasing efficiency are urgent priorities.

The absence of well-targeted donor support acts as yet another constraint. For example, in the area of civil service and expenditure reforms, the Government has identified the need to retrench employees. However, these employees need to be compensated and the Government requires resources for this. This is an area where donors could assist, but are generally unwilling to do so. Compensation programmes therefore will rely on resources being 'fungible' from elsewhere.

4   MEDIUM TERM CONSEQUENCES AND PROSPECTS FOR SUSTAINABILITY

The previous section focused on the short-run consequences of the reforms and, in particular, on their immediate impact on public finances. The short-run effects are in fact encouraging – the macroeconomy has been successfully stabilized, government revenues have been augmented and government expenditures restrained. In contrast to stabilization, adjustment programmes should not, however, be judged solely in terms of their impact effects but rather by reference to their medium-term consequences. Will the reforms successfully diversify the revenue base to deliver a more buoyant tax structure and will they be sustained? In a recent evaluation of experience with reform programmes, Greenaway and Morrissey (1993) argue that medium-term prospects should be judged against a number of criteria: on the one hand credibility, initial conditions and political economy considerations; on the other hand sequencing and timing issues. To these should be added supply side responsiveness. We will consider the prospects for the Bangladeshi reform under these headings.

4.1   Initial Conditions, Credibility and Political Economy

A crucial ingredient to sustainability is credibility – are the reforms seen as credible by private sector agents, outside investors and outside agencies? It is too early in the Bangladesh programme to say for sure whether this is the case or not – inevitably one has to judge credibility ex post as there is no way of 'measuring' it ex ante. At this stage, all we can note is that the reforms were implemented against a backcloth of crisis and this is helpful in the sense of signalling the necessity for change to the private sector. However, although the government does appear to be committed to the programme, as we noted earlier, it has been World Bank inspired and financed. The signal this sends is one of a question regarding 'ownership' and therefore commitment. Will the reforms be sustained beyond the duration of the credit?

Credibility and sustainability are tied in with initial conditions. The fact that these were characterized by economic crisis may enhance their credibility and facilitate sustainability. More important however, they have been adopted by a new government. The initial phases were introduced by the military regime of General Ershad, but have been sustained by the democratically elected government of President Zia. The initial conditions do appear to be consistent with policy compatibility – trade liberalization has been accompanied by exchange rate depreciation. As Collier and Gunning (1992) show, this is important if the excess supply of money and resultant trade deficit associated with trade liberalization is to be neutralized. Often, in an adjustment programme, aid in the form of adjustment credits is used as a substitute for devaluation – under a range of plausible scenarios this is unlikely to be sustainable. Although credits have obviously been disbursed to Bangladesh, they have not been used to avoid exchange rate adjustment. This will contribute to a set of initial conditions which is conducive to sustainability.

Political economy factors have a crucial bearing on credibility and sustainability – in particular the degree to which lobbying in the early stages erodes the reforms or results in instrument substitution; and the extent to which systemic reforms underpin the infrastructure. Almost all reforms create gainers and losers. Highly controlled regimes, such as pre-reform Bangladesh, have large influential constituencies of agents who have secured property rights to the rents from protection. As losers from reform they invariably lobby against its introduction. If this is unsuccessful they then lobby for special treatment. Bangladesh is no exception. Lobbying efforts have been directed at making special cases for VAT exemption, cases for supplementary special duties on imports, temporary protection via statutory restrictive orders and so on. The key problem here is that once special cases are created, there is a strong incentive for others to lobby for similar treatment, and the seeds for slippage are sown. In the Bangladesh case it is unfortunate that opportunities have been provided for special treatment: special supplementary duties are available to deal with 'luxury products'; a sick industries commission has been created to ease adjustment problems; statutory restrictive orders remain available for 'temporary' reintroduction of quotas; some exceptions and exemptions from VAT have been permitted. One can make a good case for some of these – for instance luxuries do provide a justification for sumptuary taxes on equity grounds; adjustment pressures should not be neglected and so on. If however a large number of exceptions are permitted in the early stages of a rule change, the basis for the rule is eroded, the credibility of its maintenance called into question. The number of exceptions and exemptions in the (crucially important) early stages of the reform have introduced more discretion into the system than is desirable.

The role of the institutional infrastructure which underpins reform is vital and can have an important bearing on the prospects for sustainability. Two dimensions are relevant: whether existing institutions can accommodate change; and how existing and new institutions evolve with change. These are rather important in the case of Bangladesh since the fiscal reforms did actually involve new taxes, in particular the VAT. There was a technical assistance programme which preceded the introduction of VAT but this is widely regarded as inadequate in the government service. Moreover, the manpower provisions of the National Revenue Board do not appear to have altered with the reform, despite the broadening of the tax base. On political economy grounds one can make a case for a rapid introduction, since that pre-empts the mobilization of resistance and directs resources at on-the-job training. Moreover, defendants would point out that VAT has been associated with revenue enhancement. This is certainly true. Without further investment in the administrative infrastructure however, serious constraints could arise with the extension of the base of the tax. Ambitious plans are in hand to broaden and deepen the tax. It is likely that the present stock of tax officials will be inadequate for this purpose. If further revenue enhancement does not come about from the extension of the base, rate changes may be necessary; if rate changes occur this could erode commitment.

4.2 Sequencing and Timing

Medium-term consequences and the eventual sustainability of the reform programme in general and fiscal reforms in particular, will also be affected by sequencing and timing issues. Among the most important of these are: whether reforms are pervasive or narrow; sweeping or modifying; rapid or gradual; appropriately sequenced.

As we saw in Section 2 the Bangladesh reforms can reasonably be described as pervasive rather than narrow. They are not confined to one particular sector but are fairly broadly based. Having said that, however, they are not sweeping reforms. Some radical departures have been initiated (e.g. VAT), but many changes are simply modifications. Although the reforms are set within the context of a rolling programme and, as such, are phased, implementation has nevertheless been fairly rapid. Finally, the sequencing does appear to have been appropriate in that quantitative restriction (QR) elimination has preceded some of the tariff reductions; trade reforms and fiscal reforms have preceded liberalization of factor markets and the capital account.

We are now at the stage in the programme where a major privatization effort is being implemented and some consideration is being given to the liberalization of exchange controls. Clearly these are reforms which will broaden the base of the entire programme. What are the implications of all this for sustainability? In the most comprehensive cross-country analysis of liberalization in developing countries to date, Michaely et al. (1991) conclude that rapid implementation is more conducive to sustainability than staged programmes and that broadly based programmes have better prospects than those which are narrowly based.

They could find no reliable inferences regarding sequencing although Edwards (1990) and others have made a cogent case to support the view that prospects for sustainability are enhanced by having product market and fiscal reforms precede capital market reforms. The Bangladeshi reforms have thus far been a qualified success, the economy has been successfully stabilized and fiscal enhancement has occurred against the backcloth of a broadly based and appropriately sequenced programme.

Sequencing and timing do appear to have been appropriate to the circumstances in Bangladesh. Given the pervasiveness of controls prior to reform and the influence of well-entrenched interest groups, rapid implementation of a broadly based programme was undoubtedly more sensible than a gradualist piecemeal strategy. Having said that, it has to be acknowledged that to a degree it is the 'easy' stages which have been undertaken so far. VAT is confined to manufacturers and importers, with the service sector, wholesalers, retailers and small firms excluded; many of the tariffs which have been reduced were in all likelihood redundant and average nominal rates remain relatively high (and effective rates are no doubt higher still); expenditure reductions have been concentrated on capital rather than current expenditure. Since the reforms appear to have 'worked' in the sense of delivering fiscal enhancement, this may deliver more by way of government commitment, which in turn may help maintain the momentum of reform and encourage government to tackle current expenditure overruns. The next stage is somewhat tougher: extension of the VAT base; tariff cuts that do actually deliver more by way of competition to local products; public sector retrenchment to cut back current expenditure rather than capital expenditure. Longer term success depends upon the momentum being maintained; in turn this will be sensitive to the supply side response to the reforms.

4.3 Supply Side Response

The fundamental objective of adjustment lending programmes is to deliver growth which is not balance of payments constrained. To do so reforms are directed at mobilising domestic resources more efficiently and allowing relative prices to play a more important role in allocating resources. In an economy like Bangladesh where the influence of government is so pervasive, reforms which alter the balance of activity in the public sector and the accumulation of public sector resources and their use are crucial to creating an environment within which the private sector can flourish. Ultimately, however, for the programme to be successful there has to be a private sector supply side response. It is this which not only delivers growth but broadens the tax base to provide greater tax buoyancy.

Thus far the supply side response in Bangladesh has been muted. There are several possible explanations for this. First of all, stabilization of the macroeconomy was effected in part via a measure of demand deflation and import compression. This ought to be a 'one-off' effect and now that inflation is under control and public finances have been stabilized, its influence may wane. Second, it may be that the reform programme has as yet done little to alter incentive structures in the economy. As a consequence private sector invest- ment has yet to respond. A third possibility is that the reforms have altered relative prices and therefore incentives, but that the private sector has yet to be persuaded that they will be sustained. In other words, there is a question mark against the commitment of the government towards seeing the reform pro- gramme through. For perfectly rational reasons then, investors hold off from committing themselves to long-term projects. A fourth possibility is that private sector investors do actually see the reforms as credible but responses are sufficiently slow that the full effects are not yet evident. Whether it is the second, third or fourth of these which is the explanation, the message is the same – to help stimulate a private sector response, programme implementation needs to be maintained.

5   CONCLUSIONS

In recent years Bangladesh has embarked upon an ambitious and extensive programme of policy reforms. These were directed in the first instance at stabilizing the macroeconomy and subsequently at creating the conditions for sustainable growth. The programme has contained many 'standard' features of adjustment lending reforms, but also some novel and rather ambitious features. In this paper we have concentrated on the consequences of reform for the government budget constraint. Both revenue and expenditure changes have been implemented – again some standard and some novel. The programme has already succeeded in diversifying the revenue base and changing the balance of expenditures away from current and towards capital projects and there is a clearly identified extension to the programme laid out for the next few years. In the short run the broader programme has not been threatened by fiscal depletion despite an adverse macro climate dominated by slow growth. However, it is now reaching a critical stage – the planned extensions and the infrastructure to support those extensions are pre-requisites for sustainability. Sustainability is in turn a pre-requisite for the credibility and longer term success of the pro- gramme.

NOTES

1. For details of these changes see Ghafur and Chowdhury (1988).
2. For a detailed discussion of the financing patterns of the budget deficit, see Priya Basu and Machiko Nissanke, 1992 and Chapter 3 of *The Least Developed Countries 1992 Report*, UNCTAD Secretariat, February 1993.

REFERENCES

Basu, Priya and Machiko Nissanke (1992), 'Improving Domestic Resource Mobilisation for Economic Development', UNCTAD Discussion Paper.

Chowdhury, O. and M. Hossain (1988), 'Tax Structure in Bangladesh: An Overview', *The Bangladesh Development Studies*, 16, pp. 65–91.

Collier, P. and J. Gunning (1992), 'Aid and Exchange Rate Adjustment in African Trade Liberalisations', *Economic Journal*, 102, pp. 925–39.

Edwards, S. (1990), 'The Sequencing of Economic Reform: Analytical Issues and Lessons from Latin America', *The World Economy,* 13, pp. 1–14.

Falvey, R. and C.D. Kim (1992), 'Timing and Sequencing Issues in Trade Liberalisation', *Economic Journal*, 102, pp. 908–24.

GATT (1992), *Trade Policy Review: Bangladesh* (Geneva: GATT).

Ghafur, A. and H.O. Chowdhury (1988), *Financing Public Sector Development Expenditure in Selected Countries: Bangladesh* (Manila: Asian Development Bank).

Greenaway, D. (1993), 'Liberalising Foreign Trade Through Rose Tinted Glasses', *Economic Journal*, 103, pp. 208–23.

Greenaway, D. and C.R. Milner (1993), *Trade and Industrial Policy in Developing Countries* (London: Macmillan).

Greenaway, D. and O. Morrisey (1993), 'Structural Adjustment and Liberalisation in Developing Countries: What Lessons Have Been Learned?', *Kyklos*, 46, pp. 241–61.

Mansur, A. and B. Khondker (1991), 'Revenue Effects of the VAT System in Bangladesh', *The Bangladesh Development Studies*, 19, pp. 1–33.

Michaely, M., D. Papageorgiou and A. Choksi (1991), 'Lessons of Experience in the Developing World', *Liberalising Foreign Trade,* vol. 7 (Oxford: Blackwell).

UNCTAD (1993), *The Least Developed Countries 1992 Report* (Geneva: UNCTAD Secretariat).

Whalley, J. (1991), 'Recent Trade Liberalisation in the Developing World: What is Behind it and Where is it Headed?', in D. Greenaway et al. (eds), *Global Protectionism* (London: Macmillan).

World Bank (1989), *Bangladesh: Recent Economic Developments and Short-Term Prospects* (Washington DC: World Bank).

World Bank (1990), *Bangladesh: Managing the Adjustment Process – An Appraisal* (Washington DC: World Bank).

World Bank (1993), *Bangladesh: Implementing Structural Reform* (Washington DC: World Bank).

4. Structural Adjustment and Fiscal Reforms in Malawi: An Assessment

Priya Basu and Chris Milner

1 INTRODUCTION

Malawi is a small, landlocked, predominantly agricultural economy with a per capita GNP at the start of the 1990s of about $180. The economy has been relatively open compared to other African economies and during the 1970s achieved one of the highest growth rates among the developing countries. This period of strong economic growth, driven mainly by growth in the estate agriculture sector (specializing in tea, tobacco and sugar for export), came to a halt in the late 1970s and early 1980s when steep declines in the terms of trade, drought and the onset of transport difficulties through Mozambique, which forced up international transport costs, induced sharp declines in per capita income.

The economic crisis revealed severe structural weaknesses in the economy, including a stagnant smallholder agricultural sector (growing maize mainly for subsistence and some export cash crops), high import dependence in the industrial and energy sectors, inefficient public enterprises and a limited institutional capacity. To restore macroeconomic stability and address the structural weaknesses, the Government implemented a series of adjustment/reform programmes during the 1980s, with World Bank and IMF support. Tax reform, import liberalization and reform of the agricultural and financial sectors were key elements of the structural policies. Although the adjustment effort began at the start of the 1980s, it was hampered by a new set of unfavourable external developments – including a further sharp terms of trade deterioration, the closure of the rail link through Mozambique and a substantial influx of refugees from Mozambique. This has necessitated a series of stabilization and adjustment efforts during the 1980s with the most substantive structural policy reforms coming in the post-1987 period. Although these reforms have not yet been completed, they are sufficiently advanced and the agenda of implementation sufficiently clearly defined to warrant some assessment of the progress to date.

The focus in this paper is on the fiscal aspects of the reform programmes in the post-1980 period, and in particular on the relationship between fiscal and other, including trade, policy reforms. We are interested in a number of aspects of this relationship. How did the trade policy reforms which were required as part of the structural adjustment programme affect the country's fiscal position? How successful have fiscal reforms been? How has fiscal reform affected the implementation of other elements of the reform programme? Finally, we consider how much structural adjustment has been achieved, and what role trade and fiscal policy reforms have played in the adjustment.

1.1 Structure of the Case Study

In order to address these issues the remainder of the paper is organized as follows. In Section 2 we review the main features of the post-1980 reform programme in Malawi, giving attention to the context and objectives of the broader structural adjustment reforms and to their content and sequencing. Section 3 provides a more detailed description and analysis of the fiscal reforms. The impact of these reforms, and of other factors, on government revenue and expenditure are evaluated in Section 4. This in turn provides a basis for investigating in Section 5 the questions raised above, with the aim of assessing the effectiveness of the reforms in general and the fiscal reforms in particular. The lessons to be drawn from the reform experience and the longer term viability of the reforms are discussed in Section 6.

2 MALAWI'S ADJUSTMENT PROGRAMMES: 1981–93

Unlike many developing countries, Malawi had not pursued a highly interventionist and inward-oriented strategy in the post-independence period up to the 1980s. Malawi was characterized by pragmatic economic management, which given its narrow resource base and the small size of the organized domestic market necessitated a relatively open economy. But the economy was fragile because of the dependence on imported goods and a small range of exports to generate the foreign exchange required to purchase them, combined with a narrow (physical and human) resource base, high land density and a growing population. This fragility was exposed by a number of external shocks in the 1980s.

Arguably the impact of these shocks was intensified by the period of debt-led growth and investment in the second half of the 1970s. Access to foreign lending in this period disguised fundamental weaknesses in Malawi's fiscal system which were later to become apparent and to be exacerbated by the impact of the external shocks. By 1981 debt servicing consumed about 34 per cent of current expenditures, compared with approximately 15 per cent in 1977–8, and this put strong upward pressure on current expenditures at a time when the budget was already under strain as a result of the external shocks. As a consequence Malawi was forced to turn to the multilateral agencies for both temporary financial relief and long-term adjustment finance.

2.1 Objectives of the Adjustment Strategy

The Government's principal development objectives were and are to increase the rate of economic growth so as to achieve sustained increases in per capita incomes, within the context of macroeconomic stability and poverty reduction. These objectives are outlined in the Statement of Development Policies, 1987–96 and in four successive Policy Framework Papers (PFP).

The Government initiated a broadly based adjustment effort in 1981, with the emphasis on tackling the immediate problems caused by the external shocks and on regaining macroeconomic stability. The major elements of the adjustment programme during the period up to the mid-1980s, which was initiated within the context of three Structural Adjustment Loans (SALs) from the World Bank and arrangements with the IMF, were the reduction of fiscal deficits, the restructuring of public sector enterprises and the reform of smallholder agricultural pricing and marketing policies. With the onset of a second set of external difficulties in the mid-1980s, the adjustment programme was expanded as indicated by the Four PFPs which have been agreed with the World Bank and IMF since 1988. This extended adjustment programme – supported by an Industry and Trade Policy Adjustment Credit (ITPAC) and an Agricultural Sector Adjustment Credit (ASAC) from the World Bank and other bilateral donors, and by successive arrangements with the IMF – covered further adjustments in fiscal and agricultural policy and the restoration of a relatively open trade and foreign exchange regime. The sequencing and content of these reforms are discussed in greater detail below.

Since the end of the 1980s the scope of the adjustment programme has been expanded to encompass further objectives. This reflects increasing awareness of the extent of poverty and the accompanying structural deficiencies of the economy, arising out of the limited human resource base and limited economic participation in formal economic activity. A 1992 credit for the Entrepreneurship Development and Drought Recovery Programme (EDDRP) facilitated policy reforms which focus on improving the investment environment, increasing access to financial capital and enhancing human capital development.

2.2 Sequencing and Content of the Reforms

The timing and extent of financial arrangements in support of the adjustment programme, outlined above in broad terms, are summarized in Table 4.1. The relative longevity of the programme and the fact that it is still ongoing make it important to ascertain with accuracy when and to what extent reforms were actually implemented. We attempt in this section to briefly outline the policy reforms across the whole range of policy instruments or areas (see Table 4.2 for a summary presentation). In Section 3 we give detailed consideration to the specific area of fiscal reforms in Malawi, and therefore exclude any discussion of these reforms at this stage.

Monetary control and interest rate management

Over the adjustment period monetary policy has become less accommodatory, and correspondingly less inflationary. Structural reforms in the monetary sector have sought to improve monetary control mechanisms, whilst at the same time increasing the competitiveness and efficiency of the financial system. The financial system is dominated by the banking sector, comprising the central bank and two commercial banks. Commercial bank interest rates have been liberalized to encourage greater flexibility, though the increased control of inflation has been a more significant factor in the return of positive real rates than the flexibility of nominal rates (which has remained limited).

Statutory reserve requirements were increased after 1989 (following revisions to the Banking Act) with the objective of focusing monetary policy on the control of reserves with less reliance on direct credit ceilings. Direct credit ceilings on commercial banks were eliminated in 1991 in line with the aim of developing a more market-oriented financial system.

Smallholder agricultural policies

Reform in this area focused initially on the annual increase of producer prices (notably of maize), following the elimination of the monopoly marketing role of the Agricultural Development and Marketing Corporation (ADMARC). This strengthening of price incentives resulted in improved performance among larger smallholders in particular. Subsequently non-price incentives to encourage participation by smallholders were strengthened under the 1990 ASAC credit. For example the licensing system which prevented smallholder production of high value cash crops was revised.

The pricing and marketing reforms have been accompanied by some growth in estate agriculture and among larger smallholders. But agricultural productivity overall has stagnated, partly perhaps because of reduced fertiliser usage but largely because of limited adoption of improved technologies and new varieties. This has constrained domestic food security and efforts to stimulate agricultural exports. The revisions to agricultural policy, following ASAC in 1990, were therefore aimed at supporting smallholders and improving land utilization.

*Table 4.1 Financing Arrangements in Support of Adjustment in Malawi,
1981–93 ($ million)*

Period	World Bank Loans and Credits	Amount of Support[a]	Purpose/area
1981	SAL I[b]	45.0	Fiscal policy Smallholder agricultural policies Public sector enterprise reform
1984	SAL II	55.0	Fiscal policy Smallholder agricultural policies Public sector enterprise reform
1986	SAL III	99.0	Fiscal policy Smallholder agricultural policies Public sector enterprise reform
1987	SAL III Supplement	55.0 (15.0)	
1988	ITPAC[c]	186.5 (107.5)	Trade and industrial policy
1990	ASAC[d]	123.6 (44.6)	Agricultural sector reform
1992	EDDRP[e]	120.0	Investment incentives Small enterprises Financial sector Capital and labour markets

Notes:
a. Including amount from bilateral sources in brackets.
b. Structural Adjustment Loan.
c. Industry and Trade Policy Adjustment Credit.
d. Agricultural Sector Adjustment Credit.
e. Entrepreneurship Development and Drought Recovery Programme.

Table 4.2 Summary of Policy Reforms in Malawi, 1981–93

Policy area	Timing	Measures
Monetary Control and Interest Rate Management	1981–92	– Greater interest rate flexibility – Revision of banking legislation for market-oriented monetary control – Elimination of direct credit controls – Moved to market-determined interest rates
Fiscal Policy	1981–	See Table 4.3 for details
Agricultural Policies (smallholder)	1981–93	– Increases in producer prices – Abolition of state marketing monopoly
	1990–93	– Lowering of administrative barriers to entry of markets – Liberalization of fertilizer market and reduction of subsidy – Redirection of R&D – Improved land-utilization in estates
Public Sector Enterprise Reform	1981–7	– Restructuring of parastatal sector – Increased tariffs for public utilities – Tightening of financial targets
Trade Policy	1988–92	– Exchange controls on imports phased out – Import and export licensing reduced substantially – Enhanced duty drawback scheme – Exchange rate adjusted periodically
	1992–6	– Tariff Liberalization and rationalization planned
Industrial Policy	1981–8 1988–92	– Phased removal of price controls – Reduced scope of industrial licensing – Elimination of authority to grant exclusive production rights
	1992–	– Simplification of procedures for business registration and company incorporation – Elimination of industrial licensing process for investments – Estate land rents adjusted more frequently
Investment Incentives	1992–	– Investment code planned – Planned establishment of investment promotion centre – Promotion of small-scale enterprises (through land-use and credit policies)
Financial Sector Reforms	1992–	– Further liberalization of financial sector planned – Development of capital market to be encouraged
Labour Market Reforms		– Review of labour market imperfections planned – Review of minimum wage legislation planned

Public sector enterprise reform
Besides the reforms to ADMARC, restructuring of the parastatal sector included reorganization of the Malawi Development Corporation (MDC), divestiture and restructuring of the quasi-public conglomerate, Press Holdings (PHL), and increased tariffs for public enterprises or agencies such as Malawi Airways and Malawi Housing Corporation. Financial performance in the parastatal sector as a whole subsequently improved, and financial targets under the PFPs have in general been attained.

Trade and exchange rate policy
In the early stages of the adjustment period Malawi's trade and foreign exchange regime was relatively open. The regime became more restrictive however, in response to the deteriorating economic situation in the mid-1980s; trade taxes were gradually increased and exchange controls on the financing of imports were introduced. Under the auspices of the 1988 and 1990s credits (ITPAC and ASAC), the Government began to phase out exchange controls on imports, and except for a small negative list, this was completed by January 1991. This period also witnessed efforts to improve the duty drawback system for exports. The need for further trade liberalization, however, is recognized under the 1992 EDDRP Credit. Under this, the Government is committed to setting tariff reform targets for 1995/6. In general the aim is to reduce the average tariff rate on non-government imports to no more than 15 per cent, with a maximum rate of 35 per cent.

The latest programme also commits the Government to the policy of maintaining the exchange rate at a level consistent with external competitiveness. Over the past decade the kwacha has been devalued several times with the nominal exchange rate falling from about 0.8 Kw/US$ in 1980 to 2.8 Kw/US$ in 1992.

Industrial policy
Early adjustment measures initiated important steps towards developing a larger and more innovative private industrial sector. Measures such as the removal of price controls and, since 1988, the reduced scope of industrial, import and export licensing have reduced the extent of government intervention. These measures have also been supported by the reforms in the parastatal sector. There was some recovery in private investment between 1988–91, but this was mainly in traditional sectors, and there remains some reluctance among policy makers to relinquish control over private sector enterprise. The 1992 EDDRP credit therefore focuses in particular on improving the investment environment for entrepreneurial activity.

The policy reforms initiated after 1992 under the EDDRP are summarized in Table 4.2 under a number of headings (Investment Incentives, Financial Sector

Reforms and Labour Market Reforms). As it is difficult at this stage to ascertain the degree of implementation or to identify any of their effects we will not discuss them any further at this stage. They are listed in Table 4.2 to emphasize that the adjustment programme is still ongoing, and to highlight where further reforms are perceived to be required.

This section has outlined the wide-ranging and sustained adjustment programme undertaken in Malawi since 1981. Probably the most comprehensive and significant aspects of these reforms have been those pertaining to fiscal policy and we turn to a detailed analysis of fiscal reforms in the next section.

3   FISCAL POLICY REFORM IN MALAWI

The pre-reform tax system, inherited from the colonial period, was one heavily dependent on direct taxes, personal and company income taxes accounting for as much as 50 per cent of total tax revenue. The income tax base was however extremely narrow, comprising a few large private firms in primary processing and distribution and workers in the public sector and large companies. Indirect taxation was raised initially primarily from customs duties (about 45 per cent of total tax revenue in the 1960s), with a rate structure designed to promote import substitution of consumer goods and to deter luxury consumption. The base for indirect taxation was broadened, however, in 1970 with the introduction of surtax (a sales tax) on the sales price of domestically manufactured goods and the duty-inclusive price of imports (by 1977 the base rate of surtax was 15 per cent, with an uplift factor of 1.2 on imports). Capital goods were exempt while registered manufacturers could qualify for a rebate of surtax paid on intermediate inputs, the amount of the rebate depending on the final product manufactured and whether the input could be sourced locally.

The various negative exogenous shocks which the economy experienced from the late 1970s combined to increase demand for government expenditure, with adverse consequences for the fiscal position. The budget deficit rose from 8–9 per cent of GDP in 1976/7 to 12–14 per cent in 1978–9. The initial response to this fiscal crisis was to raise taxes in an ad hoc manner on virtually all existing tax bases, and particularly on international trade. The basic domestic surtax rate was increased in a number of steps to 30 per cent by 1984 and income taxes were also raised. New tax bases were created with the introduction of the explicit taxation of exports in 1985.

By the mid-1980s it was increasingly evident that the above, ad hoc revenue-raising measures were not desirable in the long run, and that the tax system as a whole was in need of reform especially if adjustment to a more liberal economic environment was to be achieved. In 1985 the Government asked the World Bank for assistance in reviewing the tax system and suggesting recommendations for reform and this resulted in a report in November 1985 (Chamley et al., 1985).

3.1 Reform of Indirect Taxes

The key features of the recommended reforms of taxes on goods and services are set out in Table 4.3. Tax reform has been implemented in three stages: stage 1 in 1987–9, stage 2 in 1990–92 and stage 3 in 1992–3.

Malawi's surtax was previously based on the ring or suspension method of commodity taxation; transactions among the 'ring' of registered manufacturers were exempt and surtax only applied to sales outside the ring. Since the seller had to request documentation from the buyer to show that he was registered, it was possible to transform this arrangement into a VAT-type system of commodity taxation by reversing the procedures of the existing system. By replacing the exemption approach with a tax-credit principle all sales would become taxable (except for export sales), with sellers claiming credit for taxes paid on input purchases. This offered the possibility of reduced production distortions associated with input taxation, and the administrative advantage of removing the need to distinguish between final and intermediate goods or between tax-exempt and tax-paying producers. Thus although the government had originally resisted the introduction of value-added tax (VAT) on grounds of administrative complexity (and subsequently resisted a change of name for surtax), it accepted and implemented reforms in the April 1988 budget that introduced a VAT-type system of commodity taxation. The administrative demands imposed by the introduction of the credit mechanism were expected to be the most difficult aspect of this reform, but the nature of the existing arrangements, the analysis undertaken in the study period, prior training and procedural and documentation reforms were such that the revised surtax became operational fairly quickly. Indeed, as Table 4.3 shows, it was possible to extend the coverage of surtax within the manufacturing sector, and the wholesale and retail sectors and in stage 2 (1990–92) to the service sector.

The second key feature of the indirect tax reforms involved the rationalization of trade and domestic taxes in order to shift the revenue function of trade taxes into domestic taxation. This was to be achieved by eliminating the uplift factor on import surtax (raising the basic rate to compensate for this), and then applying the same basic (or luxury) surtax rate (and crediting system) to all formal domestic production and imports (competing and non-competing). Thus import duties could then be rationalized (i.e. the adjustment of rates, the incorporation of any additional import levies and conversion of specific into ad valorem duties) in order to satisfy protective objectives only. The expectation was that these duties could be gradually reduced as liberalization proceeded. Indeed the creation of a prototype consumption tax, with common surtax rates

Table 4.3 Summary of Taxation Reforms in Malawi, 1987–93

Tax Policy Reform	Administrative Reform
Stage 1: 1987–9	
a) Indirect	
– Shift from ring to credit surtax system	– Issuing of taxpayer identification numbers
– Rationalization of tariffs and domestic rates	– Construction of a master tax file
	– Computerization
– Expansion of surtax base	– Redesign of tax forms and documents
	– Introduction of document control system
	– Some staff training
	– Conversion to harmonised system for commodity classification
b) Direct	
– Revision of investment allowance	
– Increased company tax base	
– Introduction of provisional tax on non-PAYE income	
– Introduction of a border withholding tax on non–residents	
– Expanded withholding on bank interest for individual income taxpayers	
Stage 2: 1990–92	
a) Indirect	
– Surtax, excise and customs rates reduced	– Further staff training
– Further conversion to ad valorem excise taxes	– Extension of computerization
	– Enhancement of auditing and collection procedures
– Expansion of surtax to services	
– Development of a duty drawback system	
b) Direct	
– Decreased tax rates	
– Extension of personal income tax base	
– Introduction of taxation for capital gains, fringe benefits, foreign exchange gains	
Stage 3: 1992–3	– Further staff training
	– Development of a field audit programme
	– Further collection enhancement
	– Further computerization
	– Creation of a Tax Policy Unit

on imports and domestic production, tended to lower nominal and effective protection rates immediately.

Exports are zero-rated for surtax purposes, and refunds on taxed inputs are available through the crediting process. Similarly the intention was that the competitiveness of exports should not to be harmed through trade taxes; an improved duty drawback scheme has been developed and export taxes (introduced in 1985) have been eliminated.

There are clearly elements of efficiency improvement and fiscal (base) enhancement associated with these indirect tax reforms. But an important aim of the reforms was also to achieve greater equity (i.e. progressivity) through the reform of the rate structure. A number of the reforms have in fact been directed towards this objective. Excise and custom duties have been shifted progressively from a specific to an ad valorem basis. Ad valorem excises on goods such as alcohol and tobacco have been added in effect as luxury rates to the basic surtax, with the 'quality' of the excisable good determining the rate applied. Luxury import tariff rates have been replaced by new higher surtax rates. These higher surtax (or ad valorem excises) have been central to the attempt to increase equity within the indirect tax system.

3.2 Reform of Direct Taxes

As pointed out earlier, company taxes were a major source of direct and total tax revenues. At the time of the fiscal study the statutory nominal company tax rate was 50 per cent. Chamley et al. (1985) estimated that this translated into an average effective tax rate of 39 per cent and a marginal effective rate of 43 per cent in the manufacturing sector and 58 per cent in non-manufacturing. The disparity between nominal and marginal rates in the case of manufacturing was owing to generous investment allowances (which varied between sectors) and the ability of firms to pay tax with a lag of at least one year.

The reforms of company taxation were aimed at increasing neutrality (i.e. reducing inter-sectoral and asset biases) and in expanding the tax base. Thus the collapsing of all investment-related allowances and credits into a uniform, initial allowance of 40 per cent began in April 1988, which had the effect of raising the allowance for a number of assets. Similarly the base of company taxation has been increased in a number of ways: a withholding tax was imposed on sales by firms in the tobacco and transport sectors, state-owned enterprises have been incorporated into the company tax framework, and all firms have been placed on a current estimated payment system.

In stage 2 company tax rates have been reduced to a rate of 35 per cent, although the cuts in the nominal rate have tended to be offset by the effects of inflation; the effective tax rate being subject to upward pressure by the erosion of the real value of depreciation allowances and by the inflation of nominal capital gains on inventories.

The reform of personal income tax has been slower. In stage 1 the base was expanded by the introduction of provisional tax on non-PAYE income and by expanding the withholding system. In stage 2 the tax base was extended to include, for example, capital gains and fringe benefits. Corresponding to this broadening of the income tax base, the highest income tax rate for individuals was reduced from 50 per cent to 35 per cent.

3.3   Tax Administration Reforms

Although there have been financial constraints and a continuing shortage of technical staff, some effort has gone into raising the administrative capacity of the income tax and customs and excise departments. Indeed by stage 3 the whole focus of the reforms was on the design and implementation of modern and computerized administrative procedures. Resident advisers from the Harvard Institute of Economic Development have been in place since 1987. In stage 1 the focus of the reforms was on the essential pre-requisites of enhanced administrative capacity and efficiency, for example, taxpayer identification numbers, a master tax file, and documentation design and control. There was also some progress in computerization, in particular in the income tax department, and in the training of officials (e.g. surtax administration). These efforts continued in stage 2. Some graduate-level training has been provided abroad, and local training has included instruction programmes and practical training in assessment, audit and collection activities. As a result the backlog of income tax assessments has declined and a programme of the field audit for income tax (albeit with a small staff of auditors) has been initiated. But staffing levels and skills remain a serious problem in all areas. This constraint appears to be particularly severe in the area of income tax collection (as of January 1993 there were more than 8 500 delinquent business accounts amounting in value to Kw37 million) and the surtax division of customs and excise (where the number of registrations did not increase as expected, despite the extension of surtax to services).

3.4   Public Expenditure Management and Control

Although not specifically part of the fiscal reform package discussed so far in this section, it is appropriate to mention at this stage the ongoing pressures (within the adjustment programme) to improve the mobilization and management of public resources. Intensified fiscal discipline at the start of the 1980s had brought progress in lowering the overall budget deficit. However the deficit worsened again in 1986/7, maize purchases and expenditures due to the security situation driving up recurrent expenditures. In February 1988, the authorities introduced a new growth programme based on the Statement of Development Policies (DEVPOL) for the period 1987–96. This was followed and supported by the IMF and World Bank arrangements discussed in the previous section. A recurring feature of these programmes is the aim of strengthening the budgetary allocation process, the reviewing of allocation priorities between sectors and the controlling of expenditure in sectoral ministries. In particular, the aim has been to strengthen the role of the rolling three-year Public Sector Investment Programme (PSIP) in expenditure planning including more comprehensive control of parastatal investments involving government finances.

4   IMPACT OF REFORMS ON THE GOVERNMENT BUDGET

This section examines the impact of reforms on government revenue, expenditure and deficits. For the purposes of our discussion the adjustment period is divided into two. The first period, 1981/2–1986/7 covers the stabilization measures introduced in response to the exogenous shocks of the late 1970s. These reforms had brought about a reduction of the overall deficit by 1985/6 but they were undermined by further unfavourable developments in the mid-1980s. These developments, coupled with the fact that policy changes during the first half of the 1980s had been focused on 'stabilization' rather than on longer term 'adjustment', resulted in a sharp worsening of fiscal balances in 1986/7. The second period, 1987/8–1992/3, covers the implementation of a series of more wide-ranging stabilization and adjustment programmes. While the main thrust of fiscal policy reforms under these programmes has been on minimizing fiscal imbalances the programmes have included some fundamental reforms in the tax structure and changes to the decision-making process guiding expenditure allocation as described earlier.

4.1   Revenue and Expenditure Trends and Patterns: 1981/2–1986/7

The economic difficulties of the late 1970s and early 1980s precipitated a deterioration in the overall budget deficit (including grants), which stood at almost 12 per cent of GDP in 1981/2 (see Table 4.4). Domestic revenues stagnated and there was a decline in the inflow of foreign grants as a proportion of GDP. Under pressure to reduce the budget deficit the Government cut public expenditures, which appeared to be an easier and quicker solution to the problem than efforts to mobilize additional revenues.

Total expenditures as a percentage of GDP declined from 35.6 per cent in 1981/2 to 31.4 per cent in 1985/6. Development expenditures and extra-budgetary expenditures bore the brunt of these cutbacks, while recurrent spending actually increased over this period (see Table 4.4).[1]

Table 4.4 Central Government Budgetary Operations in Malawi, 1981/2–1991/2^a (% of GDP)

	82	83	84	85	86	87	88	89	90	91[b]	92[c]
1. Total revenue and grants	23.8	23.0	22.3	23.0	25.1	24.8	23.7	27.1	26.5	22.8	22.5
1.1 Revenues	20.0	19.6	19.9	20.7	22.7	22.5	21.2	21.2	22.6	20.6	19.2
1.1.1 Tax	16.2	16.7	16.6	17.3	19.1	17.8	16.3	18.4	19.2	17.5	16.6
1.1.2 Non-tax	3.8	2.9	3.3	3.4	3.6	4.7	4.8	2.8	3.4	3.1	2.6
1.2 Grants	3.8	3.3	2.3	2.3	2.4	2.3	2.5	5.9	3.9	2.3	3.4
2. Expenditure	35.6	32.2	30.1	29.5	31.4	36.4	29.9	30.1	29.5	27.0	24.9
2.1 Recurrent	21.0	21.0	20.1	21.4	21.8	25.6	22.4	19.6	21.9	20.9	19.8
2.2 Development	11.2	11.2	10.0	8.1	8.2	8.7	7.5	9.6	6.7	6.1	5.1
2.3 Extra-budgetary	3.3	.	.	.	1.3	2.1	.	0.9	0.8	.	.
3. Deficit before grants	-15.6	-12.5	-10.2	-8.8	-8.7	-13.9	-8.7	-9.0	-6.9	-6.5	-5.7
Overall deficit	-11.7	-9.2	-7.8	-6.4	-6.3	-11.5	-6.2	-3.1	-2.1	-4.2	-2.3
GDP at market prices (K million)	1 103.8	1 244.0	1 435.9	1 707.7	1 949.9	2 191.2	2 756.5	3 552.3	4 388.2	5 069.9	6 144.3

Notes:
a. Fiscal years.
b. Actual.
c. Revised.

Source: Economic Report, Malawi Government, various issues (1980–92).

There are a number of reasons for this pattern of expenditure reduction in Malawi. First, public enterprises in Malawi suffered a fiscal crisis in the early 1980s, resulting in a decline in investment by the statutory bodies (commercial parastatals) during the first half of the 1980s, which accounted for almost half of the overall decline in investment over that period. Development loans to public enterprises by the Central Government also declined, reflecting the Government's efforts to reduce expenditure by the statutory bodies. Second, a large part of development (capital) expenditure in Malawi has tended to be foreign financed. A decline in grant inflows into Malawi during the first half of the 1980s therefore led to a fall in development spending. Third, programmes have at times set capital budget targets that in hindsight seem ambitious and unrealistic in relation to the implementation capacity of the country. Fourth, bureaucratic and administrative delays in the recipient country, lack of government funds to finance the domestic part of the costs, and delays in the release of counterpart funds of commodity aid by different donor agencies have also often led to shortfalls in capital spending. Finally, governments may find it easier to meet overall fiscal targets by reducing capital expenditures than by cutting wages and salaries, or by raising taxes. Moreover, a large part of the recurrent budget tends to be non-discretionary, for example, contractual interest payments on foreign debt.[2]

In contrast to the decline in capital spending, current expenditures continued to display an expansionary trend. A breakdown of current expenditures by functional classification and economic type suggests that increases in current spending during the period 1981/2–1985/6 were fuelled mainly by the rising public debt (both domestic and foreign) and increases in grants and subsidies to public and private bodies (see Tables 4.7 and 4.8 below). Debt servicing requirements were raised by the appreciation of the US dollar and higher interest rates on dollar denominated loans. Revisions to civil service salaries also contributed to the expansion of current expenditures.

Fiscal policy during the first half of the 1980s focused relatively little on revenue enhancement, although some changes were introduced to income taxes. 1983 saw the abolition of personal allowances/deductions and the withholding tax (limited to corporate dividends and interest payments) was introduced in 1985. These changes, coupled with the good tobacco and tea yields and generally buoyant prices in 1983/4, resulted in an increase in revenues from income and profit taxes. Some increase was also seen in revenues collected from individual income and profit taxes, and the surtax. As a result tax revenues as a share of GDP rose by nearly 3 percentage points between 1981/2 and 1985/6.

Non-tax revenues suffered a small decline over the period, owing mainly to the financial crisis in most of the parastatals, and the share of foreign grants in GDP also fell from 3.8 per cent in 1981/2 to 2.4 per cent in 1985/6. Despite this government revenue (including grants), rose from 23.8 per cent of GDP in 1981/2 to 25.1 per cent in 1985/6 (see Table 4.5).

Table 4.5 *Major Tax and non-Tax Revenues: Malawi, 1981/2–1992/3 (% of GDP)*

	82	83	84	85	86	87	88	89	90	91[a]	92[b]	93[c]
Tax revenue	16.2	16.7	16.6	17.3	19.1	17.8	16.3	18.4	19.2	17.5	16.6	16.3
1. Tax on income and profit	5.6	6.4	6.5	6.9	7.9	7.7	6.6	7.8	8.0	7.3	6.8	6.8
– Companies	3.1	3.6	3.7	4.2	5.2	4.7	3.5	4.7	4.7	4.4	4.1	3.9
– Individuals	2.5	2.7	2.8	2.6	2.7	2.9	3.1	3.1	3.3	2.9	2.7	2.9
2. Taxes on property	–	–	–	–	–	–	–	–	0.0	0.0	–	–
3. Taxes on goods and services	6.0	5.9	6.0	6.5	6.4	6.4	6.6	7.3	7.7	6.8	6.5	7.0
– Accommodation and refreshments	–	–	–	–	–	–	–	0.1	0.1	0.1	0.1	0.1
– Surtax	4.9	4.7	4.7	5.4	5.3	5.4	5.8	6.3	6.7	5.9	5.7	6.2
– Excise duties	0.8	0.9	0.9	0.7	0.7	0.6	0.5	0.6	0.6	0.6	0.5	0.5
– Licences	0.3	0.3	0.3	0.3	0.3	0.3	0.2	0.3	0.2	0.2	0.2	0.2
4. International trade taxes	4.5	4.2	4.1	3.9	4.7	3.7	3.1	3.2	3.5	3.2	3.5	3.8
5. Stamp duty	–	–	–	–	–	–	–	–	0.1	0.1	–	–
Non-tax revenue	3.8	2.9	3.3	3.4	3.6	4.7	4.8	2.8	3.4	3.1	2.2	3.2
1. Treasury fund receipts	0.2	0.3	0.2	–	0.1	0.2	0.3	0.3	0.4	0.3	0.3	0.4
2. Rents	0.2	0.2	0.1	0.2	0.3	0.3	0.3	0.2	0.2	0.2	0.2	0.2
3. Departmental receipts	2.5	2.1	2.5	2.4	2.6	2.8	2.2	1.2	2.4	2.1	1.4	1.7
4. Other	0.9	0.3	0.4	0.7	0.5	1.3	2.0	1.0	0.4	0.4	0.2	0.9

Notes:
a. Actual.
b. Revised.
c. Estimates.

Source: Economic Report, Malawi Government, various years (1980–92).

As a consequence of the trends in government expenditures and revenues described above, the overall deficit (including grants) was reduced from 11.7 per cent of GDP in 1981/2 to 6.3 per cent in 1985/6. But the following year was marked by a reversal in budgetary trends. Total expenditures increased, owing to large extra budgetary expenditures associated with food stocking and the security situation combined with a sharp growth in debt service. The expansion in expenditures resulted in a worsening of the overall deficit to 11.5 per cent of GDP in 1986/7.

4.2 Recent Fiscal Reforms and their Impact: 1987/8–1992/3

The Government introduced a new growth programme in February 1988 based on the Statement of Development Policies (DEVPOL) and supported by a 15-month stand-by arrangement with the IMF. This was followed by a three-year structural adjustment programme covering the period April 1988 to March 1991, supported by arrangements under the IMF's ESAF, the World Bank's Industrial and Trade Policy Credit (ITPAC) and an Agricultural Sector Adjustment Credit (ASAC), and significant donor-cofinancing. Structural adjustment during the period July 1991 to June 1992 was financed by a fourth annual arrangement under the ESAF, which was extended by six months to the end of 1992, and by another 12 months to the end of 1993. Fiscal reforms have formed an important component of the overall adjustment programme and have entailed the close monitoring of government expenditures and reduction of the overall deficit in order to permit the transfer of financial resources to the private sector, thereby reducing macroeconomic imbalances while supporting the recovery of private investment. Major efforts have also been made to mobilize revenues, and tax reforms have formed an important part of the Government's policy agenda since 1987. It is worth mentioning that the initiative for tax reforms was largely indigenous, and was started before the donor-supported adjustment process began.

Impact on revenues
Malawi embarked on an ambitious programme of tax reform in 1987, with the objectives of improving revenue generation, efficiency, equity and ease of administration. The details of these reforms were presented in Section 3. This section provides an assessment of their impact on the level and structure of revenues.

The reforms in indirect taxes aimed to shift the burden of taxation towards consumption rather than production-based taxes. Together with increasing levels of imports associated with liberalization (and the consequent increases in surtax revenues collected from imports) the reforms led to a rise in the contribution of taxes on goods and services to GDP, from 6.4 per cent in 1986/7 to 7.7 per cent in 1989/90. This was accompanied by a small reduction in the contribution of international trade taxes. The corporation tax reforms did not have any immediate revenue impact, although taxes on individual incomes registered an increase from 2.9 per cent of GDP to 3.3 per cent between 1986/7 and 1989/90, reflecting the restructuring of salary scales in the public sector. Thus, the overall contribution of taxes on income and profit increased from 7.7 per cent of GDP to 8.0 per cent in 1989/90 (see Table 4.5).

During the period 1987/8–1989/90 there was an overall increase in the share of tax revenues to GDP, from 17.8 per cent to 19.2 per cent. In addition to improved revenue mobilization, the tax reforms also resulted in a change in the tax and revenue structure. There was a trend towards a greater reliance on taxes, which more than offset the declining contribution of non-tax revenues. Among the different types of taxes, the reliance on indirect taxes increased; within indirect taxes, the contribution of the surtax increased, which more than compensated for the falling contribution of revenues from international trade taxes (see Table 4.5).

In comparison with the major changes of 1987/8–1989/90, there were relatively few tax reform measures introduced in 1990/91. The budget presented in March 1990 reduced the company tax rate from 50 per cent to 45 per cent for companies incorporated inside Malawi; this was further reduced to 40 per cent in 1991/2. The rationale behind reducing the rates was to increase compliance, and although this may prove to be the case in the medium to longer term, the short-run effect was a decline in corporate taxes from 4.7 per cent of GDP in 1989/90 to 3.9 per cent in 1992/3. A new business tax on turnover was also introduced in 1990/91. Rate reductions were also applied to the individual income tax, with the top marginal rate of income tax being cut in line with the company tax rate. This was accompanied by a tightening of the taxation of fringe benefits. In 1991/2, the system of fringe benefits was modified such that the tax is now levied on the company rather than the employee. Nevertheless, a decrease in these taxes as a percentage of GDP also occurred in the early 1990s (see Table 4.5).

As regards indirect taxes, a more efficient system of duty drawbacks has recently been introduced. The surtax base has been further expanded to include certain utilities and services, and phased reductions in surtax exemptions have been implemented. Despite these changes, revenue from the surtax as a proportion of GDP fell sharply after 1989/90, reflecting mainly stock accumulation related to the import liberalization programme, and to a lesser extent, weaknesses in tax administration.

Although efforts have been made towards improving tax administration, the tax reform programme since 1987 has focused primarily on structural changes in the tax system, rather than on administrative reform. Structural changes did result in some short-term gains in revenue, as discussed above. However, declining trends in both tax and overall revenues over the past three years indicate that the gains achieved were temporary and that tax administrative reforms are a precondition for any further improvements in revenue mobilization.

Impact on expenditure

Fiscal policy since 1987 has stressed the need to contain expenditures and total budgetary spending declined from 36.4 per cent of GDP in 1986/7 to 25 per cent in 1991/2, before recovering to 31.4 per cent of GDP in 1992/3. The decline in government spending was a result of significant cuts in both recurrent and development expenditures.

Current spending as a percentage of GDP fell from 25.6 per cent in 1986/7 to 19.8 per cent in 1991/2, a decline which mainly reflected a significant reduction in public debt servicing over the period: the share of public debt servicing in total recurrent expenditures dropped to 27.1 per cent in 1991/2 from 47.5 per cent in 1987/8. Debt servicing was cut as a result of the reduction in the budget deficit as well as an increase in external concessional lending. After increasing considerably in 1987/8, owing to salary revisions effected in July 1986, current expenditure allocated to wages and salaries declined in the following three years under the impact of the Government's austere wage policy. The other categories of current expenditure whose share in total current spending saw a decline over the period 1986/7 to 1991/2 included defence expenditures, social services and grants and subsidies to public bodies (mainly statutory bodies). The latter reflected the Government's efforts since 1987 to achieve a comprehensive restructuring of the parastatal sector, comprising reorganization, divestiture, cost reduction, and regularization of financial flows, which has led to an improvement in the financial performance and operating efficiency of the sector. The focus of parastatal reform in the late 1980s was on restructuring ADMARC, which was largely completed by 1991/2.

Expenditures on the development budget continued to decline as a percentage of GDP in the period 1986/7–1991/2 (see Table 4.6). Spending on agriculture and natural resources and on transport and communications were reduced while social services as well as 'other services' both experienced a significant increase in investment. While this was consistent with the Government's policy of raising public investment in priority social sectors, it should be added that *actual* development spending on social services has been consistently below the budgeted targets. In contrast, *actual* development expenditure on transport and communication has generally been above the approved ceilings. Furthermore, a closer examination of the development budget reveals that the share of 'gross consumption' (i.e. resources for salaries and wages, and goods and services) has risen considerably since the mid-1980s. This suggests that a growing portion of activities listed under the development budget actually belong under the recurrent budget. As the bulk of these activities are donor funded, it would seem that external aid is increasingly being allocated to recurrent activities.

The generally restrictive trends in public expenditure over the period 1986/7 to 1991/2 were reversed in 1992/3 when recurrent expenditures as a percentage of GDP rose to 25 per cent, around 5 percentage points higher than in the previous year. Furthermore, the ratio of development spending to GDP also recorded an increase in 1992/3 for the first time in over a decade.

The steep increase in recurrent spending was attributable mainly to important salary and wage revisions, in accordance with the decision that wage policy should provide for appropriate and more regular increases in remuneration of the civil service, to redress wage compression and restore competitiveness. But it was also partly owing to the drought and the two devaluations in 1992, both of which exerted further upward pressures on budgetary expenditure. At the same time, the relative share in total recurrent spending of debt servicing declined (see Table 4.7).

Consistent with the Government's wage policy, the wage bill rose to 26.4 per cent of total current spending in 1992/3, as compared to 22 per cent in 1990/91. This was also reflected in the increase in the relative importance of 'general services' (general administration, defence and justice) in the recurrent budget, particularly that of general administration which occurred because of the rapid expansion in public employment over recent years (government employment grew twice as fast as private sector employment in the early 1990s) and the large wage awards granted in 1992.

It appears from Table 4.8 that the wage bill is gradually crowding out the other budgetary categories. The balance between budgetary allocations to 'salaries and wages' and 'other goods and services' (e.g. fuel, maintenance, training, subsistence allowance, transfers, and so on) has been moving in favour of the former in recent years and this may have a detrimental effect on the quality of public services, especially as the data suggest that the cuts in the operations budget are unevenly distributed among the various sectors and ministries, and do not reflect any priority towards essential social services or the rural population.

Impact on the overall budget balance
Against a background of rising external finance, the enhanced revenue mobilization, combined with recurrent expenditure restraint and the Government's inability to increase development spending, resulted in a substantial improvement in the central Government's financial position over the period 1986/7 to 1989/90. The overall budget deficit (including grants) fell from 11.5 per cent of GDP in 1986/7 to 2.1 per cent in 1989/90; excluding grants, the domestic deficit was reduced from 13.9 per cent to 6.9 per cent of GDP over the same period. The lower deficit together with the availability of foreign financing allowed the Government to significantly reduce its net credit from the banking system. The domestic deficit was further reduced to 6.5 per cent and 5.7 per cent of GDP,

Table 4.6 Central Government Development Expenditures by Main Heads, 1981/2–1992/3 (% of total development expenditure)

	82	83	84	85	86	87	88	89	90	91	92	93
Agriculture and natural resources	22.4	21.9	26.1	20.7	16.1	26.6	27.6	21.1	18.7	20.0	25.1	19.0
Social services[a]	10.9	16.8	18.7	20.1	14.7	12.9	12.2	16.3	16.2	22.6	31.3	25.0
Transport and communication	39.6	25.6	23.5	36.5	40.6	37.9	33.4	47.9	46.3	39.1	15.7	28.0
Other services[b]	27.1	35.7	31.6	22.6	28.5	22.6	26.7	14.7	18.7	18.3	27.9	26.0
Loans to public enterprises	3.4	3.8	0.5	1.8	3.8	2.6	1.1	2.4	0.7	4.2	4.2	0.4

Notes:
a. Includes education, health, community and social development.
b. Includes power, government buildings, housing, water and sanitation, finance, commerce and industry, works organization, miscellaneous.

Source: Economic Report, Government of Malawi (1985–93).

Table 4.7 Functional Classification of Central Government Recurrent Expenditures, 1981/2–1992/3 (% of total recurrent expenditure)

	82	83	84	85	86	87	88	89	90	91	92	93
General services	31.7	32.3	32.9	27.8	33.7	28.0	28.3	33.4	32.0	37.7	34.3	38.0
General administration	12.4	14.6	17.5	12.1	15.7	11.1	13.1	17.9	18.6	23.8	23.4	27.0
Defence	9.6	7.3	7.8	7.3	9.0	8.8	7.7	7.6	6.7	5.8	5.4	5.8
Social services	22.3	20.3	21.6	20.4	20.6	22.2	20.5	22.5	21.2	22.5	17.6	19.3
Economic services	17.1	19.1	18.8	16.7	18.0	16.5	16.1	18.2	16.3	15.2	25.1	13.9
Unallocable services	46.7	35.0	35.8	49.4	49.6	50.5	53.4	47.8	42.8	37.9	34.0	38.8
Public debt	40.1	29.7	28.4	43.2	43.4	44.5	47.5	45.1	36.7	30.2	27.1	30.8

Source: Economic Report, Government of Malawi (1985–93).

Table 4.8 Economic Classification of Central Government Recurrent Expenditures, 1981/2–1992/3 (% of total recurrent expenditure)

	82	83	84	85	86	87	88	89	90	91	92	93
Salaries and wages	24.9	26.1	26.5	23.4	24.6	23.5	26.5	23.2	22.7	22.4	23.7	26.4
Other goods and services	40.4	39.4	37.1	35.4	36.4	37.1	32.9	39.8	38.7	44.8	44.1	44.9
Interest on debt	22.4	22.9	19.3	29.0	21.9	27.2	29.3	23.2	24.5	16.8	13.6	12.8
Grants and subsidies	9.1	9.6	15.0	9.2	10.2	9.5	8.9	8.8	8.1	8.6	8.2	9.7
– to public bodies	7.4	8.3	12.0	6.9	7.4	7.1	6.3	6.1	6.4	6.9	5.0	6.8
– to private bodies	0.6	0.4	0.9	0.7	1.1	0.8	1.6	1.2	0.8	0.9	1.1	1.2

Source: Economic Report, Government of Malawi (1985–93).

respectively, in 1990/91 and 1991/2, owing mainly to cuts in expenditure, despite falling revenues as a proportion of GDP.

In many respects, 1992/3 marked a second watershed in Malawi's fiscal performance (the first watershed being 1986/7). The budget deficit, both including and excluding grants worsened. The reasons for this included temporary but substantial delays in balance of payments support and foreign grants from bilateral donors in 1992;[3] a considerable expansion in recurrent expenditures, and to some extent, in development spending; and finally, the failure of tax revenues to perform as buoyantly as expected.

5   ASSESSING THE IMPACT OF REFORM

Given that the primary focus of this paper is on the fiscal aspects of Malawi's reform programme, we turn first to a direct assessment of the effectiveness of the fiscal reforms. The relationship of the fiscal reforms to the wider adjustment programme should not be ignored, however, and in the second part of the section we present an assessment of the impact of the structural adjustment programme, and of the role of fiscal reform within that programme.

5.1   Fiscal Performance

Extent to which objectives have been satisfied
Table 4.9 attempts to evaluate the performance/outcomes of the fiscal reform programme against the objectives that it intended to achieve. Throughout the period 1981–93, fiscal policy has been aimed at the final objective of minimizing fiscal imbalances through reducing and maintaining the budget deficit at a non-inflationary and sustainable level. Intermediate objectives during the period 1981/2–1986/7 have included (1) improving the efficiency of the tax system; (2) improving the expenditure allocation decision-making process; and (3) strengthening the assessment of the public sector investment programme. The period post-1987/8 has seen the inclusion of additional intermediate objectives, including (4) improving tax administration; and (5) strengthening of non-tax revenues.

The Government was largely successful in reducing the fiscal deficit during the decade 1981/2–1991/2, with a temporary interruption in 1986/7. The period witnessed an 80 per cent reduction in the overall deficit while the deficit excluding grants was also lower by around 63 per cent. As noted above, expenditure cuts made the major contribution to deficit reduction.

With regard to the intermediate objectives, on the revenue side, the tax structure experienced fundamental reforms as a result of the tax reform process implemented since 1987. The reforms were, however, not primarily designed with a view to enhancing revenues, and have tended to be fairly revenue neutral

Table 4.9 Summary of Reform Objectives and Outcomes

Objective	Objective	Strategies and Measures	Outcome/Status/Timing
Reduce overall deficit to non-inflationary and sustainable level	A. Revenues: – improve allocative efficiency of tax system – improve administrative efficiency of tax system – strengthen non–tax revenue performance	– tax reforms (structural reforms) including introduction of VAT–type surtax – strengthen government audit capabilities to improve tax compliance – restore substantial payments into petroleum stabilization fund	– 1987/8–91/2 fundamental overhauling of tax structure revenue neutral outcome – 1991/92 – ongoing. No significant results visible in terms of revenue outcome – 1991/2–92/3. Ongoing marginal increases in non-tax revenues.
	B. Expenditures: – improve budgetary allocation process	– develop proposals to shift donor financing to current expenditure – strengthen expenditure control process in line ministries – review expenditure priorities in key economic and social sectors and revise expenditure allocation to meet sectoral targets	– 1990/91–92/3 completed increasing proportion of development budget allocated to current activities – 1991/2 – ongoing. No visible outcome in terms of containing expenditures – 1991/2 – ongoing. Some increase in current spending allocated to social services.

in their impact albeit with an expansion of the tax base (in principle at least). Furthermore, improving tax administration only featured strongly in the reforms as late as 1991/2. The relative absence of administrative reforms reduced the effectiveness of the structural reforms.

With regard to the intermediate objectives concerning expenditures, total current spending was reduced, owing to a drop in interest payments. Little control was, however, achieved on the discretionary element of current expenditures (i.e. net of interest payments on debt), which continued to grow.

Nevertheless, by 1991/2, the Government had succeeded in achieving a low budget deficit to GDP ratio, and the process of fiscal stabilization was perceived as having been completed. Furthermore the analysis presented in the previous section suggests that some additional gains have been made over the last decade. Notable among these is the reduction in public debt; the improved financial control and performance of the parastatal sector, as reflected in the considerable decline in budgetary transfers to the sector; and significant changes in the structure of taxes, including the introduction of the value-added type surtax, reflecting an improvement in allocative efficiency and a reduction in distortions in production, trade and investment.

The fiscal outcome in 1992/3 indicates however that many of the gains achieved are fragile, and also that the effective and efficient implementation of the reforms remains constrained by several factors. Notable among these is the poor quality and levels of staffing, personnel recruitment and training, and the consequent inadequate administrative capacity in Government departments required to fully implement many of the reforms. While the civil servants at the top (the permanent secretary level) are well trained and committed, efficient implementation of the reforms has been impeded by several factors discussed below.

Top level civil servants are constantly moved from heading one ministry/department to another. There is a lack of trained and 'trainable' middle- and junior-level personnel. Despite successive wage increases, Government salaries remain low in comparison to the private sector, and the Government has difficulty in attracting college graduates. Most new entrants tend to be high school graduates. The selection procedure is over-centralized with local departments generally having little say in a candidate's selection. Moreover, the large waiting period between the selection of a candidate for employment and the actual starting date of employment creates major disincentives to join the Government service.

Finally, many Government departments, particularly in the field offices and at the local level, tend to be severely understaffed, and pay little attention to staff training and development. Staffing in the tax related departments, for instance, has not kept up with the broadening of the tax base, and staff expansion has, in general, been unplanned and ad hoc. In particular the number of

staff available to deal with registration, collection and verification of the surtax
is insufficient.

Training of personnel is generally confined to those working in head offices,
while the needs of those working in the field tend to be neglected. The level of
training provided appears in general to be inadequate.[4]

The effectiveness of the tax reforms in enhancing revenue mobilization has
also been impeded by the inadequate nature of information flows regarding
potential tax-payers, especially with respect to those eligible to pay the newly
introduced surtax. When the new surtax was introduced in 1989, not only were
tax collectors relatively unprepared to deal with it, but there was limited
awareness among the public regarding the surtax. Potential manufacturers liable
to pay this tax were not properly informed about the procedural details connected with it. More recently, the services sector has been included in the surtax
net, and there was practically no information sent out to registered services from
whom the Government expects to collect the tax.

Poor planning and coordination of the budget acts as a further major constraint to the effective implementation of fiscal reforms. At present, the recurrent budget is drawn up by the Ministry of Finance, while the Ministry of
Economic Planning is in charge of the Development budget, with apparently
little coordination between the two ministries. Moreover, long-term planning of
budgets does not exist. This creates inefficiencies, often resulting in overspending, and mismatching between recurrent and development expenditures, as well
as imbalances within each budget. Development expenditure has been falling
vis-à-vis recurrent spending while within the development budget, there is a
growing imbalance in favour of current expenditures at the expense of fixed
capital formation. Within the recurrent budget there is evidence of a growing
imbalance in favour of wage-related expenditures at the expense of operations
and maintenance activities.

5.2 Economic Performance and Structural Adjustment

The improvement in macroeconomic performance in 1987 is evident from
Table 4.10. After negative growth in 1986 and stagnation in 1987, GDP grew
consistently by more than 3 per cent per annum in the 1988–91 period, restoring
per capita GDP growth to a positive rate. The real growth rate in the smallholder
agriculture sector was in double digits. Moreover inflation fell sharply after
1988; from over 30 per cent to 12 per cent in 1990/91. The improved performance in output and price stability helped to support a recovery in investment; the
gross investment ratio rising from 12 per cent in 1986 to around 19 per cent by
the start of the 1990s.

The more stable monetary and financial conditions prevailing after 1986
combined with the structural reforms are likely to have contributed to the
recovery in output. But, despite the successful implementation of a wide range

Table 4.10   Some Key Macroeconomic Indicators, 1987–92
          (Percentages)

	1987	1988	1989	1990	1991[a]	1992[b]
Growth rate	0.5	3.3	4.1	4.8	7.8	–4.0
(GDP factor cost)						
CPI change	26.8	31.4	15.7	11.5	11.9	13.4
Current account/GDP	–5.1	–9.1	–13.4	–8.5	–10.8	–17.0
Exports/GDP	23.5	22.0	16.9	22.6	22.6	25.4
Imports/GDP	24.6	27.2	25.0	26.0	29.1	29.1
Gross investment/GDP	15.4	18.7	20.2	19.1	19.0	19.8
(including private	(7.7)	(9.7)	(10.7)	(10.8)	(10.6)	(12.9)
fixed I/GDP)						

Notes:
a. Estimated.
b. Projected.

Source: World Bank Report No: P-5461-MAI (World Bank, 1992).

of medium to longer term adjustment reforms, the fragility of the Malawian economy and its susceptibility to shocks remains evident in the 1990s. The supply response to structural adjustment so far has not been adequate to sustain growth in the face of the 1992 drought for example. Indeed even without the effects of the 1992 drought, which necessitated food imports on an unprecedented scale, balance of payments deterioration was evident after 1987. Over the period 1987–91 export growth was slower than import growth, with little diversification out of the traditional exports of tobacco, tea and sugar and limited development of the potential for manufactured exports.

About half of the population is estimated to be still living below the poverty line, with limited opportunities to raise their incomes given the relatively low levels of human capital and the country's poor natural resource base. Labour has already borne a significant part of the burden of the stabilization efforts, as real wages have declined. Commitment to adjustment is not likely to be maintained in the longer term without greater attention to poverty alleviation, while clearly some considerable time will be required to enhance Malawi's stock of human capital.

What is evident from the above assessment, and the description in Section 2 of the nature of the structural adjustment programme in Malawi (especially after the mid-1980s), is that there has been a high degree of policy reform (or at least of notional implementation thereof) but that the achievement of the longer term objectives has not yet been completed. Major steps in satisfying intermediate objectives – increasing the efficiency of the fiscal regime, liberalizing the industrial licensing and the import regime, improvement of the price signalling mechanism through the removal of import controls, and the reduction of government interference in the process of private sector investment – have been achieved. As well as requiring more time, the achievement of long-term goals appears to depend crucially on human resources development and a change in attitudes towards 'control' of the economy on the part of political policy makers and senior administrators. Despite a stated commitment to the fostering of entrepreneurship and individual initiative, the tendency to 'control' on economic and political grounds remains a strong feature of the policy environment in Malawi.

6.   LESSONS FROM THE FISCAL REFORM EXPERIENCE AND SOME RECOMMENDATIONS

Access to external resources is obviously important for a country like Malawi, but improvements in the mobilization of domestic resources is also vital. Fiscal policy issues remain central therefore to the process of structural adjustment in Malawi.

6.1   Improving Resource Mobilisation

Malawi's fiscal position points to the urgent need for policy changes directed both at mobilizing greater revenues, and also at further rationalizing the structure and management of public expenditures. Furthermore, fiscal reforms must be properly phased, sequenced and implemented in a manner that is coordinated with other macroeconomic reforms.

Building human capacities

A single obvious conclusion emerging from the above review of constraints is the crucial need for building up human capacities for the better administration of revenues and expenditures.

As regards revenues, there is a need for a simple, manageable, and well-administered tax system. The tax reforms implemented so far have met with some success. However, it is felt that too much emphasis has been placed on reforming the tax structure, with comparatively little attention given to administrative reforms. In this context, it is crucial that in future, the reform of the tax structure and tax administration be more carefully coordinated. Better tax administration would involve the following:

- Training of personnel, both at the managerial level and the level of tax collectors. Training courses should be provided to surtax collectors, to enhance their understanding of the intricacies involved in the new VAT-type surtax. Training in auditing is also necessary.
- Improving staffing levels is also crucial to the successful implementation of the reforms.
- There is a need to improve the quality of staff recruited in tax departments, particularly in the Customs and Excise Department. This would require developing a more attractive incentives package so as to encourage more graduates to join the Government.
- Enhanced information flows are also essential. These would include better information in relevant tax departments regarding taxpayers, both individuals and firms, which could be achieved through computerization. At present, there exists a dual system of information flows – manual and computerized. The computerization of the surtax system has begun in collaboration with the HIID team based in the Customs and Excise Department in Blantyre but progress has been slow. The Income Tax Department based in Blantyre also received some computer equipment, most of which became obsolete before they received any training in the use of the equipment. Enhanced information flows are also necessary in other areas, notably, in improving the awareness of taxpayers with regard to newly introduced taxes such as the reformed surtax.
- There is need for improving working conditions of the staff in the tax departments, and for providing them with better working facilities, essential furniture, fixtures and vehicles.

As in the case of revenues, better expenditure management would require building up human capacities in budget planning, and in the monitoring and control of expenditures. Training in auditing and computing is also necessary.

Maintaining the pace of reforms and avoiding 'reform regress'
As regards tax structure, the reforms currently underway are clearly in the right direction. Reforms in the surtax are likely to improve efficiency and minimize distortions and it is important that the pace of reforms is maintained. The surtax base has been recently expanded to include certain utilities and services, and the Government must make every effort to include as many services as possible under the surtax net. Furthermore, in the medium term, it will be necessary to shift the levying of the surtax from its current manufacturing/import stage to the retail stage. Enforcement, implementation and minimizing tax evasion are three areas for immediate concern. Furthermore, reforms in tax structure must be coordinated with other macroeconomic and sectoral reforms.

The reform of the budgeting and expenditure control system is also underway. There is an urgent need to improve coordination of recurrent and development budgets, and of central government and local government budgets. This would require improvements in accounting, flash reporting, better information flows, and computerization. The Government should strengthen the role of the rolling three-year Public Sector Investment Programme in expenditure planning.

Second, priorities and programmes for recurrent and development spending should be reviewed periodically. In this context, efforts towards more efficient and effective social sector spending need to be continued. On the development budget, it is believed that a stricter control and monitoring of contracts involving the purchase of equipment and the hiring of labour, so as to minimize rent-seeking, would release considerable resources. Project selection and approval also merit greater care.

6.2   External Support

Donor support is essential for the successful implementation of the adjustment programme. Bilateral support was frozen after last year's Consultative Group meeting. In this context, the results of the recent referendum, leading up to multi-party elections are expected to have a positive impact in the medium term on the human rights situation, and it is hoped that the support of bilateral donors will be resumed.

NOTES

1.   A similar trend has been observed in several other adjusting countries including Bangladesh and Tanzania. For a detailed analysis of country experience see Nissanke and Basu, 1992.
2.   See Nashashibi et al., 1992.
3.   Bilateral donor support was temporarily frozen after the 1992 Consultative Group meeting, on the grounds that the Malawi Government under Life President Banda had been involved in severe and widespread human rights violations.
4.   When the new surtax was introduced in 1989, staff at the customs and excise department who were supposed to collect and administer this tax received only six weeks of training, involving a three-week training course in the new surtax credit system, two weeks training in accounting and one week in verification. This was simply not enough to familiarize officials with the intricate details of the complex surtax credit system. Moreover, anecdotal evidence suggests that even those personnel who receive training in certain areas are not necessarily assigned to relevant ministries for long periods of time. We were told that the Harvard Institute of International Development (HIID) in collaboration with UNDP financed the advanced training of selected officers from the tax department for a training programme in tax administration at Harvard. Upon their return to Malawi, however, these officers were moved to other unrelated ministries.

REFERENCES

Chamley, C., R. Conrad, Z. Shalizi, J. Skinner and L. Squire (1985), *Tax Policy for Malawi*, 2 vols (Washington DC: World Bank), processed.

Chirwa, Gilbert B. (1990), 'Reflections on the Long-Term Perspectives Study for Sub-Saharan Africa, with Particular Reference to Malawi', in *The Long-Term Perspective Study of Sub-Saharan Africa*, vol. 1, *Country Perspectives* (Washington DC: World Bank).

Nashashibi, K., S. Gupta, C. Luiksila, H. Loria and W. Mahler (1992), 'The Fiscal Dimensions of Adjustment in Low Income Countries', *IMF Occasional Paper* 95, Washington DC.

Nissanke, Machiko and Priya Basu (1992), *Improving Domestic Resource Mobilization for Economic Development in Less Developed Countries*, UNCTAD Secretariat.

Shalizi, Zmarak, and Lyn Squire (1988), *Tax Policy in Sub-Saharan Africa: A Framework for Analysis Policy and Research Series* 2 (Washington DC: World Bank).

5. Fiscal Adjustment in The Gambia: A Case Study

Priya Basu and Norman Gemmell

1 INTRODUCTION

The Gambia is a country of only 11 300 square kilometres, with a population of around 890 000 (making it one of the most densely populated countries in Africa). It stretches east from Africa's Atlantic coast along both banks of the Gambia river and is totally surrounded by Senegal apart from a narrow stretch of coastline at the river estuary. The World Bank estimates its per capita GDP at $230 in 1989, population growth has been rapid, at around 3.4 per cent per annum in recent years, and the country's illiteracy and infant mortality rates are high. The economy's production structure is heavily based on agriculture (23 per cent of GDP) and services; the manufacturing sector accounts for less than 7 per cent of GDP. Groundnuts and other crops continue to be The Gambia's main exports but tourism became a major source of foreign exchange earnings during the 1980s. Quantitatively of more significance however is the large entrepot trade which has emerged in recent years, with Senegal and Mauritania the main destinations for re-exports (mainly food and clothing products). Even official statistics, which are known severely to under-record this trade, indicate that re-exports constituted over 55 per cent of total exports in 1990/91.

Like many African countries, The Gambia's economic performance deteriorated substantially in the late 1970s and early 1980s following the world oil shocks, with declines in per capita GDP, growing current account and government budget deficits, and accumulating foreign debt arrears. As a precondition for IMF and World Bank stabilization and structural adjustment loans, The Gambia undertook major and comprehensive economic reforms in 1985 with further reforms in the later 1980s leading to the Programme for Sustained Development (PSD) initiated in 1990. Fiscal reforms were prominent in these programmes. A significant improvement was observed in the late 1980s and early 1990s in the Gambian economy in terms, for example, of improved growth performance, reduced inflation and lower government and trade deficits.

Various writers (e.g. Hadjimichael et al., 1992; IMF, 1990; Radelet, 1992) have attributed much of this improvement to the reform packages.

Our interest in this study is in the fiscal aspects of the Gambian economy during the 1980–92 period, focusing particularly on the inter-relationships between fiscal and other reforms, and on the interactions between fiscal policy variables and macroeconomic indicators such as GDP, inflation and the balance of payments. For example, did the trade policy reforms which were required as part of the conditions for IMF and World Bank loans to The Gambia from 1985, ease or worsen fiscal constraints? How successful were the fiscal reforms in particular? How did they contribute to the social dimensions of adjustment?

We address these issues in this study. The main features of the reform programmes are outlined in Section 1. Section 2 concentrates on fiscal aspects and reviews the main patterns and trends in key tax and expenditure variables before, during and after reform. Section 3 discusses the objectives which the reforms sought to achieve and explores their impact on the Gambian economy. Given the methodologies available, this exercise is necessarily circumspect and 'suggestive' rather than conclusive. Nevertheless, it is possible to learn some lessons from the Gambian experience which can inform and improve future fiscal policy in The Gambia and other LDCs undertaking similar adjustment programmes. These lessons are reviewed in Section 4.

2   THE GAMBIAN ECONOMIC REFORMS

By the early 1980s the Gambian economy displayed several problems common to African economies following the external shocks of the 1970s. These shocks, together with heavy public sector involvement in the economy, were associated with severe balance of payments problems and fiscal deficits. Despite access to three IMF Standby Facilities in the early 1980s and efforts to stabilize the external balance, by the mid-1980s underlying external imbalances had assumed major proportions, with a current account deficit equal to 21 per cent of GDP, rising external debt service arrears, and a severe fall in gross foreign exchange reserves. In addition foreign donors and lenders were refusing to provide further assistance. Inflation rates had also risen to as high as 70 per cent per annum.

The Gambian government introduced an Economic Recovery Programme (ERP) in mid-1985 in response to the crisis. The programme was designed by a task-force appointed by Minister of Finance Sisay, comprised primarily of Gambian bureaucrats and technocrats, and two expatriates – an economic adviser in the Ministry of Finance, and an economist from the World Bank. Economic reform programmes have, of course, become common features within the 'conditionality' terms attached to structural adjustment loans (SALs) from the World Bank to many developing countries. Though the ERP was one of the most sweeping reform programmes attempted on the African continent, its major objectives (to redress internal and external imbalances) and the methods employed to achieve these objectives, were very similar to those of standard IMF and World Bank supported stabilization and structural adjustment programmes.[1] We discuss some of the reasons for this when considering the objectives of reform in Section 3.1 below.

IMF conditions for stabilization loans frequently stipulate exchange rate, monetary policy and fiscal reforms with the short-term aim of reducing excess aggregate demand and the associated balance of payments and inflationary problems. So-called 'supply-side' reforms have been advocated as longer term solutions to these and other problems (such as prolonged or 'structural' fiscal and current account deficits). Supply-side reforms typically involve measures to improve public and private sector efficiency, such as liberalizing foreign exchange, financial, and key product markets from government controls, public sector wage restraint, privatization of parastatals, and measures to minimize tax 'distortions' and enhance revenue collection. As detailed below, many of these features figured prominently in the Gambian reforms.

2.1 Reform Measures

Table 5.1 lists the major components of reform in The Gambia undertaken in the 1985 ERP and the 1990 PSD. Dates in parentheses indicate when specific actions were initiated. The ERP in particular was comprehensive and wide-ranging and included all of the 'typical' reform measures mentioned above. The introduction of a floating exchange rate, the liberalization of the foreign exchange market and the raising of interest rates (followed closely by Central Bank decontrol of interest rates) were among the earliest measures adopted. Major trade and tax policy reform was undertaken between 1986 and 1988 with export taxes and duties removed in 1986 and import tax abolished in 1988 (it was replaced by a sales tax in the same year). The rationalization of import duties towards a structure involving fewer and less dispersed rates of duty was begun and this process has been continuing under the PSD with taxes on imports being moved towards rates of 10 per cent, in line with the domestic sales tax rate. Nevertheless a number of higher rate import duties, ranging up to 87 per cent, remain in operation.

To rectify The Gambia's large and persistent budget deficits prior to 1985, the ERP sought to reduce expenditures 'across the board' with a 20 per cent cut in public sector employment and a wage freeze for the remaining employees. Because significant contributions to the deficits were attributable to subsidies made to loss-making parastatals, a privatization programme was initiated early in the ERP, which reduced the number of parastatals from 21 in 1985 to seven in 1992, with a further two to be privatized in 1993. Almost all of the remaining parastatals were required to enter into 'performance contracts' with the government which allowed greater financial supervision by the Ministry of Finance and through which parastatals were expected to become net contributors to the government budget within a short period. 'Performance audits' for parastatals were also introduced, undertaken by external auditors such as the UK Crown Agents.

Although trade tax reforms were initiated early in the ERP these were not primarily motivated by revenue-raising concerns but by objectives of trade liberalization and reductions in price distortions (both consumption and production) in the economy. Indeed, as occurred in other SAL recipients, a systematic assessment of the budgetary implications of trade tax reforms within the ERP does not seem to have been undertaken. Instead, enhancement of tax revenues was primarily sought through improvements in tax administration and collection procedures for other taxes.

The 1990 PSD sought primarily to reinforce reforms begun under the ERP. As we report below, with persistent budget deficits (inclusive of grants) perceived to be largely eliminated by 1989, fiscal reforms concentrated on refining and improving tax accounting procedures, redoubling efforts to widen tax bases, and pursuing tax evasion loopholes with the objective of minimizing the vulnerability of the budget to future changes in foreign grants. On the expenditure side, the PSD emphasized greater priority to 'social' services such as health and education with small increases in their relative expenditure allocations. The government also authorized a household survey on the 'Social Dimensions of Adjustment' (SDA) to monitor social status and provision, and the social impact of expenditure policies. The first preliminary report of the SDA was made in 1992. Despite the apparent contradiction, the PSD also introduced user charges in the education and health sectors which comprised charges for some school books and drugs at health clinics, as part of efforts to increase non-tax revenues.

2.2   Financing the Reforms

Table 5.1 also indicates the main external finance made available by the World Bank, the IMF and other donor institutions which helped to finance some of the reforms; the finance generally being conditional upon reform implementation and/or success. Following a number of stand-by facilities from the IMF before 1985 (the last of which was cancelled in April 1985) which had failed to deliver improvements in The Gambia's external imbalances, the SAF/ESAF loans in 1986 were conditional mainly on major monetary and foreign exchange reforms. Tax and other public/private sector reforms were principally seen as longer term, 'structural' measures and were required to satisfy World Bank SAL conditionality. However the complete package of reforms, and the conditions for continued donor support, were agreed between all three parties – The Gambian government, the IMF and the World Bank – with short-term and long-

Table 5.1 Key Features of the Economic Reform Programme (ERP) and the Programme for Sustained Development (PSD)

The ERP (initiated 1985)	The PSD (initiated 1990)
Fiscal Reforms:	– Increase public infrastructure (1990)
– Abolition of export taxes (1986)	– Preparation of Public Expenditure Programmes for education, health, etc. (1991)
– Rationalization of import duties (1986)	– Computerization of customs and income domestic taxes/duties (1988) tax admin. (1992)
– Abolition of import tax (1988)	– Corporate tax rate reduced: 75 per cent to 50 per cent and index of income tax brackets (1992)
– Rationalization or abolition of misc.	– Broaden tax bases especially for income and sales taxes (1990)
– Introduction of sales tax (1988)	– Measures to improve tax collection and compliance
– 20 per cent cut in public sector employment	– Discretionary duty waivers abolished (1992)
– Freeze public sector wages (1986)	
– Reduce total public expenditure	
– Improve/clarify budget accounting	
– Simplify income tax schedule (1988)	
Other Public Sector Reforms:	– Further parastatal privatization
– Privatization of parastatals (1985)	– Introduction of 'user charges' (1986) in education and health sectors (1992)
– Parastatal 'Performance Contracts'	– Priority public expenditure on 'social (1986) sectors': education, health, housing (1990)
– Major admin. reforms of Ministries	– Extension of performance contracts
	– Improve public sector management (1992)
	– Liberalization of Gambian groundnut market
	– GPMB monopoly eliminated (1990)

114

Table 5.1 (contd...)

The ERP (initiated 1985)	The PSD (initiated 1990)
Trade and Financial Reforms: – Reform of trade taxes (see above) – Floating (devaluation) of exchange rate (1985) non-concessional) borrowers – Liberalization of foreign exchange market (1986) – Decontrol of domestic interest rates (1985) – Establish targets for money supply control (1986)	– No government guarantees for private – Privatization of foreign exchange bureaux (1992) – Abolition of credit ceilings (1990)

External Finance:	Facility (period)	Amount (source) (SDR million)	Co-financing (source) ($ million)
	SAL (Aug'86)	14.2 (World Bank)	
	SEF (Sept'86–Oct'87)	5.1 (IMF)	
	SAF (Sept'86–Nov'88)	12.0 (IMF)[a]	
	ESAF (Nov'88–Nov'91)	20.5 (IMF)	9.0 (ADF); 4.5 (UK)
	SAL (June'89)[b]	17.9 (World Bank)	6.0 (ADF); 2.5 (Netherlands)

Notes:

a. SDR 3.4 million not purchased.

b. Second tranche due 1990/91 delayed due to reform 'slippage'.

SEF = Standby/Extended Facility; (E)SAF = (Extended) Structural Adjustment Facility; SAL = Structural Adjustment Loan; ADF = African Development Fund.

115

term reforms expected to be mutually reinforcing. As Table 5.1 indicates, this support was substantial, amounting to over SDR 32 million under (IMF) SAF/ ESAF arrangements and over SDR 20 million in (World Bank) SAL support. In 1985/6 total aid amounted to SDR 38 million (or 19 per cent of GDP) and averaged SDR 52 million in the five years to 1990/91 (or 25 per cent of GDP) (see Hadjimichael et al., 1992, pp. 5–6).

By disbursing these grants and loans in several tranches, following regular reviews of reform implementation and success, the IMF/World Bank was able to exert considerable pressure on the government to pursue these reforms vigorously. In fact, some tranches were delayed, because of lags (relative to agreed timetables) in implementation, or achievements of certain 'targets' (see Section 3.1).

2.3 Sequencing of Reforms

The sequencing of various elements in the reform packages is noteworthy. Given the severe external and internal disequilibria facing the economy, among the first corrective measures to be adopted were those aimed at reducing these macroeconomic imbalances through a devaluation of the exchange rate and a lowering of money supply growth. Reductions in fiscal deficits, initially via expenditure pruning, and the associated reduction of domestic credit creation to finance the public sector borrowing requirement were also expected to contribute to improvements in the balance of payments and inflation. Macroeconomic stabilization was seen as a pre-requisite for more sustained improvements in GDP growth rates and budget deficits. To achieve these latter objectives tax reforms were phased in over 1986–8, a series of privatizations were initiated and public sector administrative reforms were pursued. Each of these measures was perceived as an important step towards the longer term objectives of maintaining low fiscal deficits, enabling future increases in public expenditure to be tax-financed, improving public sector efficiency and allowing private producers and consumers to respond to market-driven price signals.

An important early reform was the temporary raising of groundnut prices paid to farmers, despite the fact that this entailed an increase in subsidy. The rationale behind the price increase was firstly to protect poor farmers from the initial adverse effects of liberalization and secondly to improve producer incentives following a series of production shortfalls owing primarily to adverse weather conditions in the early 1980s. However, measures were subsequently taken to lower domestic groundnut prices to world levels because of the budgetary implications of maintaining high producer prices and the perverse incentives provided to farmers by the divergence of domestic and world prices.

Privatization was also begun early in the reform timetable which is atypical of other African reform programmes. In The Gambia's case this was seen as important because parastatal subsidies represented an unusually large share of the fiscal deficit so that without early privatization it would have been much more difficult to cut public expenditure quickly. It is also notable that the ERP contained almost no measures aimed specifically at distributional or poverty issues. This reflects the fact that the preoccupation of the government and the lending institutions in the early 1980s was to rectify major disequilibria and inefficiencies in the economy. However, partly because of inequalities exacerbated by the ERP, the 1990 PSD paid more attention to reforms aimed at improving distributional aspects as reflected, for example, in various 'social sector' measures.

3 TAXATION AND PUBLIC SPENDING: PATTERNS AND TRENDS, 1981–91

By the early 1980s, the Gambian economy was facing a major fiscal crisis. The overall budget deficit (including grants) amounted to around 12 per cent of GDP and the domestic budget deficit (which excludes grants) was as high as 18 per cent of GDP in 1981/2.[2] It was clear that domestic revenues had not been able to keep pace with the expansion of public expenditures. The latter mainly reflected the rapid growth in government consumption expenditures, associated in part with the doubling of the civil service during the late 1970s.

At the same time, unfavourable weather conditions and inadequate price incentives caused groundnut production to fall. The export of groundnuts had generated the major share of the country's foreign exchange earnings, and up until the early 1980s, taxes levied on the export of groundnuts had also accounted for around 5 per cent of total government revenue. The decline in groundnut exports thus had a negative impact on both the balance of payments and domestic revenue. Furthermore, growing uncertainties emerged in the early 1980s regarding the future availability of foreign aid and concessional finance from abroad. Faced with this economic crisis, the government initiated efforts towards fiscal reform in the early 1980s, but these reforms were of an uncoordinated and unsustainable nature, involving piecemeal changes. As noted earlier, it was not until 1985 that the government formally embarked on a programme for economic recovery.

3.1 Major Trends in the Government's Resource Position: 1981–91

1981/2–1984/5: the pre-reform period
The government's fiscal position, as measured by the size of the budget deficit, experienced an improvement during the 1981/2–1984/5 period. The overall budget deficit was reduced to around 7 per cent of GDP in 1984/5 while the domestic deficit fell to around 12 per cent of GDP. The improvement in the

fiscal deficits – by 5–6 per cent of GDP compared to the levels recorded in 1981/2 was, however, brought about primarily through a reduction in government spending, and not through a sustainable increase in domestic revenues. Total government expenditure as a percentage of GDP fell from 45 per cent in 1981/2 to 31 per cent in 1984/5. The burden of spending cuts was borne mainly by the recurrent budget, which fell by 13 percentage points during this period (from 30 per cent of GDP in 1981/2 to 17 per cent in 1984/5), while development (capital) expenditures declined by around 1 percentage point.

Government revenues including grants also fell considerably, declining as a percentage of GDP from 32 per cent in 1981/2 to 23 per cent in 1984/5, mainly because of a large reduction in grants from 12 per cent to 4 per cent of GDP. Domestic revenues remained broadly constant in this period, fluctuating between 17 per cent and 20 per cent of GDP, although the non-tax element of domestic revenues showed a small but steady decline. Thus despite the reduction in the deficit attained during the first half of the 1980s there were two reasons for the government's continued concern regarding its fiscal position: the deficit was still too high, and the improvement which had occurred had been brought about through expenditure reduction rather than domestic revenue expansion and not therefore in a sustainable manner.

1985/6–1989/90: The ERP period
Fiscal adjustment was accorded high priority under the ERP. The main objective was to minimize fiscal imbalances, and the principal measure initially utilized to achieve this was again expenditure restraint. Austere fiscal policies resulted in a considerable improvement in the government's deficit position during the second half of the 1980s, with the overall budget deficit falling to around 2 per cent of GDP in 1989/90. An overall surplus was in fact recorded during three years: 1985/6, 1986/7 and 1988/9. The domestic budget deficit also improved during the period to 8 per cent of GDP in 1989/90 (see Table 5.2).

Alongside the restraint on public expenditures, an increase in the mobilization of domestic revenues and a recovery in foreign grants (particularly in the first two years of the ERP) also contributed to the reduction in the overall budget deficit; these developments are examined in more detail below. The general trends in public finance over the second half of the 1980s therefore pointed to an improvement in the fiscal position; and although a larger deficit was incurred in 1987/88 this was owing to a combination of specific factors discussed below.

1990/91–1991/2: The PSD period
The Programme for Sustained Development (PSD), which was launched in 1990, sought to reinforce the economic policies pursued under the ERP. The government continued its tight fiscal stance and initial estimates for the fiscal

Table 5.2 Revenues and Expenditures, 1980/81–1991/2 (% of GDP)

	81	82	83	84	85	86	87	88	89	90	91	92
1. Domestic revenue + grants	25.4	32.1	20.1	24.8	23.0	24.8	32.8	29.7	29.9	27.4	26.4	(22.4)
2. Domestic revenue	19.5	19.8	17.3	20.6	18.9	19.3	22.0	20.1	22.9	20.9	21.0	(20.6)
3. Tax revenue	17.0	17.2	15.2	18.7	17.4	17.6	20.5	18.5	21.1	19.6	19.6	(19.2)
4. Non-tax revenue	2.5	2.6	2.1	1.9	1.4	1.7	1.5	1.7	1.8	1.3	1.4	(1.4)
5. Grants	5.9	12.3	2.8	4.2	4.1	5.4	10.8	9.6	7.0	6.4	5.4	(1.9)
6. Total expenditure	39.2	44.7	28.6	32.9	30.7	19.8	32.0	37.2	30.0	29.5	30.8	(25.8)
7. Recurrent expenditure	22.3	29.7	21.4	21.5	16.7	13.9	21.1	26.4	21.8	22.1	23.5	(20.6)
8. Development expenditure	16.9	14.9	7.2	11.4	14.0	5.9	10.8	10.8	8.2	7.4	7.4	(5.2)
9. Overall deficit (1–6)	-13.9	-12.6	-8.5	-8.1	-7.7	5.0	0.9	-7.5	-0.1	-2.0	-4.5	(-3.4)
10. Domestic deficit (2–6)	-19.8	-17.9	-11.3	-12.3	-11.8	-0.5	-10.0	-17.0	-7.1	-8.5	-9.9	(-5.2)
11. Capital revenue	0.0	0.0	0.1	0.0	0.0	0.3	0.0	0.2	0.2	0.3	0.3	(0.1)
12. Change in arrears	0.0	0.0	0.0	3.3	3.3	-3.2	-0.9	-0.3	-1.3	0.0	0.0	(0.0)
13. Special provisions	.	.			.		10.5	8.0	0.0	4.7	1.6	(1.6)

Notes: Figures in brackets are from the Central Statistical Division, Government of Gambia.

Source: Gray et al. (1992).

year 1990/91 suggested further improvement in the government's overall resource position, with an overall budget surplus of around 1.3 per cent of GDP
and a domestic deficit of 4 per cent of GDP (see Hadjimichael et al., 1992).
However revised estimates from the Ministry of Statistics suggest that both
budget deficits (as a percentage of GDP) increased slightly in 1990/91 (see
Table 5.2) as a consequence of both expenditure increases and some decline in
revenues. Public finances are however healthier than might at first appear
because some overseas grants due in 1990/91 and 1991/2 were delayed owing
to implementation failures associated with some reforms, but will be released in
due course.

3.2 Government Revenue

The share of overall government revenue (including grants) in GDP declined
between 1981/2 and 1991/2 (see Table 5.2).[3] After falling to an all-time low of
20 per cent of GDP in 1982/3, revenues rose steadily, especially after 1984/5,
reaching 33 per cent of GDP in 1986/7, but then declined again between 1988/
9 and 1991/2. A major contributor to these trends in overall revenue was the
fluctuation of foreign grant inflows. As a proportion of GDP, grants generally
declined in the period preceding the ERP, increased in the period after 1985 but
fell somewhat thereafter.

Domestic revenues fluctuated around 19 per cent of GDP in the first half of
the 1980s, rose to 23 per cent in 1988/9 and experienced a small decline in the
subsequent two years. On average domestic revenues were higher by about 3
percentage points (at 21 per cent of GDP) after the introduction of the ERP
compared with the pre-ERP period. A number of factors contributed to this
increase, in particular the rise in tax revenues, which account for around 90 per
cent of domestic revenues in The Gambia (see Table 5.3). Tax revenues
increased from an average of 17.5 per cent of GDP during 1981/2–1985/6 to
around 21 per cent during 1986/7–1990/91.

An important component of the increase in the tax/GDP ratio during the
second half of the 1980s/early 1990s was the introduction of the *national sales
tax* (at a 10 per cent rate) in July 1988 as part of an effort to broaden the tax base
and reduce reliance on international trade taxes. Though notionally based on
sales, in practice the tax is typically levied at the manufacturer/importer stage,
and comprises a sales tax on domestically manufactured goods as well as on
imports.[4]

The main 'domestic' source of sales tax revenue is the foreign tourist
industry (though this may be more accurately seen as an export tax). International package tours – the main tourism source – were zero-rated when the
sales tax was first introduced, but a rate of 6 per cent was imposed in 1989/90
and was subsequently raised to 10 per cent. Despite this, sales tax revenue from
tourism currently accounts for only around 2 per cent of domestic revenue. The

Table 5.3 Structure of Revenues, 1980/81–1991/2 (% of total domestic revenue)

	81	82	83	84	85	86	87	88	89	90	91[a]	92[b]
Tax revenues	87.5	86.9	87.6	90.6	92.5	90.9	93.2	91.7	91.9	93.6	93.2	93.3
Taxes on income	21.8	16.3	14.2	13.2	15.9	14.6	12.3	13.0	12.9	13.8	12.5	11.6
1. Income tax – personal	9.6	5.7	6.5	7.5	6.5	4.8	4.8	4.3	4.8	5.3	5.2	4.2
2. Income tax – companies	11.1	9.4	4.8	4.8	8.3	7.2	6.8	7.8	7.1	6.8	6.7	6.4
Domestic taxes on goods and services	4.7	4.4	4.5	5.2	9.6	5.2	5.2	6.8	27.2	35.8	38.5	38.1
1. Excise duties	1.2	1.9	1.6	2.2	6.5	1.6	2.5	1.2	0.3	0.1	0.1	0.0
2. Motor vehicle and road tax	1.7	1.5	2.0	1.4	1.0	1.3	0.9	1.0	0.9	0.8	0.8	0.9
3. Entertainment, etc.[c]	0.9	0.5	0.7	0.8	1.0	0.8	0.5	0.2	0.5	0.0	0.0	0.0
4. Telecommunications[d]	–	–	–	–	–	0.1	0.4	0.4	0.5	–	–	–
5. National sales tax	..	..	–	..	..	..	..	..	23.9	32.3	34.6	35.2
Taxes on IT	60.4	65.7	70.1	71.4	65.9	70.4	75.1	71.3	51.3	43.2	42.0	43.4
1. Import duties	53.7	57.8	64.7	56.1	53.6	59.0	63.2	58.7	47.8	42.8	41.9	43.4
2. Import tax	5.8	3.3	4.6	6.1	6.6	7.5	9.8	9.8	1.6	–	–	–
3. Export duties	0.6	4.1	0.4	8.4	4.1	3.4	1.6	2.5	1.2	0.2	0.1	0.0
Non-tax revenues	12.5	13.1	12.4	9.4	7.5	9.0	6.8	8.2	8.1	6.4	6.8	6.7
1. Fines, fees, other receipts	8.1	8.4	8.2	8.3	4.6	8.3	5.2	6.0	5.1	5.3	–	–
2. Incentives, dividends and prop. income	3.5	4.1	3.3	0.6	2.4	0.4	1.4	2.0	2.7	0.8	–	–

Notes:
a. Revised figures.
b. Estimates.
c. Until 1988/9, this includes: entertainment tax, hotel bednight tax, casino machine tax, casino and gaming licences, hotel, retaurant and tourist licenses, and ad valorem taxes on hotel bills. After 1988/9, hotel bednight taxes and ad valorem taxeson hotel bills were discontinued.
d. This comprises the GAMTEL 10 per cent surcharge.

Source: Table 5.2.

121

government also intended to target telecommunications, insurance services and air tickets but encountered severe problems in enforcing these taxes. Thus, by 1990/91, domestic indirect taxes (sales tax on domestically produced goods plus other domestic duties/excises) accounted for only around 10 per cent of domestic revenue which nevertheless represents an improvement over previous years.

A more important source of revenue has been the sales tax levied on imports (e.g. on the fuel imports by the Gambia Utilities Company (GUC) and the Gambia Public Transport Corporation (GPTC)) which accounted for 26 per cent of domestic revenue in 1990/91. Sales taxes on imports accounted for the bulk of the increase in tax revenues in 1988/9.

Taxes from international trade have declined in relative importance in recent years, but they remain the primary source of revenue.[5] Trade taxes fell from 16 per cent of GDP in 1986/7 to 9 per cent in 1991/2 (see Table 5.4) while their share of domestic revenue fell from 75 per cent to 43 per cent in the same period (Table 5.3). These developments reflect the changes in tariff structure through the lowering of duty rates, the elimination of the 6 per cent import tax at the time when the sales tax was introduced and the process, which was started in 1986/7, of phasing out export taxes, including the elimination of the export tax on groundnuts in 1989/90. However, the loss in revenue due to these measures has been almost wholly offset by the gains in revenue from sales tax on imports; although these are officially classified under the item 'domestic taxes on goods and services', sales taxes on imports act more like a tax on international trade than a domestic sales tax. Furthermore, in recognition of the expected losses in revenue from tariff reforms the government extended customs duties on fuel purchases to the GPTC (at the full rate) and the GUC (at 25 per cent of the normal rate) in 1989/90.

An interesting feature of the post-ERP fiscal developments was the substantial rise in trade taxes (by over 3 percentage points of GDP) in the first two years following the introduction of the reforms. This almost certainly reflects the effects of the large depreciation of the dalasi in 1985.

Direct taxes (personal and corporate income taxes) are a relatively unimportant source of domestic revenue in The Gambia, as in other LDCs. Reforms were introduced in the income tax system during 1988/9, with a view to improving the efficiency of the system and curtailing widespread tax evasion. The number of personal income tax brackets was reduced from 12 to five, and the marginal tax rate for the highest bracket was reduced from 75 per cent to 50 per cent and then to 35 per cent. The complex system of allowances was also rationalized with the introduction of a unified standard allowance. Despite these reforms, little improvement was achieved in revenue generation. It is possible that improvements in collection and administration, and the widening of the tax base, were offset by the increase in the threshold level of taxable income. It also

Table 5.4 Trends in Major Taxes (as % of GDP) Current Prices, Net Prices, 1981/2–1991/2

	82	83	84	85	86	87	88	89	90	91	92
1. Income and property	3.6	2.1	2.7	2.9	2.8	2.7	2.6	2.9	2.9	2.6	2.4
1.1 Company tax	2.1	0.8	0.9	1.5	1.4	1.0	1.6	1.6	1.4	1.4	1.3
1.2 Personal income tax	1.3	1.1	1.5	1.2	0.9	1.5	0.9	1.1	1.1	1.0	0.9
2. International trade	14.6	12.1	14.7	12.4	13.6	16.5	14.3	17.2	14.4	8.9	8.9
2.1 Import duty	12.8	11.2	11.6	10.1	11.4	13.9	11.8	10.9	8.9	8.8	8.9
2.2 Import tax	0.7	0.8	1.2	1.2	1.4	2.2	1.9	0.4	0.0	0.0	0.0
2.3 Export duty/tax	0.9	0.1	1.7	0.8	0.0	0.0	0.0	0.3	0.0	–	–
3. Tax on production, service, expenditure	1.0	0.8	1.1	1.8	1.0	1.1	1.4	6.2	7.5	8.1	7.8
3.1 Excise duty	0.4	0.2	0.4	1.2	0.3	0.5	0.2	–	–	–	0.0
3.2 Roads and motor vehicles	0.2	0.3	0.3	0.2	0.2	0.2	0.2	0.2	0.2	0.2	0.2
3.3 Fishing	–	–	–	–	0.1	0.1	0.6	–	0.5	0.6	0.4
3.4 Hotels and tourism	0.1	0.1	0.2	0.2	0.2	0.1	–	0.1	0.5	0.5	–
3.5 Telecommunications	–	–	–	–	–	–	–	0.1	0.2	0.2	–
3.6 Civil aviation	–	–	–	–	–	–	–	–	0.7	0.6	–
3.7 National sales tax	0.0	0.0	0.0	0.0	0.0	0.0	–	5.4	6.8	7.3	7.2

Source: Table 5.2.

appears that lowering the highest tax bracket did not have the expected positive impact on compliance, at least in the short run.

Non-tax revenues declined as a proportion of GDP in the period to 1984/5 but have remained relatively stable since (at around 1.7 per cent), although they have failed to regain the levels attained in the early 1980s (see Table 5.2). Increasing these non-tax revenues has become an important fiscal objective in recent years by, for example, the introduction of user charges in the education and health sectors. What emerges from the above analysis of revenue structure is that gains in domestic revenue achieved during the ERP and the first year of the PSD were the result of a combination of factors, the most important being the introduction of the sales tax on imports in 1988 and the effects of currency depreciation on import taxes. To a lesser extent, increased revenue generation resulted from sales taxes levied on domestically produced goods, the introduction of the corporate profits tax and a small increase in non-tax revenues from the sale of fixed assets. Nevertheless, revenue gains during the period 1981/2– 1990/91 as a whole were modest: domestic revenues (as a percentage of GDP) in 1990/91 were only about 2.5 percentage points higher than a decade earlier. On the other hand, the domestic deficit improved from about 20 per cent of GDP in 1980/81 to under 10 per cent of GDP in 1990/91 with the 'sustainable' deficit (i.e. when capital revenues are included and 'special provisions' are excluded) undoubtedly less than this. It follows that the improvement in the government's fiscal position over the 1980s as a whole was achieved largely through expenditure pruning, with increased tax revenues making a modest contribution after 1985. In this sense, The Gambia is not atypical of adjusting countries elsewhere in sub-Saharan Africa.[6]

3.3 Government Expenditure

Total expenditures as a percentage of GDP have displayed considerable fluctuation during the 1980s. They suffered a sharp decline from 45 per cent to 31 per cent of GDP between 1981/2 and 1984/5 (see Table 5.2). In the first year of the ERP (1985/6), expenditures were cut further, to 20 per cent of GDP, but then recovered in the following two years to reach 37 per cent in 1987/8, before falling back to around 30 per cent in 1988/9 and 1989/90. The first year of the PSD witnessed a small increase in expenditures, to almost 31 per cent of GDP in 1990/91, though provisional figures for 1991/2 suggest that this higher level may not be sustained.

The burden of expenditure cuts during the first half of the 1980s was borne mainly by recurrent expenditures, which decreased by around 16 percentage points of GDP between 1981/2 and 1985/6. The main categories of recurrent spending to be cut during this period included expenditures on wages and salaries of government employees and current transfers (subsidies) to parastatals (see Table 5.5).

The government achieved the cuts in wage and salary expenditures by introducing major changes to public employment in 1986. Following an audit of civil service workers, about 25 per cent of the civil service workforce was retrenched, involving over 2 500 casual and low-grade workers, and almost 1 000 established employees. In addition many vacant posts were eliminated from the roster, an embargo was introduced on the creation of new posts, the filling of vacancies was restricted, and civil service salary levels were temporarily frozen. Consequently expenditure on wages and salaries fell from around 29 per cent of total expenditures in 1985/6 to 14 per cent in 1986/7.

The government introduced major cuts in spending on the social sectors, especially in the education and health budgets. As a percentage of total expenditures social sector spending declined from 34 per cent to 20 per cent between 1981/2 and 1985/6 (see Table 5.6).

On the other hand, the share in total government spending of expenditure on economic services, both current and capital, and particularly on agriculture and infrastructure, expanded considerably during the first half of the 1980s though capital spending as a whole declined in relation to GDP by around 5 percentage points. The main items on which capital spending was cut included capital transfers to parastatals, and expenditure on building and civil works.

It is often argued that it is easier politically for governments to cut capital spending (rather than current spending) because there are fewer, or less influential, 'interest groups' to defend the former. However, in The Gambia much of government income in the form of aid inflows is tied to capital spending on specific projects so that cutting such spending would also lead to reduced government income. Furthermore, the government has entered into long-term commitments for such projects with donors who may re-evaluate their future project financing if the government were to appear willing to sacrifice these projects to satisfy short-term budgetary constraints.

In 1986/7 and 1987/8, total expenditures expanded substantially. The expansion was however mainly due to 'one-off' increases in current expenditure on special budgetary support to cover losses incurred by the Gambia Produce Marketing Board (GPMB) and the GUC, and to provisions for the liquidation of other parastatal debts, which amounted to around 9 per cent of GDP in both years (see Hadjimichael et al., 1992, p. 21). Furthermore, net lending rose markedly in 1986/7, when the government established the Managed Fund, consisting of non-performing government-guaranteed loans of the Gambia Commercial Development Bank (GCDB), which were consolidated and transferred to the government in January 1987.

Following these 'extraordinary' expenditures, government spending declined again in 1988/9 by about 7 percentage points of GDP. Recurrent spending decreased from 26 per cent of GDP in 1987/8 to around 22 per cent in 1988/9 mainly owing to a further fall in transfers to parastatals and households, and a further cut in social spending. Capital expenditure fell from 10.8 per cent to 8.2

Table 5.5 Structure of Government Expenditures (by economic type), 1981/2–1990/91 (% of total)

	82	83	84	85	86	87	88	89	90	91[a]
1. Recurrent	66.6	74.7	65.4	54.5	70.1	66.1	91.0	72.6	74.9	70.0
1.1 Wages and salaries	22.4	30.4	28.5	25.4	29.4	13.9	11.3	17.1	18.8	14.4
1.2 Maintenance	3.0	4.6	4.5	4.0	3.5	2.6	2.4	2.4	3.0	2.5
1.3 Transfers and subsidies[b]	5.0	6.8	9.9	6.3	8.7	19.2	11.8	8.5	7.6	6.7
1.4 Acquisition of fixed capital assets	0.9	0.9	1.4	1.0	0.9	0.4	1.7	1.8	2.3	1.3
1.5 Debt service charges	4.2	13.2	4.8	3.6	9.3	13.4	18.1	26.3	25.1	29.9
2. Capital/Development expenditure	33.4	25.2	34.6	45.5	29.9	33.9	28.9	27.4	25.0	22.0

Notes:
a. Estimates.
b. Includes transfers and subsidies to: households, parastatals, non-profit institutions, local authorities, and abroad. Pre-84/85, transfers to parastatals took the form of 'subsidies'; post-84/85, they took the form of 'transfers'.

Source: Table 5.2.

*Table 5.6 Expenditure by Functional Classification, 1981/2–1990/91
           (% of total)*

		81/2	85/6	89/90	90/91
1.	General public services	34.1	22.6	23.3	21.9
	1.1 Public administration	..	12.6	12.2	11.6
	1.2 External affairs	..	2.6	3.4	3.0
	1.3 Public order, defence	6.5	7.4	7.7	7.3
2.	Social services	34.0	19.8	17.8	22.3
	2.1 Education	14.7	10.3	10.3	12.9
	2.2 Health	5.9	5.6	6.2	6.4
3.	Economic services	29.2	45.8	24.9	18.6
	3.1 Agriculture, etc.	9.7	20.2	4.8	5.9
	3.2 Mining, manuf., constn	1.1	0.3	1.9	1.8
	3.3 Infrastructure	17.4	22.4	15.1	9.4
	3.4 Hotels and tourism	0.9	0.3	0.4	0.3
4.	Public debt services	..	7.5	30.7	31.9
5.	Pension and gratuities	..	2.5	2.4	2.0

per cent of GDP though this primarily reflected delays in the execution of two large foreign-financed projects. Expenditure on building and civil works remained high reflecting the construction of the Banjul–Serekunda highway, but development expenditures on the health and agriculture sectors fell substantially.

From 1988/9, total expenditures remained relatively stable. There was a further small reduction in spending in 1989/90 in line with the government's policy of expenditure restraint, though the first year of the PSD (1990/91) saw a slight increase in both current and capital expenditures, the former owing to a rise in civil service salaries and a moderate increase in spending on health and education.

4   ASSESSING THE IMPACT OF REFORM

In order to analyse the effects of the reform programmes on the Gambian economy we would, ideally, like to compare the actual post-reform situation with a 'counterfactual' post-reform situation in which all other potentially relevant variables remain unchanged. The construction of such a counterfactual would however require sophisticated economic modelling which is beyond the scope of the present study. An alternative is to compare actual pre- and post-reform periods. In doing so, however, it is important to try to identify other (non-reform induced) changes which might have affected the 'targets' of reform. In this section we first consider the objectives of the reform packages in terms of the 'intermediate' variables (e.g. budget deficits) and 'final' variables (e.g. GDP growth) which the reforms were designed to affect. Post-reform changes in these variables can then be assessed to identify the extent to which these resulted from the policy reforms or from exogenous changes in other causal variables.

Of course, interdependencies among relevant exogenous variables and between these and policy variables can be complex, and different instruments of reform can have various mutually enhancing or inhibiting effects. It may be expected, for example, that weather-induced changes in groundnut production in The Gambia could affect GDP growth independently of, but possibly simultaneously with, reforms designed to increase growth. Similarly, the removal of trade taxes as part of a reform package could affect one objective of reform beneficially (e.g. improve private sector efficiency) but adversely affect some other reform objective(s) (e.g. by raising budget deficits). Disentangling these various interactions is necessarily imprecise and the quality of available data in The Gambia is fairly limited. Our attempts to assess policy reform impacts in this section are therefore, for the most part, qualitative rather than quantitative, but are based on as much available data as possible.

The methodology which we follow in the remainder of this section is:

- to identify the objectives of reform;
- to examine the extent to which the intermediate and final objectives of reform were achieved in the post-reform period; and then
- to consider the extent to which this can be attributed to the policy reforms (especially fiscal reforms) or to changes in other factors over the same period.

In Section 4, we consider some of the factors which lay behind The Gambia's reform successes and failures and their implications for reform elsewhere.

4.1 Reform Objectives

Table 5.7 lists a number of intermediate and final objectives associated, to differing degrees, with the two major reform initiatives in 1985 and 1990. The intermediate objectives consist of those policy reforms which are considered to be necessary in order to facilitate the achievement of the final objectives. The final objectives listed are common policy objectives of almost all governments seeking to raise the living standards of their populations and they figure prominently in all IMF/World Bank adjustment programmes. It is noteworthy however that poverty/inequality-reducing objectives were not prominent in ERP documents. Rather, anticipated changes in poverty/inequality associated with the ERP were seen as factors which might constrain the policies adopted to

Table 5.7 *Intermediate and Final Objectives of Reform*

Type of Reform	Intermediate Objectives	Final Objectives
Fiscal/Public Sector Reforms	– Eliminate budget deficits – Increase tax revenue – Diversify tax base – Improve public sector efficiency – Improve private sector incentives and diversify private economic activities – Discourage 'high cost' domestic production – Create competitive product markets (e.g. groundnuts)	– Reduce income inequality and poverty – Increase income growth
Trade and Financial Reforms	– Minimize trade distortions – Improve money supply control – Create competitive markets for domestic and foreign currency	– Reduce/remove balance of payments deficits and foreign debt arrears – Reduce inflation

achieve the other final objectives. Social and poverty-related objectives were much more prominent in the PSD.

The intermediate objectives listed in Table 5.7 are commonly found in ERP and PSD documents emanating from the government of The Gambia, from the donor institutions, and from commissioned reports assessing the implementation and outcomes of the reform programmes. These objectives are also standard to many IMF/World Bank structural adjustment and stabilization packages associated with loan agreements with LDC governments. This suggests that, although the Gambian government had a strong input into the drafting of the reform agreements and initiated them voluntarily, much of the content originated from the lending agencies.

A major difference with the Gambian case, however, seems to be that several Gambian officials (most notably Minister Sisay) understood and accepted the need to achieve these intermediate reform objectives and genuinely sought to implement them. This contrasts with many other reforming countries where these conditions were not satisfied – governments were often reluctant to implement certain aspects of reform designed to meet these objectives (for a variety of reasons) but gave lip service to them as a means of acquiring loans.

Despite a number of implementation problems which delayed the disbursement of some loan tranches to The Gambia, the government's commitment to reform gained it considerable credibility with the IMF and World Bank which facilitated subsequent loan and reform agreements. The government's recent request for further voluntary technical assistance from the IMF despite graduating from the ESAF highlights the generally positive attitude within the government towards IMF-sponsored reform objectives and prescriptions for implementing them.

Finally an important aspect of all the reform objectives above was their sustainability: the reforms were intended to be long-lasting and even developed further beyond the immediate period during which the reforms were required as part of loan conditionality. Reforms designed to achieve stabilization objectives, though often short-term in nature (in the sense that they required rapid implementation) were expected to be maintained if future balance of payments crises or inflationary episodes were to be avoided. For similar reasons, reforms undertaken over longer periods were seen as essential for improvements in the supply side of the economy which would need continued monitoring and adapting in the light of experience if the full benefits of adjustment were to be reaped beyond the initial reform period. Such measures as administrative reform, increased tax collection efforts and public expenditure planning were seen as measures which should be part of ongoing government activity.

It would seem that the relatively good performance of The Gambia (by the standards of other African countries) in terms of the extent of reform 'slippage' or 'regress' can also be partly attributed to the government's high degree of commitment to the reform programme. A recent assessment by IMF economists reports that reforms in The Gambia were 'implemented broadly on schedule' (Hadjimichael et al., 1992, p. 6); where slippages were observed these can be attributed largely to exogenous factors or to mistakes which are an inevitable part of the learning process.

4.2 Meeting Reform Objectives

Given the objectives outlined above, a key question is: how far were the intermediate objectives listed in Table 5.7 achieved? We consider these in turn below.

Intermediate objectives

Fiscal/public sector objectives On the fiscal side considerable progress was made in reducing the overall government budget deficit as noted in Section 2.1 above. Though the Gambian government is seeking to achieve budget surpluses excluding grants, their reliance on these grants is likely to persist for some time. This does not currently represent a serious problem since the country can expect to continue to receive significant levels of concessional finance to fund development projects.

It is important to recognize that, following the experience of the early 1980s, eliminating the budget deficit by cutting expenditures without raising tax revenues was not a viable long-term option. Not only would immediate increases in tax revenues reduce the necessary expenditure cuts in the short run but, by putting in place mechanisms to enhance revenue generation in the longer term, the reforms were attempting to provide a sustainable financial basis for funding public expenditures in later years. As demonstrated in Section 2.2, substantial increases in tax revenues were achieved in the first two years after the 1985 reform, but thereafter tax/GDP ratios stagnated or even declined. Revenue data also indicate that government revenues actually fell in real terms, by around 6 per cent from 1987/8 (three years after the first reforms) to 1991/2. However this was mainly owing to a large drop in non-tax revenues (much of which is accounted for by the ending of stabilization of exports (STABEX) support in 1988) while real tax revenues were almost 40 per cent higher in 1991/2 compared with 1987/8.

Another fiscal objective was the rationalization of the tax system and diversification of tax revenues in order to reduce the sensitivity of overall tax revenues to large short-term fluctuations in specific taxes. With its heavy reliance on import taxes prior to 1985, tax revenues in The Gambia were strongly influenced by import levels which, during balance of payments crises, could fall dramatically over short periods. Considerable progress was made towards rationalizing the tax system with the elimination of export taxes, the removal of various import duties and domestic excise taxes, and reductions in the number of tariff rates between 1985 and 1988. The introduction of the sales tax in 1988 also served to rationalize indirect tax rates towards a uniform rate of 10 per cent. Though rates other than 10 per cent were initially allowed for certain goods and services (e.g. tourist hotels and package tours, some imports), timetables for convergence of these tax rates to 10 per cent were established.

A major objective of the introduction of the sales tax was the broadening of the indirect tax base to minimize the revenue volatility associated with tariffs and excises. However, since the bulk of sales tax revenues are raised on imports together with the output of a small number of large domestic enterprises, the degree of base-broadening achieved so far must be considered relatively small. For practical reasons it would be difficult to collect the sales tax at the retail or wholesale levels and therefore, other than for imported goods, sales tax is generally collected at the producer level. Given the problems of identifying the large number of small-scale producers and commercial traders in The Gambia, these are effectively exempt from sales tax liability. Essentially, the vulnerability of tax revenues to changes in the balance of payments remains, though the removal of export taxes on groundnuts has removed one source of revenue volatility.

Fiscal objectives would seem therefore to have been only partially achieved so far. Moreover there are signs that improvements following major reform efforts are difficult to sustain. Nevertheless, with the privatization in 1993 of two parastatals (GPMB and GUC) which have continued to be a burden on fiscal finances, only five major parastatals will remain. This should allow fiscal deficits to be both smaller and more stable in the future as 'special provision' items are eradicated and some previously privatized companies begin to pay dividends to the government (where it retains minority shareholdings).

The Gambia's success at improving public sector efficiency also appears to be mixed. Tax and customs administration (which have had to cope with various and substantial changes in tax structures since 1985) remain important concerns. Different taxes are still collected by a variety of ministries with complex administrative and legal links to the Ministry of Finance and Economic Affairs which administers the government budget. The extensive use of discretionary tax and duty waivers also seems to have hindered collection efforts, although this may improve with the ending of such waivers in 1992 and 1993. A clear example of enhanced public sector efficiency is the improved performance of parastatals which have entered into 'performance contracts' with the government, and the privatized firms in which the government retains equity. The success of these measures is evident from the near elimination of government subsidies to such firms (with the exception of the GUC which seems to have been resistant to efforts to raise efficiency).

Private sector objectives The intermediate objectives of improving private sector efficiency, discouraging high-cost domestic industry, creating competitive markets, and diversifying the economy, are difficult to observe and measure directly.[7] Success in meeting these objectives might rather be inferred from their expected impact on the 'final' objectives of increased growth rates, reduced un(der)employment and an improved trade balance, which we discuss below. Two points are worth stressing at this stage however. Firstly, the removal of trade barriers such as tariffs is often advocated to raise efficiency by redirecting resources away from domestic import-substituting industries which are viable at tariff-protected prices but not at world prices. These gains are likely to be small in The Gambia since, even in the presence of tariffs, there was little domestic production of import substitutes especially in the industrial sector. This is not to deny that efficiency gains from reform occurred in some markets (such as in the groundnut market). However the inefficiency evident there before reform probably resulted more from government-guaranteed monopoly positions and market controls in general than specifically from trade restrictions.

Secondly, it is widely acknowledged that, since the dismantling of trade restrictions from 1985, there has been a significant re-direction of The Gambia's trade towards Senegal and other neighbouring states, with a rapidly expanding re-export trade (to circumvent Senegalese trade protection against (non-Gambian) imports). In addition Gambian groundnut production is increasingly being exported to Senegal for processing (and re-export) because the Senegalese government continues to offer higher prices (to subsidize poor farmers) while prices in a liberalized Gambia now broadly reflect world levels. One consequence of this is that under-recording of exports and groundnut production has almost certainly increased since 1985 (since these goods no longer pass through the GPMB or the customs posts at ports – the main recording mechanisms). This obviously hampers attempts to assess the consequences of trade and fiscal reforms. It also hinders assessment of the degree of diversification of the economy – in particular whether dependence on groundnuts has been reduced.

The degree of under-recording of groundnut production and exports is likely to vary from year to year but has probably been greater since the 1985 reforms and especially after 1986. Though care must be taken when drawing conclusions about trade diversification, the available evidence suggests that diversification of the production structure has so far been limited, especially in industrial sectors. Within agriculture there appears to have been some diversification towards fishing activities with increased exports of smoked fish.

The growth of the re-export trade, especially with Senegal, has undoubtedly produced significant gains for the Gambian economy. However it has also raised the vulnerability of the economy to policy changes outside The Gambia. In particular, liberalization in Senegal involving either reductions in tariffs and other trade restrictions or the removal of groundnut subsidies could seriously weaken the balance of payments and tax revenues (via taxes on the imports of re-exports) in The Gambia. Liberalization in Senegal does not seem likely in the near future but, given widespread shifts in policy in this direction in African countries in recent years, the effects of possible policy shifts in Senegal in the long term should not be ignored. In addition, it should be recognized that as the re-export trade grows the Senegalese authorities may become more sensitive to its role in their economy and could move to amend the 'free trade' agreement with The Gambia which (together with Senegalese import taxes) currently creates the incentive for Senegalese imports to be channelled through The Gambia.

Another feature of the post-reform period in The Gambia is the considerable expansion of the (private) services sector in the form of tourism and tourism-related activities. Both of these seem likely to have been assisted by trade and exchange rate reform, particularly the large depreciation of the dalasi in 1986 following liberalization of the foreign exchange market. However, though tourist numbers generally expanded during the 1980s the largest increase occurred before 1985.[8] To the extent that reform encouraged such activities, fiscal reform seems unlikely to have been important. Nevertheless, the tourism sector has provided a source of tax revenues since it was brought into the sales tax base.

The effects of trade and financial policies on the reform objectives are not the primary focus of this study. However these policies may interact with fiscal aspects of reform and, since they are often designed to help achieve the same final objectives, the relative importance of each should be considered. In terms of the intermediate objectives in Table 5.7 it is generally recognized that money supply aggregates, following large initial fluctuations after the liberalization of the exchange rate in 1986, have been less volatile compared with the pre-1985 period. But, as Hadjimichael et al. note: 'deviations from the initial program targets for . . . monetary aggregates have been caused primarily by exogenous factors – such as weather developments . . . and shortfalls or delays in external assistance – and to a lesser extent by domestic policy slippages' (1992, p. 29).

Trade/financial objectives Finally, the government's reform target of a competitive foreign exchange market has perhaps been the most obvious success of all the intermediate objectives of the 1985 reforms. Achieving a competitive domestic money market appears to have been less successful so far but nevertheless significant reforms have occurred since 1985. The floating of the dalasi and the removal of controls on private foreign currency holdings, as well as precipitating a large devaluation of the currency, has enabled a flourishing foreign exchange market with only insubstantial differences between official bank and informal market exchange rates. The government has encouraged an expansion of the number of private banks operating in The Gambia, including privatizing the government-owned commercial bank. It is, however, difficult to assess how competitive these markets have become not least because assessing the degree of monopoly power in the banking sector has proved notoriously difficult even in developed countries and this is no less so in The Gambia. The banking system is still dominated by a small number of mainly foreign-owned banks and, as interest rates have risen since liberalization, the bank's margins between lending and deposit rates have also widened – a phenomenon often attributed to monopoly power. However, such a response might be anticipated in a market freed from government controls and is not necessarily incompatible with increased competition and efficiency. The larger interest rate spreads may reflect increased lending risks which are often associated with radical reform programmes and the uncertain prospects for the servicing of bank debt by newly privatized companies.

Final objectives
The ultimate test of the success of a policy is whether it meets its final objectives; in this case faster and sustained economic growth, balance of payments equilibrium, paying off foreign debt arrears, lower inflation and reduced income inequality and poverty. All of these contribute directly to improvements in society's welfare.

Economic growth A commonly used method to assess the growth effects of the 1985 reforms has been to compare pre- and post-1985 growth rates. We address this by asking two questions. (i) Did the growth rate increase after 1985? (ii) How far can any observed changes be attributed to the reforms in general and fiscal reforms in particular?

Tables 5.8 and 5.9 show growth rates for GDP and some of its components between 1980/81 and 1991/2. Table 5.8 indicates that GDP growth, averaged over two or three years after 1985, exceeded average growth rates for two or three years prior to 1985. Indeed any post-1985 average exceeds the two or three year average before 1985 though the margin is not very large. If four or five year averages are considered before 1985, the post-1985 performance does not look particularly good. Table 5.9 confirms that these high (four and five year) averages before 1985 essentially result from very large increases in groundnut production in 1981–3. The post-1985 evidence does, however, suggest a more consistent growth performance, with positive growth rates being achieved every year.

While there is clearly some improvement in growth rates after 1985 compared with the immediate pre-reform period, the evidence does not seem to support the view, expressed by a number of previous studies, that reform was associated with significantly improved growth performance. There are a number of reasons for this. Firstly, initial estimates of GDP growth in the three years 1986/7–1988/9 suggested an average annual rate of around 5 per cent, but more recent (1991) revisions have scaled down estimates for these years to around 3 per cent. Secondly, to assess the growth-enhancing effects of reform from 1985, we would ideally like to compare actual experience with the counterfactual post-1985 experience had there been no reform. Though this latter case can never be known with any precision, there were signs of deteriorating

Table 5.8 GDP Growth before and after the ERP (% per annum)

Pre-ERP:		Post-ERP:		No. of
Period	GDP growth	Period	GDP growth	years
1984–5	1.6	1985–6	4.1	1
1983–5	–3.3	1985–7	3.4	2
1982–5	2.7	1985–8	2.9	3
1981–5	6.7	1985–9	3.2	4
1980–85	4.0	1985–90	3.6	5
		1985–91	3.4	6
		1985–92	3.5*	7

Note: * Provisional estimate.

Table 5.9 Growth Rates for Aggregate GDP and Agricultural Sub-Aggregates, 1980/81–1991/2
(Growth per annum)

	81	82	83	84	85	86	87	88	89	90	91	92*
Real GDP (at mkt. prices)	-7.9	19.8	14.6	-8.2	1.6	4.1	2.8	1.7	4.3	5.2	2.3	4.0
Real agricultural GDP	-12.6	38.3	-5.4	-27.9	10.7	3.9	7.5	-0.0	-1.2	7.3	-14.0	5.4
Crop production	9.5	44.2	21.3	-27.5	7.3	0.8	7.1	-1.0	-5.5	12.9	-22.6	6.7
Groundnut production	-20.0	36.3	38.5	-29.8	7.5	-33.5	45.6	9.1	-18.3	32.7	-42.3	8.0

Note: * Provisional estimate.

economic performance in The Gambia leading up to 1985 with unsustainable balance of payments deficits, worsening debt arrears and so on. In the absence of corrective action it is likely that this would have impacted adversely on GDP growth after 1985, producing growth rates less than those actually observed.

Overall, therefore, there is some evidence that improved growth perform-ance coincided with the ERP, but how far was the former caused by the latter? Despite considerable research effort, robust hypotheses and reliable evidence on the causes of economic growth in general remain elusive, with the role of government policy being particularly difficult to assess. In the case of The Gambia it has been argued that, owing to heavy reliance on crop production, and groundnuts in particular, the country's GDP growth rate is mainly influenced by fluctuations in the output of these sectors, which in turn are determined by largely exogenous factors – weather and international commodity prices. Table 5.9 shows annual growth rates during 1980/81–1991/2 for real GDP, real agricultural GDP, and overall crop and groundnut production. Inspection of the data suggests substantial co-movement between the four series and the correla-tion coefficients between GDP growth rates and the other three variables are high – 0.858, 0.742 and 0.740 for agriculture, crops and groundnuts respec-tively, for 1980/1–91/2 overall (see Table 5.10). This would seem to confirm that developments in these activities (which might reasonably be treated as essentially exogenous, though policy towards them may have some influence) will strongly impact on GDP growth in general. However, similar correlations over the seven year post-ERP period are 0.906, 0.543 and 0.508 suggesting that for groundnut and total crop production at least, the correlation is weaker than for the period as a whole. The higher correlation coefficient between agricul-tural and total GDP in the later period mainly reflects the diversification noted earlier into non-crop agricultural activities such as fishing. Both these develop-ments might suggest some role for policy reform in the growth process – by counteracting adverse changes in crop production and by encouraging fish-related exports. Years of negative growth in agricultural activities also provide an interesting pre- and post-reform comparison. In 1980/81 and 1983/4 reduc-tions in groundnut output of 20 per cent and 30 per cent respectively fed through into GDP growth rates of negative 8 per cent in both years. In 1988/9 and 1990/91 however, despite similar or greater recorded reductions in groundnut pro-duction, The Gambia managed to maintain positive GDP growth of 4.3 per cent and 2.3 per cent respectively. In both these post-reform years negative crop growth was offset by strong growth in fisheries, tourism and tourism-related activities. While there were some specific fiscal reforms which may have contributed to this – such as the removal of export taxes – trade and financial reforms seem likely to be of greater significance. Nevertheless, since trade and fiscal reforms were designed to be mutually reinforcing (for example, through simultaneous reductions in fiscal and foreign trade deficits) a precise demarca-tion may be inappropriate.

Fiscal Reforms in LDCs

Table 5.10   Correlations of Sub-Aggregate Growth Rates with GDP Growth

	1980/1–1991/2	1985/6–1991/2
Real agricultural GDP	0.858	0.906
Crop production	0.740	0.543
Groundnut production	0.742	0.508

Balance of payments and debt objectives   The post-ERP period has been
associated with clear and substantial improvements in The Gambia's current
account deficit and a reduction in debt arrears. All arrears were paid off by 1990
and recent current account deficits have been covered by inflows of foreign
capital, moving the overall balance of payments into surplus, while foreign
exchange reserves rose from the equivalent of about one week of total imports
in 1986 to the equivalent of five months of imports by the end of 1992. This
turnaround in the balance of payments has been accompanied by a fall in the
share of groundnuts in total (recorded) exports (from 30–40 per cent in the early
1980s to 12–14 per cent in the 1990s), and a rise in the contribution of income
from tourism (from 25–35 per cent in the early 1980s to almost 50 per cent in
the 1990s). As noted earlier official data suggest that the share of re-exports in
total exports has been fairly stable or slightly rising since 1985 though this fails
to capture unrecorded re-exports.

How much of this undoubted success can be attributed to reform? The short
answer is probably 'quite a lot'. Of course, the condition for The Gambia to
receive substantial inflows of foreign assistance from the IMF, the World Bank
and other aid agencies was the undertaking of many of the reforms outlined
above. In an analytically trivial, but practically important, sense, therefore,
reform (or the willingness to pursue reform) directly affected the country's
external position by providing the trigger for concessional inflows. This in turn
increased the willingness of private creditors to extend debt rescheduling and
additional credit. Continued political commitment to reform in the post-1985
period by the Gambian government has also been required to ensure continued
foreign inflows. It is important to recognize that some foreign inflows were
contingent on commitment to, rather than simply the success of, reform so that
improvements in The Gambia's external position was not necessarily dependent
on successful reform elsewhere in the economy.

Considering economic, rather than 'accounting', aspects of the improved
external position, a reasonable tentative conclusion would seem to be that the
floating of the exchange rate and liberalization of the foreign exchange market
were especially important for the balance of payments improvement and the
growth of tourist inflows, while the trade tax reforms provided an additional
stimulus to the re-export trade. According to IMF estimates the effective

exchange rate for the dalasi depreciated by 57 per cent in nominal terms and by 44 per cent in real terms during 1986. Since 1986 improvements in the current account have been associated mainly with increased invisible, rather than visible, exports. The effects of devaluation on visible exports have been limited probably because The Gambia's major merchandise exports are agricultural commodities with low price elasticities of supply. Travel (tourism) income, which is the main invisible export, may however be more price responsive so that depreciation of the dalasi is likely to have significantly improved The Gambia's competitive position as a destination for tourists especially relative to other African destinations.

The buoyancy of the re-export trade, even prior to 1985, was essentially a function of differences in import duty rates between The Gambia and its neighbours. The progressive decrease in Gambian duties from 1986 relative to those of other countries is likely to account for the increase in this activity so that in this respect fiscal reform has probably been crucial.

Inflation objectives The Gambia's inflation performance broadly reflects the patterns of money supply growth noted earlier, namely sharp rises immediately after liberalization of the foreign exchange market in 1986 (with annual inflation reaching 46 per cent in 1986/7) followed by declines in subsequent years to 5 per cent in 1990/1, but rising to about 12–13 per cent in 1992. Though the Gambian authorities have concentrated on money supply growth as the main intermediate target for policy to reduce inflation, fiscal policy is also likely to have been important. In particular it must be doubtful whether inflation would have fallen to the same extent had fiscal policy not achieved such large reductions in the budget deficit. Success in reducing the budget deficit in recent years has enabled the government to make net repayments to the domestic banking sector, which helped to limit money supply growth. However, inflation in The Gambia is clearly not simply determined by domestic monetary factors, but exogenous changes in groundnut prices and delays in foreign assistance payments (necessitating further domestic borrowing by the government) are also important. It has also been suggested that inflation increases in late 1989 partly reflected the budgetary consequences of a large rise in public sector wages in 1989 after several years of restraint (see Hadjimichael et al., 1992).

Social objectives Social (equity and poverty) objectives received little attention in the ERP which was aimed essentially at improving efficiency in the Gambian economy. More explicit attention has been given to social aspects in the PSD but the likely social consequences of the main efficiency-enhancing reforms do not appear to have been considered in any detail. This partly reflects the fact that data which would enable an assessment of social impacts to be made are sparse. Attempts to rectify this have been addressed recently with the initiation of two household surveys – a household expenditure survey and a social dimensions of adjustment (SDA) survey seeking information on such aspects as education and health status, nutrition, housing and employment status. Though a preliminary report of the latter survey is available this clearly cannot yet provide information on changes in social factors and empirical evidence on the social impact of the ERP or PSD is therefore both limited and tentative. Nevertheless it is possible to consider the direction of likely social consequences of some aspects of the reform programme.

Effects of groundnut market reforms Groundnuts in The Gambia are grown predominantly by small-scale farmers who, together with farm workers, represent the bulk of the rural poor. In the early years of reform, prices of groundnuts were raised to discourage cross-border sales and this might be expected to have helped poor farmers. However the subsequent liberalization of the groundnut market led to substantial falls in groundnut prices as they moved towards world levels. The extent to which this harmed rural farmers is difficult to predict because cross-border sales are known to have increased as farmers sought to benefit from the higher prices available in Senegal. However the combination of a rapidly growing rural population, poor harvests and declining groundnut prices in the late 1980s almost certainly lowered the living standards of the rural poor. The conclusion of Hadjimichael et al. (1992) that 'these adverse effects reflected entirely the impact of unfavourable weather and the collapse of groundnut prices on world markets, and could not be attributed to the reform measures implemented by the authorities' surely underestimates the effects of reform. Since a crucial aspect of reform was the reduction of Gambian groundnut producer prices to world levels, government policy surely bears some of the blame for the declining living standards which ensued. On the other hand, the removal of the GPMB's monopoly on groundnut exports in 1990 could be expected to have benefited groundnut farmers who could now legally seek the highest possible prices for their produce.

Effects of foreign exchange liberalization The effects of the depreciation of the dalasi on the living standards of farmers following foreign exchange liberalization is uncertain. To the extent that the rural poor spend on non-tradeable goods (e.g. housing, some foodstuffs) but are dependent on tradeables such as groundnuts for their income, their living standards would be raised by depreciation, which increases the relative price of tradeables. The reverse would hold for poor farmers growing non-tradeable produce such as fruit and vegetables in order to purchase imported foodstuffs such as rice and flour.

Effects of public/private sector reforms For the urban population, the encouragement of private sector development has probably served to help small traders and producers who are strongly represented among the poorer sections of the urban population. However, notwithstanding some urban–rural migration following public sector retrenchment in 1985, increasing rural–urban migration has been a persistent feature in The Gambia in recent years, and this has put pressure on the urban infrastructure (e.g. housing, electricity and water/sewage services). As a consequence the failure of public enterprise reform significantly to improve the performance of the Gambia Utilities Corporation may have adversely affected the access of the urban poor to essential services.

Effects of social sector spending As part of a restructuring of public expenditures in the PSD the share of education expenditures in total spending is targeted to rise from 20 per cent in 1989/90 to 22 per cent in 1992/3 with smaller increases for health spending.[9] However recent estimates suggest that the outturn in 1991/2 and 1992/3 might be under 19 per cent. Moreover recent small increases in education and health spending have arisen against a background of reduced relative expenditures on these items since 1985 as a result of difficulties controlling other types of expenditure (e.g. provision for parastatal losses) during attempts at overall cutbacks in government spending. An important contributor to the health status of the poor is the quality of drinking water and sewerage services. Government spending on these activities has not received particular priority and has tended to fluctuate in relative importance depending on the timing of individual development projects. The continued poor performance of the GUC has probably also had adverse effects on the public health of poorer sections of the population.

A number of features of the PSD however are encouraging for the future social consequences of reform. In addition to the process of monitoring the social status of the population mentioned earlier, increased priority within the education sector is being given to primary education. This is essential if The Gambia's very low literacy rates are to improve especially for poor rural dwellers. Attempts are also being made to reduce the number of 'unqualified' teachers. This is designed to reverse a problem worsened by the 1985 reforms when public sector wage cuts increased difficulties in recruiting suitably qualified teachers especially in rural areas. Within health expenditures, priority is being given to provision of rural health centres.

A more systematic way of determining spending priorities is also incorporated in the PSD. This includes public expenditure programmes designed to formulate specific plans for most of the main functional classifications of public spending. This should enable better monitoring and implementation of explicit social objectives. A similar strategy is being followed for capital spending via public investment programmes. Of itself this has little direct impact on social objectives but, by identifying key areas where donor assistance is required to assist with major development investments, it can help to focus attention on socially valuable projects and encourage concessional inflows to finance them.

Effects of non-tax revenue-raising measures Finally, one aspect of the PSD which may carry adverse distributional consequences is the introduction of user charges in education and health sectors. At present these involve modest charges for school books and drugs but there is also a wider tendency to attempt to shift the financial responsibility for other aspects of education from the public purse to parents (e.g. school uniforms). While it is often the case that small user charges can help substantially to curtail the inefficient use of resources when these are provided entirely free of charge, the distributional impacts of these in The Gambia are largely unknown but are likely to be potentially important. Drug charges to patients, for example, have been introduced to curtail rising government expenditures on drugs. This does not seem to have been accompanied by a systematic assessment of alternative methods of achieving greater spending control. Alternative arrangements which exclude patients who can afford to purchase drugs privately, rather than the lowest income patients, from free public services may be capable of achieving the same objective but with fewer adverse distributional effects.

5   LESSONS FROM THE GAMBIAN REFORM EXPERIENCE

The Gambia's experience with structural and stabilization reforms is noteworthy in at least three respects: (i) the reforms were drafted by the government and were undertaken voluntarily; (ii) the reforms were associated with a considerable improvement in several macroeconomic variables, and (iii) they met with little overt political opposition or social unrest. In each of these respects the reform experience of The Gambia differs from that of many other LDCs. Though the improvement in The Gambia's economic performance since the mid-1980s, and the contribution of the various reform measures, may have been exaggerated in some respects, the country can justifiably be regarded as one of the more successful economies in Africa over that period. A number of useful lessons may be learned which have implications for future Gambian development and for other LDCs, though the relevance of these lessons for other countries would need careful assessment in each case.

5.1   Administrative Issues

Despite a political regime in The Gambia which was generally in agreement with IMF/World Bank prescriptions for reform, administrative constraints hampered, and continue to hamper, the implementation of various aspects of reform. Tax administration in particular has proved persistently difficult owing to poor accounting and auditing practices in both the private and public sectors, legal loopholes in tax laws which delay or reduce tax collections, diverse government agencies and ministries which collect tax and non-tax revenues (but withhold them from the Ministry of Finance), and the existence of legal discretionary duty waivers which inhibit objective tax assessments. As a result fiscal reforms designed to produce a less distortionary tax structure are unlikely to achieve maximum effect without administrative reform as a pre-requisite. Administrative reform and the training of personnel should be facilitated by the adequate provision of the technical assistance by lending agencies to the government concerned.

It is difficult to assess how well the Gambian authorities have coped with the administrative aspects of reform implementation since intercountry comparisons of this sort are very difficult to make and improvements over time in some aspect of administration often lead to other administrative constraints being highlighted. However, it is noteworthy that the Gambian government accepted the need, early in the reform period, to tackle administrative reform, and progress has been made, for example, on administering treasury bill auction markets, and on monitoring tax collections. In addition, as administrative failures have appeared, attempts have been made to rectify them. For example some (remaining and recently privatized) parastatals have refused to pay their assessed tax liabilities to the Treasury because, they argue, some subsidy payments due from the Treasury remain outstanding. This highlighted legal inadequacies in the contractual arrangements between the government and these firms and in privatization laws to which the government is responding by amending necessary legislation. It is important that such 'learning-by-doing' gains from reform are exploited.

In The Gambia, administrative problems, especially in fiscal affairs, remain. This is evident from (i) the government's difficulty in maintaining and increasing tax revenue collections relative to GDP; (ii) recent recommendations for improvements in customs and income tax practices; and (iii) the government's request for continued technical assistance from the IMF.

Finally, restoring and maintaining macroeconomic stability requires careful demand management. Given the fairly long reaction and implementation lags which characterize budgetary policy (even in developed countries), demand management requires accurate and early information pertaining to the receipt of tax and other revenues. The reform process has highlighted major problems for demand management in The Gambia in that relevant information on revenues is sometimes only provided to the Ministry of Finance up to twelve months after these have been paid to the collecting agency. A system of monthly revenue transfers from revenue-collecting agencies to the Ministry of Finance is currently being implemented to help resolve this. This serves to emphasize the importance of reform of the administrative aspects, as well as the more obviously 'economic' aspects, of tax administration if economic gains (such as successful macroeconomic management) are to be fully realized.

5.2 Political Issues

Three political factors appear to have contributed to The Gambia's success. Firstly, the government has been stable with free elections returning the same party to power several times and with continuity in the Presidency. The government has cooperated with the aid agencies which advocated the reform programme and has made genuine attempts to implement reforms. Commitment from the top of the political hierarchy and willingness to respond to the advice of technical assistance teams has undoubtedly assisted the process.

Secondly, the absence of reform in neighbouring countries has been crucial for the expansion of re-exports and the growth of the foreign tourist industry, both of which have been important ingredients in the balance of payments improvements and increases in customs revenues. It suggests that political conditions, and changes in these conditions, in other countries can influence the country undertaking reform in fundamental ways, including the optimal form and timing of particular reforms within an overall programme.

Thirdly, a distinguishing feature of the Gambian reforms was the absence of major political opposition or social unrest. One possible reason for this may have been the absence of significant subsidies to the poor in the form of food or housing subsidies, prior to reform. As a consequence some of the more socially painful measures were largely avoided in The Gambia, whereas in several other reforming countries, removal of subsidies has been an important part of fiscal reform. A related aspect is the extent to which the Gambian government was able to ameliorate the adverse effects of reform and compensate losers, especially those in rural areas who traditionally provided much of the ruling party's support. Thus, as noted earlier, two of the major groups who stood to lose from the reforms – groundnut producers and retrenched public employees – were 'compensated' by initial increases in groundnut producer prices and efforts to relocate retrenched workers (e.g. via urban–rural migration).

5.3 Reform Regress

Despite overall compliance with reform there is nevertheless a tendency for initial reforms to regress over time suggesting that continued supervision of reforms and willingness to extend or adapt reform measures in the light of experience will enhance success. Some of this regress can result from unforeseen effects of new policies. For example, the removal of import tariffs on efficiency grounds may reduce government revenue and necessitate the imposition of alternative tax handles which may have economic effects similar to those which the reforms were designed to remove. Thus, the primary objective of customs and inland revenue officials/advisers is often the maximization of tax revenues, while Treasury/Ministry of Finance staff/advisers may attach higher priority to the objective of removing tax-induced distortions from the economy.

Reform designers therefore need to be aware of possible conflicts between revenue-raising and incentive-creating objectives.

Some regress from initial reform commitments can also occur, as discussed in Section 3.1, because governments are not convinced of the need for some reforms, or consider them too costly to implement in political and/or economic terms, despite agreeing to the reforms with donor agencies. Implementation of reforms therefore lapses if donor agencies do not adequately monitor them or penalize non-implementation. In general The Gambia's good record on maintaining reforms has probably been strongly influenced by the contribution of Gambian politicians and officials to drafting the initial reform packages agreed with the donors and the voluntary nature of the Gambian government's compliance. Where dilution of reforms has been observed in The Gambia these can be attributed mainly to some of the 'incompatibilities' of certain aspects of the reform programmes, adverse incentives at the administrative level, or because the government feels in the light of experience that some reforms are not yet practicable at the administrative level (though it may not have persuaded the lending agencies of this). An example of this last case can be found in the persistent calls by the donor agencies for the government to improve its tax collection efforts. These calls are often followed by the announcement of some measures designed to improve tax collections but which are not vigorously pursued subsequently.

5.4   Public Current versus Capital Spending

As in other LDCs, the recurrent budget in The Gambia is mainly financed from domestic sources of (tax and non-tax) revenue while the development budget is funded by overseas concessional finance. Reform in The Gambia enabled the resumption of large concessional inflows for new development projects. Most development (capital) projects however have recurrent spending implications arising from subsequent running and maintenance costs. This inevitably places additional demands on the recurrent budget though the recurrent implications are often not considered by aid donors and would not normally be funded by them anyway. Since many of these projects are proposed by donors rather than the Gambian government there is a tendency to accept donors' proposals as a kind of a 'free good' – the true cost of which is the foregone spending when public finances are diverted to cover project running and maintenance costs.

Two consequences can follow from this. Firstly, the rapid influx of external assistance after reform may have exceeded the economy's absorptive capacity for such investments leading to failed or underperforming projects (relative to expectations). This can produce unanticipated financial burdens on the government and, via reputation effects, discourage private investors and future aid. Secondly, tax revenues may have to be redirected either to maintain projects or cover their financial losses.

5.5   Reform and Growth

The Gambian government (and governments in other LDCs undertaking reform) have been criticized for laxity in implementing reforms as GDP growth
rates decrease again after a few initial post-reform years of increased growth. In
The Gambia's case at least, this criticism ignores two important factors. Firstly,
neither the initial increase nor the subsequent fall in growth rates are entirely
due to reform efforts. As shown earlier, the effects of the reforms on economic
growth are limited by the impact of exogenous changes in agricultural output.
Secondly, at the point of initiating economic reform, LDC economies are
usually experiencing severe economic difficulties including misallocation and
underutilization of resources, and macroeconomic disequilibria. It might therefore be expected that significant gains can be made in economic performance
initially by removing the more obvious and serious obstacles, but once this has
been achieved there are likely to be diminishing returns to subsequent reforms
as the economy approaches a more optimal allocation and utilisation of
resources. Some decline in reform-induced growth rates is therefore to be
expected.

5.6   The Role of Parastatals in Reform

A major source of fiscal deficits, and the main form of transfer expenditures, in
The Gambia before reform were the parastatal enterprises most of which were
making operating losses and receiving direct subsidies from central government. Given limits to the number of enterprises that can be privatized in any one
year, the government established 'performance contracts' as a means of 'com-
mercializing' them. These explicit contracts between different departments
within the public sector seem to have worked well in most cases to eliminate
parastatal losses despite limited overt sanctions for underperforming firms.
Because parastatal subsidies were the major form of transfer payments, privatization began early in the reform process. This took a variety of forms including
selling off shares in tranches over a number of years. The Gambia therefore
provides an interesting counterpoint to the common argument that
privatizations are often best delayed in the reform process – because improving
incentives in other sectors is more important and because of limited financial
markets on which to sell equity. This latter aspect does not seem to have caused
serious problems in The Gambia.

5.7   Public Expenditure Restraint

As noted earlier, cutbacks in public expenditure through wage reductions and
freezes were regarded as essential requirements in The Gambia (as elsewhere)
in order to reduce budget deficits. In cases where civil servants are among the

best paid employees in the country this may have only a limited impact on the labour market. In certain sectors in The Gambia however, such as in the education and health sectors, wage restraint created recruitment problems and declining staff quality as the public sector lost competitiveness in the labour market compared to alternative employment sources. One implication of this is that the effects of expenditure cuts on the labour market and the performance of the public sector need to be carefully considered. These effects may take some years to emerge.

5.8   Domestic and Trade Taxes

Almost all LDC reform packages involve efforts to shift the tax burden away from trade taxes towards domestic indirect taxes. Several studies have noted with approval that such a change in the tax structure in The Gambia occurred during the post-1985 period, especially with the introduction of the sales tax in 1988. However, in the case of countries like The Gambia where domestic production of import substitutes is very limited, the change in tax structure is more apparent then real. Thus, the replacement of various import tariffs and duties by a sales tax in 1988 was little more than a renaming exercise since (i) the sales tax is still levied on imports at the customs point; (ii) sales tax on imports accounts for about 80 per cent of sales tax revenue with the remaining 20 per cent mainly coming from a few large enterprises (taxed at the production level); and (iii) a fairly large number of imports continue to be liable for both sales tax and specific import duties.

5.9   Taxes and Redistribution

Tax reforms in The Gambia were mainly motivated by efficiency considerations with little attention to distributional implications. But an obvious effect of the move towards more uniform (indirect) tax rates is the reduction of high taxes on luxury items which will have adverse distributional effects unless previous smuggling of such items was commonplace. However, in the search for a more efficient tax system, the case for uniform taxes does not generally rest on theoretical arguments but on administrative considerations, and some difference in rates may achieve both more efficient and more equitable taxation.

5.10   Size

Finally has The Gambia's small size been important for reform success? It is difficult to assess this though the smallness both of the total population and the country's land area clearly served to reduce the absolute numbers of 'losers' from reform with the associated political and economic difficulties this would have caused. Similarly monitoring and implementing reforms is easier when this essentially involves a 'city state' – which approximately describes The Gambia, with its small inhabited land area overall and with two-thirds of its population in Banjul. While smallness may make implementation of reforms easier it has the disadvantage that the diversity of economic activities in which the country has a comparative advantage is likely to be limited. Reform attempts to reduce the economy's vulnerability to exogenous shocks by diversifying its production structure and export trade can therefore be expected to be less successful in such economies.

A key aspect of The Gambia's small size is that it was relatively easy for the political commitment to reform, accepted at the presidential and cabinet levels, to be filtered down to those responsible for reform implementation at lower political and administrative levels. Thus, the blame for failed implementation was hard to avoid at lower levels creating powerful incentives for improved performance when there was genuine commitment to reform higher up the political hierarchy.

NOTES

1. The Gambia's experience with fiscal adjustment in particular does not seem to be unique. For example, short-term improvements in budget deficits but without sustained increases in revenue mobilization have been observed in World Bank and IMF sponsored adjustment programmes in a number of LDCs. For an analysis of the experience of 18 LDCs in sub-Saharan Africa and Asia, see Basu and Nissanke, 1992.
2. The overall deficit is defined as total revenue including overseas grants less total expenditure and the domestic deficit as total revenue excluding overseas grants less total expenditure.
3. Overall revenues are defined as total government revenues, both tax and non-tax, plus grants from abroad, while domestic revenues are defined as total government revenues excluding grants from abroad.
4. The sales tax on domestically produced goods is effectively a production tax rather than a consumption tax, though in bars/restaurants it is levied at the consumption stage.
5. The high reliance on international trade taxes typifies the tax structure of most sub-Saharan African LDCs, where they account, on average, for 40 per cent of revenue. The reasons for this include the size of the international trade base, the non-availability of alternative 'tax handles' and the relative ease of collection of taxes on international trade. See Shalizi and Squire (1990).
6. Basu and Nissanke (1992) provide an analysis of the impact of fiscal adjustment on public expenditure and revenue patterns in 18 sub-Saharan African and Asian LDCs. See also Nashashibi et al. (1992).
7. Measures such as Domestic Resource Costs Ratios (DRCs) and other 'efficiency'-related indices can be calculated given sufficiently disaggregated industry-level data both before and after reform. Such data are not readily available in The Gambia and reliable DRC calculations are costly (in terms of research time) to produce.
8. For example, the number of air chartered tourists (the main form of tourism to The Gambia) rose over 70 per cent from 26 745 in 1982/3 to 45 861 by 1984/5; reached 47 021 by 1989/90 and 63 131 by 1991/2.
9. The assessment of education spending priorities is further complicated by changes in definitions for expenditure shares with debt interest and transfers sometimes included and sometimes excluded from total expenditure share targets and outcomes.

REFERENCES

Basu, P. and M. Nissanke (1992), 'Improving Domestic Resource Mobilization for Economic Development', mimeo (Geneva: UNCTAD).

Gray, C., M. McPherson, J. Owens and C. Zinnes (1992), *Taxes and Private Sector Activity in The Gambia. Overview and Recommendations for Change.* Cambridge, MA.: Harvard Institute for International Development for the Economic and Financial Policy Analysis Project, Ministry of Finance and Economic Affairs, The Gambia.

Hadjimichael, M.T., T. Rumbaugh and E. Verreydt (1992), 'The Gambia: Economic Adjustment in a Small Open Economy', Occasional Paper, no. 100 (Washington: IMF).

IMF (1990), *World Economic Outlook*, A Survey of the Staff of the International Monetary Fund, Washington, DC.

Musgrave, R.A. (1969), *Fiscal Systems* (New Haven, Conn.: Yale University Press).

Nashashibi, K., S. Gupta, C. Liuksila, H. Lorie and W. Mahler (1992), *The Fiscal Dimensions of Adjustment in Low Income Countries* (Washington: IMF).

Radelet, S. (1992), 'Reform without Revolt: the Political Economy of Economy Reform in The Gambia', *World Development*, 20(8) (August), pp. 1087–99.

Shalizi, Z. and L. Squire (1990), 'Tax Policy in Sub-Saharan Africa', *Policy and Research Series* (Washington: World Bank).

Tanzi, V. (1987), 'Quantitative Characteristics of Tax Systems', in D. Newbury and N. Stern (eds), *The Theory of Taxation for Developing Countries* (Oxford: Oxford University Press).

6. The Fiscal Impact of Adjustment in Tanzania in the 1980s

Priya Basu and Oliver Morrissey

1   INTRODUCTION

Under the leadership of President Julius Nyerere, Tanzania adopted an independent, socialist-oriented, development strategy from independence in 1961. In the 1970s the economy was hit by a series of external shocks, which, combined with internal constraints and weaknesses, led to severe economic imbalances. By 1980, Tanzania displayed many of the economic problems that beset numerous developing countries and that contributed to the introduction by the World Bank of Structural Adjustment Loans (SALs) whereby the Bank, usually in conjunction with the Fund (IMF), granted external financing support conditional on the recipient's undertaking an agreed programme of economic adjustment. In the 1980s, Tanzania adopted a series of programmes that could be defined as 'adjustment programmes' (although the Bank was not directly involved in the first of these). This paper evaluates the success of adjustment in Tanzania, paying particular attention to tax reforms and their effect on internal revenue-generating capacity.

Section 2 provides a brief overview of Tanzania's economic performance, tracing the present problems back to their sources in the 1970s. Section 3 then reviews the adjustment programmes of the 1980s in terms of the chronology of reforms proposed in each. The remainder of the report provides an evaluation of adjustment. Section 4 addresses the tax reforms and their revenue impact, paying special attention to trade taxes. Section 5 turns to the expenditure side of reforms, especially the impact on health and education. Section 6 offers an evaluation, concentrating on the sequence in which, and the extent to which, reforms were actually implemented, which provides pointers to why the reforms have had limited success. Section 7 provides a conclusion, and considers the prospects for Tanzania in the immediate future.

2   OVERVIEW OF THE TANZANIAN ECONOMY, 1970–90

Tanzania had a per capita GNP of $110 in 1990 and over the 1965–90 period averaged annual GNP per capita growth of minus 0.2 per cent (World Bank, 1992). Between 1965 and 1990, agriculture's share of GDP rose from 46 to 59 per cent, and industry's share fell from 14 to about 12 per cent. Tanzania has however made relatively good progress in social development, with a creditable record on child welfare, education and the reduction of rural–urban disparities.

Tanzania inherited a British tax system on independence and maintained a fairly lean government administrative system, and hence a relatively small budget, until the formation of the East Africa Community (EAC) with Uganda and Kenya in the Arusha Declaration of 1967. This change had important fiscal implications as the basic aim was to reduce the reliance of EAC members on foreign finance. First, the previous owners of assets then nationalized had to be compensated, at a high cost to public spending (banks were also nationalized so that no international commercial banks were based in Tanzania after 1967, and have only began to return in 1992). Second, a large portion of the development budget was redirected towards directly productive enterprises (essentially, parastatals). The failure of parastatals to generate adequate surpluses implied that these changes imposed a burden on the recurrent budget and reduced development spending. Consequently, a number of measures were undertaken to increase tax revenue in this period: a sales tax was introduced in 1969; an income tax in 1973; and there were major adjustments to sales and import taxes in 1976 (Osoro, 1992a).

A variety of factors in the late 1970s combined to generate large budgetary and balance of payments deficits in Tanzania. These included the collapse of the EAC in 1977, the brief war with Idi Amin's Uganda in 1978, which cost some $500 million, the second oil price shock in 1979, and the fall in world prices for agricultural commodities. Following the dissolution of the EAC, Tanzania closed its border with Kenya until 1983; this was detrimental to agricultural trade (much of which was through Kenya) and research (which relied on the EAC). The principal internal factors which exacerbated the impact of external shocks were: weak incentives to agricultural producers, whose output was controlled by government marketing boards; the inefficiencies in marketing and distribution systems, which constrained the ability of agriculture to respond to any favourable price changes; expansionary fiscal policy with increasing deficits which led to an accumulation of debt (see Table 6.2 below) and money supply growth; and the ubiquitous overvalued exchange rate.

While the adjustment programmes discussed in the next section addressed many of these internal factors, the data presented in Tables 6.1 and 6.2 indicate the mixed success achieved. Table 6.1 presents data on a range of macroeconomic indicators; Table 6.2 presents data on revenues and fiscal balances. A number of points relevant to our subsequent discussion can be made here.

Table 6.1 Macroeconomic Indicators, 1976–91

Year (Calendar)	GDP (fc) 1976 prices TSh mill. (1)	GDP growth 1976 base % p.a. (2)	GDP pc 1976 base Index (3)	Agri/ GDP share % (4)	Manuf/ GDP Share % (5)	Exports 1976 prices TSh mill. (6)	Exports real growth % p.a. (7)	Imports 1976 prices TSh mill. (8)	Imports real growth % p.a. (9)	Balance 1976 prices TSh mill. (10)	CA Share/GDP % (10)/(1)
1976	21 652	..	100.00	41.8	13.0	5 297.00	..	541.00	..	−180.00	−0.83
1977	21 739	0.40	100.61	43.3	12.8	4 760.91	−10.14	5 557.83	−4.85	−58.37	−0.27
1978	22 002	1.21	99.31	43.8	13.5	3 611.83	−24.12	7 363.00	32.48	−2 805.87	−12.75
1979	22 739	3.35	99.54	45.6	12.0	3 632.77	0.58	6 909.42	−6.16	−2 302.43	−10.13
1980	23 419	2.99	98.70	44.4	10.9	3 464.02	−4.65	6 932.41	0.33	−2 878.76	−12.29
1981	23 301	−0.50	95.20	46.3	10.2	3 181.03	−8.17	5 392.99	−22.21	−1 303.40	−5.59
1982	23 439	0.59	92.76	50.3	8.3	2 051.24	−35.52	3 998.70	−25.85	−1 552.19	−6.62
1983	22 882	−2.38	87.80	52.3	7.8	1 867.97	−8.93	3 201.97	−19.92	−992.28	−4.34
1984	23 656	3.38	87.96	52.8	7.6	1 913.54	2.44	4 099.83	28.04	−1 806.68	−7.64
1985	24 278	2.63	89.33	56.6	6.2	1 674.12	−12.51	4 007.29	−2.26	−1 720.62	−7.09
1986	25 070	3.26	90.02	59.7	6.1	2 596.16	55.08	6 592.95	64.52	−1 656.52	−6.61
1987	26 345	5.09	90.63	58.9	7.4	3 477.83	33.96	9 104.79	38.10	−1 915.23	−7.27
1988	27 460	4.23	91.69	62.7	5.3	4 385.48	26.10	15 689.89	72.33	−7 083.60	−25.80
1989	28 376	3.34	93.22	61.7	4.5	6 233.75	42.15	16 557.38	5.53	−4 871.21	−17.17
1990	29 368	3.50	94.05	58.3	4.6	7 545.98	21.05	20 582.42	24.31	−6 089.82	−20.74
1991	30 484	3.80	94.82	62.5	3.6	6 484.53	−14.07	17 736.96	−13.82	−3 343.78	−10.97

Table 6.1 (contd...)

Notes:

(1) GDP at factor cost, 1976 prices.
(2) GDP at factor cost, 1976 prices (annual percentage growth rate).
(3) Index of GDP percentage, 1976 = 100.
(4) Agriculture, Forestry, Fisheries and Hunting as percentage of GDP.
(5) Manufacturing as percentage of GDP.
(6) Exports of goods and non-factor services (merchandise and other), current prices converted to constant 1976 prices using the GDP deflator derived from (1) and current prices of GDP figures.
(7) Annual percentage change in exports (6).
(8) Imports of goods and non-factor services (merchandise and other), current prices converted to constant 1979 prices using the GDP deflator (as for (6)).
(9) Annual percentage change in imports (8).
(10) Surplus of the Nation on current account; measured as (exports + factor income + current transfer receipts) − (imports + factor payments + current transfer payments) in current prices, converted to constant 1979 prices using GDP deflator.

CA: Current account balance (10) as a percentage of GDP (1).
TShs: Tanzanian Shillings.

Source: Taken or derived from Bureau of Statistics (1992).

153

Table 6.2 Fiscal Indicators, 1973/4–1989/90

Year (fiscal)	Tax Revenue % Exp (1)	Total Revenue % Exp (2)	Recurrent Expend. % Exp (3)	Devpmnt Expend. % Exp (4)	Deficit (2)−[(3)+(4)] % Exp (5)	External L&G % Exp (6)	External Msupp % Exp (7)	Domestic Bank % Exp (8)	Domestic Non-Bank % Exp (9)	External Finance % GDP (10)
1973/4	59.37	71.50	65.89	34.11	−28.50	11.38	0.00	12.42	4.56	..
1974/5	51.09	63.79	64.03	35.97	−36.21	16.78	0.00	13.48	5.86	..
1975/6	60.36	65.65	62.27	37.73	−34.35	17.27	0.00	9.55	5.63	..
1976/7	65.50	77.13	59.17	40.83	−22.87	19.00	0.00	−2.15	3.88	5.68
1977/8	56.76	64.61	64.61	35.39	−35.14	21.71	0.00	1.64	3.72	6.70
1978/9	43.16	52.22	63.59	36.41	−47.78	18.61	0.00	22.32	3.48	7.10
1979/80	47.10	53.82	64.03	35.97	−46.18	16.10	0.00	19.44	4.66	5.92
1980/81	54.64	59.56	68.05	31.95	−40.44	12.57	0.00	19.59	5.04	4.11
1981/2	50.16	53.27	71.82	28.18	−46.73	9.76	6.30	17.82	4.36	5.50
1982/3	55.78	65.38	77.15	22.85	−34.62	9.61	9.69	21.82	4.45	5.77
1983/4	65.38	69.07	77.44	22.56	−30.93	3.16	5.91	21.51	3.77	2.78
1984/5	66.79	70.22	77.10	22.90	−29.78	5.74	4.56	11.98	4.74	2.22
1985/6	60.74	64.35	81.34	18.66	−35.65	5.04	5.20	15.21	2.69	2.35
1986/7	55.59	59.10	77.72	22.28	−41.00	11.73	15.06	3.12	5.38	7.30
1987/8	54.62	59.59	79.37	20.63	−40.37	6.94	16.57	3.32	3.02	6.79
1988/9	54.26	61.75	83.37	16.63	−38.25	9.13	17.93	−3.84	2.31	8.68
1989/90*	52.57	58.27	83.66	16.34	−41.78	8.76	31.27	−1.63	1.74	..

154

Table 6.2 (contd...)

Notes:

*   Indicates revised budget figure.

(1) Total tax revenue as a percentage of total government expenditure.

(2) Total recurrent revenue [(1) + non-tax revenue] as a percentage of total expenditure [(3) + (4) = TE].

(3) Total recurrent expenditure as a percentage of TE.

(4) Development expenditure as a percentage of TE.

(5) Overall deficit [total revenue (2) – TE] as a percentage of TE.

(6) External financing in the form of loans and grants as a percentage of TE.

(7) External financing in the form of import support as a percentage of TE.

(8) Domestic financing through bank borrowing as a percentage of TE.

(9) Domestic financing through non-bank borrowing as a percentage of TE.

(10) External finance [(6) + (7)] as a percentage of TE.

Source: Derived from Bureau of Statistics; Lyakurwa (1992).

Table 6.1 shows that Tanzania achieved positive GDP growth for most years throughout 1976–91; however, GDP per capita tended to decline from 1977 to 1983 (by over 10 per cent in real terms) and rose rather slowly over 1984–91. It will be convenient to distinguish four periods (which will be the focus of our analysis in later sections): 1977–80, the 'base' period; 1980–82, the 'crisis' period; 1982–86, the first adjustment period; and 1986–90, the second adjustment period. The nominal exchange rate remained relatively stable during the first two periods but devaluation was clearly a major feature of adjustment from 1986. Trends in the balance of payments do not reflect the sub-divisions so simply: there was a significant deterioration in 1978–80, some recovery in the mid-1980s but further deterioration after 1988. Agriculture's share in the economy has tended to rise steadily, but this is often as much a reflection of the consistent shrinking of manufacturing's share as of real growth in agriculture.

The real value of exports (which are predominantly agricultural primary commodities) more than halved during 1977–83, varied erratically in the mid-1980s and then recovered, although it was not until 1989 that real exports exceeded their 1976 value. Import values also more than halved in the early 1980s, but then began to rise significantly, increasing by almost three times in real terms over the decade 1980–90. As a consequence, the current account deficit in real terms became vary large in the late 1970s, then stabilized until it widened quite dramatically in the late 1980s.

Poor export performance leading to balance of payments deficits was at the root of Tanzania's economic problems. To some extent this reflects poor policy and inefficiency in Tanzania – underutilization of productive capacity and disincentives to agricultural exports, although external factors, notably deteriorating terms of trade, were also important. Agricultural marketing policies contributed to the decline in volumes of agricultural exports. Real agricultural producer prices, especially of export crops, declined steeply during the 1970s, 'such that by 1984 official producer prices were on average some 46 per cent below their 1970 level in real terms' (Ellis, 1988, p. 73). The detrimental impact this had on import capacity was made worse by other aspects of domestic policies: cost-plus price controls encouraged overinvoicing of imports to justify price increases and industrial policy discriminated against agriculture but supported largely unproductive investment in manufacturing. There was a reallocation of resources from the private to public sectors (Collier, 1991).

Aid receipts were important to Tanzania and rose from an annual real value of around $300 million in 1975–7, to $500 million and more for most of the 1980s, surpassing $1 billion in 1990 (OECD, 1992). While aid accounted for about 10 per cent of foreign exchange in 1970, this figure had reached 30–40 per cent in the early 1980s and surpassed 50 per cent over 1987–90 (White and Wuyts, 1993). It would appear that this aid was badly utilised, with negative rates of return on the majority of agricultural and industrial projects, partly owing to poor domestic policy but also owing to misconceived projects (on aid to agriculture see Lele and Jain, 1991). In the early 1980s, aid in the form of commodity import support was administered by the Treasury which favoured the (relatively inefficient) parastatals (White and Wuyts, 1993). Furthermore, conflict among donors, and between donors and the government, undermined their ability to promote policies that would utilize aid more effectively (Collier, 1991).

Table 6.2 reports relevant public finance data, showing that the budget deficit reached almost half of expenditure by 1978/9, but was cut back to around 30 per cent in the mid-1980s, before rising again. Domestic bank financing of the deficit was very high in the early 1980s; as part of the reforms, bank borrowing was eliminated by the late 1980s, and the government made net repayments after 1988. External financing remained significant throughout: it was slowly rising in the pre-crisis period, when it seems to have been directed to development spending; and reached almost 20 per cent of expenditure in 1982/3, following the introduction of import support. External financing fell to about 10 per cent of expenditure over the mid-1980s, when development spending also began to fall, but was over 20 per cent after 1986/7 (with import support dominant). Reliance on donor support is undesirable, and 'a much larger degree of fiscal self-reliance must therefore be an essential objective of any policy reform' (Tax Commission, 1991, p. 4). This aspiration underlies the adjustment programmes adopted in the 1980s; its reiteration by a government commission in 1991 indicates the limited success of the adjustment process.

3   REVIEW OF ADJUSTMENT PROGRAMMES, 1980–90

The Tanzanian government was under no illusions regarding the severity of its economic problems as the 1970s came to a close, and perceived the need for external financial support, but adopted a 'go it alone' strategy. It did enter into negotiations with the IMF, and a stand-by arrangement was agreed in September 1980. The first attempt at adjustment was the National Economic Survival Programme (NESP) adopted in 1981 and reviewed in Section 3.1. This was not a success but was quickly followed by the Structural Adjustment Programme (SAP), reviewed in Section 3.2, intended to cover the period 1982/3 to 1984/5. This was followed by the Economic Recovery Programme (ERP) launched in June 1986, reviewed in Section 3.3, which, unlike the SAP, had fairly extensive Bank and Fund support. Finally, as discussed in Section 3.4, the Economic and Social Action Programme (ESAP, sometimes called ERP II) was launched in 1989, again with Bank and Fund support. Thus, Tanzania has had some form of adjustment programme in operation throughout the 1980s.

3.1   National Economic Survival Programme: 1981–2

The NESP, adopted in 1981, was essentially a short-term, crisis alleviation, approach based on the internal mobilization and utilization of resources. Export taxes were abolished in the 1981 budget, with the intention of stimulating exports (which were primarily agricultural), but any potential revenue loss was offset by increases in rates of sales tax and import duty. The hoped-for rise in export earnings never materialized; in fact, the value of exports declined in the face of falling world commodity prices in the early 1980s, and only a severe contraction of imports in 1982–83 allowed a reduction in the current account deficit, which had risen to over 10 per cent of GDP in the late 1970s (Table 6.1). Increasing overheads on marketing boards proved a burden on the government budget, and the current budget deficit peaked over the period 1978–82 (Table 6.2). The NESP was unsustainable; a major problem was a failure to address the underlying foreign exchange constraint. Thus, by 1982–3, Tanzania was in even deeper trouble.

3.2   Structural Adjustment Programme: 1982–5

The SAP was more coherent than the NESP and was intended to restore external and fiscal balance, contain inflation and stimulate a recovery in output growth (the latter to be facilitated by expanding agricultural output and increasing capacity utilization and efficiency in industry). The outcomes however were disappointing. Real GDP growth was actually negative in 1983. During 1982–4, investment and savings fell, the BOP current account deficit failed to improve and although agricultural output and the supply of foodgrains to the local market did increase, manufacturing output fell (Table 6.1). The current budget deficit was reduced but borrowing from domestic banks increased and external financing fell (Table 6.2). The Tanzanian shilling was devalued by almost 40 per cent following the 1984 budget and agricultural producer prices were increased in real terms, although food and input subsidies were removed.

As the SAP period drew to a close, it was apparent that the foreign exchange constraint remained unresolved. Given the need to secure more substantial external support, the government adopted a more 'liberal reformist' approach consistent with that advocated by the Bank and the Fund. The 1984 budget was a turning point, representing an attempt by the government to demonstrate to donors that it was willing to institute changes. In particular a trade liberalization which directly addressed the foreign exchange constraint was implemented. This included the lifting of a variety of import controls and the introduction of 'own-funds' imports. While there were restrictions on the goods which could be imported, own-funds meant that importers who produced the funds to finance the required goods would be allowed to import and pay for them, thus avoiding the effective rationing of foreign exchange by the Bank of Tanzania (the central bank). The issue of parastatal reform, the initial mooting of privatization, was also raised in 1984. A programme of tax reform commenced in 1985, when import duties and sales tax rates were reduced (see Section 4 for details).

3.3 Economic Recovery Programme: 1986–9

The ERP was launched in June 1986 and was, in its design and intentions, responsive to donor ideas regarding market-oriented economic reforms, trade liberalization, privatization and a reduction of government intervention. The government had specific objectives for achieving positive per capita GDP growth; lowering inflation and raising real interest rates to positive levels; reducing the BOP deficit largely through increased agricultural exports; and reducing the budget deficit to permit net repayment of domestic bank credit. Real per capita growth rates were sustained after 1986 and agriculture also expanded (Table 6.1) but the BOP deficit deteriorated after 1988. Moreover the current budget deficit widened and although net bank repayments were made in 1988 and 1989 this was at the cost of a dramatic increase in the importance of external financing, from 10 per cent of expenditure in 1985/6 to 40 per cent in 1989/90 (Table 6.2). External financial support was prominent in the ERP and included loans from the IMF and World Bank.

Major devaluations of the currency, the Tanzanian shilling (TSh) began in 1986, and by August 1987 the nominal exchange had been devalued by 300 per cent (from 17 TSh per $1 to 68 TSh per $1). The move towards an equilibrium exchange rate was allied to the gradual removal of restrictions on trade and access to foreign exchange. Import licences were made freely available for certain commodities, some import restrictions were removed (reflecting a general policy of shifting from QRs to tariffs), and there was a general move from a 'positive list' of those goods that could be imported to a 'negative list' of those that could not (a list which has been shortened each year). Both the own-funds and export retention schemes, whereby those earning foreign currency can use it to meet import needs, were simplified and widened in scope to allow easier access to foreign exchange for imports. An open general licence (OGL) system, allowing ready access to import licences for a limited range of raw materials and spare parts, was introduced in 1988 and was to be expanded to cover access to nearly all imports by 1990.

The principal reforms embodied in the agreement between the Bank and the Tanzanian government for the ERP are given in Table 6.3, with some indication of the extent to which they were implemented. It is clear that compliance was highest regarding conditions attached to the exchange rate, trade liberalization and fiscal policy. There was much less success in sectoral adjustment policies: although 338 out of 400 price controls were removed (Lele, 1991), agricultural efficiency was not notably improved; there was some improvement in control over parastatals, but no success in increasing industrial productivity.

Table 6.3 Reform Objectives and Implementation in ERP, 1986–8

Policy area and objectives	Implementation
1. Exchange rate	
real devaluation (immediately)	21% devaluation 87/8
maintain equilibrium rate (annual)	delay but progress
remove exchange restrictions (gradual, by 1989)	OGL Feb. 1988
abolish retention scheme (review by mid-1988)	gradual (1)
2. Trade liberalization	
rationalize tariff system (gradual, by 1989)	good progress
allow imports free of QRs (introduce, 1988–90)	OGL Feb. 1988
3. Fiscal policy and public spending	
improve tax collection efficiency (annual)	good progress (2)
restrain public sector wage bill (annual)	complied with
redirect expenditure to priority (annual)	complied with
repair transport infrastructure (priority)	complied with
medium-term financial strategy (by 1989)	complied with
restrain external debt burden (annual)	complied with
4. Public enterprises	
review performance (by 1988)	reviewed
increase productivity (restructure by 1989)	no progress
limit borrowing (restrict by 1990)	complied with
5. Money and financial sector	
limit money/credit expansion (annual)	no progress (3)
positive real interest rate (by July 1988)	little progress
review financial system (by 1988)	slow progress
6. Industrial policy	
improve foreign exchange allocation (by 1988)	progress (OGL)
allocate capital for rehabilitation (annual)	complied with
improve efficiency and capacity utilization (review)	slow progress
7. Energy policy	
8. Agriculture	
improve efficiency of marketing boards (by 1988)	little progress (3)
increase producer prices for export crops (annual)	not achieved
(to 60–70% of export price *or* by real 5% per annum)	
9. Other	
eliminate most price controls (gradual, by 1989)	complied with (4)
liberalize domestic distribution (gradual, by 1989)	complied with

Notes:

Most of the reforms identified above were agreed between Tanzania and the Bank (and often the Fund); where reviews were proposed, the Bank and/or Fund were usually involved. These reform objectives formed part of the Bank's Policy Framework Paper, 1987–90 and were monitored in the context of the Multisector Rehabilitation Credit approved in 1989. The latter constituted the core external funding for the ERP.

(1) The progress was to reduce retention rates from 50 per cent to 35 per cent by January 1989; retention for traditional exports abolished in 1989 and whole scheme to be terminated in 1990, once an equilibrium exchange rate has been attained.

(2) Reform of tariffs and sales taxes; increases in excises; elimination of exemptions for commercial imports; some strengthening of administration.

(3) Constraint not achieved because of rapid growth of credit to marketing boards, which crowded-out other sectors. Performance of boards reviewed; export crop marketing to be liberalized in 1989; food crop marketing to be gradually put on a commercial basis.

(4) 388 out of 400 price controls were relaxed.

A number of studies of tax reform, involving both local academics and consultants working for the Bank and the Fund, were undertaken over the period 1985 to 1987 and were fairly quickly reflected in policy. Initially the focus was on tariffs, and studies were informed by the need to generate revenue while recognizing the internal demands for protection, but later studies considered reforms of the domestic Sales Tax. Major reductions and rationalizations of both import duties and domestic sales taxes were announced in 1988 and 1989 (see Table 6.5 below). The range and levels of tariffs were reduced, and most specific sales taxes were converted to ad valorem taxes while marginal tax rates on personal income were reduced. A Tax Institute was established about 1987, to train tax administrators with technical assistance from the UNDP.

The economic performance in 1987/8 suggested that the ERP was having some effect. Economic growth increased, attributable largely to increased agricultural production (which seems to have been in response to domestic policy, notably higher producer prices). However, inefficiencies in processing, transporting and marketing export crops meant that potential export volumes were not attained and bank credits to marketing boards increased. Furthermore, low world prices contributed to the failure to meet export revenue targets, while also increasing the financial pressure on marketing boards (squeezed by producer prices rising faster than export prices). Consequently, the BOP deficit more than trebled in 1988, to over 20 per cent of GDP, and Tanzania was unable to meet all its external debt-servicing obligations.

3.4 Economic and Social Action Programme: 1989–92

The ESAP which was launched in 1989 as a successor to the ERP, intended to continue the momentum of the reform process and, specifically, to reduce dependence on external support, although as with the ERP, external support was provided by the Bank, the IMF and other donors. The government announced in 1990 its intention to undertake privatization, to limit government intervention to social and physical infrastructure, and to implement further reductions and rationalizations of both import duties and domestic sales taxes. Excise duty was reintroduced in 1989. The overriding aim of strengthening the tax system and mobilizing domestic revenue, given the failures of the ERP to achieve these objectives, led to the establishment of a Tax Commission in late 1989 (Section 4.3 below).

The principal reforms embodied in the ESAP are listed in Table 6.4. As under the ERP, levels of compliance were relatively good in respect of the exchange rate, trade and tax conditions, but were less successful in other areas. Frequent and significant devaluations appeared to have favoured agricultural exports and there was some success in expanding agriculture, which attained real growth rates of about 4.5 per cent in 1988 and 1989 and 6.6 per cent in 1990 (Bureau of Statistics, 1992, p. 33). Manufacturing achieved real growth in

Table 6.4　Reform Objectives and Implementation in ESAF, 1989–91

Policy area and objectives	Implementation
1. Exchange rate	
maintain equilibrium rate (annual)	devalued >21% 89/90
improve access to exchange (annual)	expand OGL (1)
abolish retention scheme (gradually phase out)	gradual (2)
2. Trade liberalization	
reduce protection/tariff levels (gradual)	good progress
continue own-funds imports	complied with
3. Fiscal policy and public spending	
rationalize/broaden tax base (gradual)	complied with (3)
reduce public sector employment (annual)	slow progress
increase emphasis on cost recovery (annual)	complied with
redirect expenditure to recovery (annual)	complied with
repair transport infrastructure (priority)	complied with
strengthen budgetary planning (gradual)	slow progress
reduce external debt burden (negotiation)	achieved
(rescheduling and cancellation)	
4. Public enterprises	
increase productivity and restructure	little progress
limit borrowing (continue policies)	complied with
5. Money and financial sector	
positive real interest rate (annual)	achieved in 1989
reform financial system (gradual)	progress
6. Industrial policy	
improve investment incentives (by 1991)	complied with
reduce controls on private sector (annual)	complied with
improve efficiency and capacity utilization (review)	slow progress
7. Energy policy	
increase power generation efficiency (gradual)	slow progress
8. Agriculture	
restructure marketing boards (from 1990)	complied with
liberalize access to inputs (by 1991)	complied with
9. Other	
decontrol domestic prices and distribution (annual)	complied with
improve delivery of social services (annual)	slow progress (4)
establish environmental priorities (review)	slow progress

Notes:

Most of the reforms identified above were agreed between Tanzania and the Bank, which monitored compliance. Many of the 'conditions' were expressed through a number of fairly specific reforms. Broadly speaking, compliance was usually attempted but not always successful in terms of achieving the objective.

(1) Import ceiling (importer per annum) doubled to $1m in June 1989, to be abolished in 1990; OGL expanded in 1990 to include most intermediate goods for a short list of restricted items.

(2) Abolished for traditional exports in 1990.

(3) Number and maximum rates of sales tax and income tax reduced; increases in excises; fewer exemptions; Tax Commission established.

(4) Emphasis was on improving the availability and distribution of key materials; e.g. importation of drugs was included within OGL from 1989, and a number of measures were proposed in 1990 to increase supply of school books.

excess of 7 per cent in 1988 and 1989 but declined by 2.5 per cent in 1990 (Bureau of Statistics, 1992, p. 34).

4 THE IMPACT OF ADJUSTMENT ON THE TAX SYSTEM

An important objective of Tanzanian adjustment was to mobilize domestic resources and reduce reliance on external assistance; hence the relevance of tax reforms which are examined below. Section 4.1 presents a brief review of the role of tax reforms within adjustment packages; 4.2 outlines the Tanzanian reforms in the 1980s, and considers the impact on revenues. The evident failure to mobilize domestic resources prompted the establishment of the Presidential Commission of Enquiry into Public Revenues, Taxation and Expenditure (referred to here as the Tax Commission) in late 1989: Section 4.3 summarizes its deliberations and recommendations. Section 4.4 offers some conclusions.

4.1 The Role of Tax Reforms in Economic Adjustment

There are at least two reasons for concentrating attention on the effects of adjustment policies on tax revenues. First, tax reforms play a complex role in adjustment packages. On the one hand, tax reductions are advocated to remove price distortions. This is especially true in respect of the rationalization of tariffs (reducing both the number of tariff rates and their levels, i.e. reducing the average tariff), which is a basic component of trade liberalization. On the other hand, governments aim to reduce the budget deficit; which is difficult to achieve through spending cuts alone (Sahn, 1992). Consequently, a fall in tax revenues can increase the deficit and undermine the adjustment programme (Greenaway and Morrissey, 1993). Second, an implicit objective of tax rationalization is to increase tax revenue. This is based on the assumptions that: first, lower tax rates in a more simple system will increase compliance and revenue; second, that a simplification of the tax system is less distortionary and will therefore raise output and expand the tax base, and third, the removal of exemptions will also boost revenue.

The principal issue for Tanzanian tax reforms was the effect on revenue; little emphasis was placed on distributional concerns, and the tax system was not seen as an efficient means of redistribution (Osoro, 1992a). While efficiency and incentive effects were implicit in the tax reforms proposed, it is unlikely that these would have convinced the government to implement reform unless they could be persuaded that revenue would increase. In line with the points made above, we should try to distinguish the elasticity of the tax system, and of individual taxes, from tax buoyancy (Osoro, 1992b). The amount by which revenue from a tax, with a given structure, changes in response to a change in its base is its elasticity. Thus, the elasticity of the tax system is how revenue from an unaltered tax structure responds to economic growth. Clearly, changing the structure of taxes (the number or level of rates; the coverage, or the exemptions) will also affect revenues. The total revenue response is termed tax buoyancy. Hence, for an individual tax or the tax system, the difference between the buoyancy (total response) and elasticity (automatic response) can be attributed to structural changes. An elasticity of at least unity is a desirable property of a tax (system) and buoyant reforms would be required to mobilize domestic resources.

Osoro (1992b) examines the elasticity and buoyancy of the Tanzanian tax system over 1979–89, and considers individual taxes – import tariffs, Sales Tax and income tax. The elasticity of a tax can be further decomposed: the 'tax-to-base' elasticity measures the direct response of revenue to a change in the base; the 'base-to-income' elasticity measures how the base changes as the economy grows. While the accuracy of such estimates is limited, a number of the findings are quite salient. First, the tax system had an elasticity of less than unity (0.80) but a buoyancy of unity, indicating that it was tax reforms that generated any overall revenue increases. Second, Sales Tax had a buoyancy of almost unity (0.96) and an elasticity of 0.7, arising because although the base was responsive to growth, the 'tax-to-base' elasticity was only 0.5, indicating the degree of revenue loss due to exemptions, avoidance and evasion. However, discretionary changes in the rate structure were revenue increasing. Third, import duty had an elasticity of about unity (0.97) and a 'tax-to-base' elasticity of 0.9, suggesting relatively efficient collection. With a tax buoyancy of 1.3, tariff changes appear to have been the principal source of increased revenue. Fourth, and finally, income tax had a 'base-to-income' and overall elasticity of 0.8, with a 'tax-to-base' elasticity and a buoyancy of about unity. Consequently, it did not contribute to increasing tax revenues.

4.2 Tax Reforms in Tanzania in the 1980s

The principal reforms to the four major sources of tax revenue – tariffs (customs duties on imports), sales tax, excise duties and income tax – over the period 1980–92 are summarized in Table 6.5. In the early 1980s, policy on tax reform was guided by the need to increase revenues (Osoro, 1992a). Hence, tax rates were increased regularly in budgets during the period 1980–86. In conjunction with, and following, a number of studies of the tax system, both the Bank and the Fund began pushing for a rationalization and reduction of taxes from 1986. These objectives were embodied in the ERP launched in 1986 (Table 6.3).

Major tariff reforms were instituted in the 1988 budget. Tariffs were simplified: the maximum rate was reduced from 150 to 100 per cent, and applied to a narrow range of luxuries; the total number of rates was reduced from over 20 to 7, and all remaining specific tariffs were converted to ad valorem rates. This simplification and reduction of rates was expected to be at least revenue neutral,

Table 6.5   Major Tax Reforms in Tanzania since 1980

Year	Tariffs	Sales	Excise	Income
1980	Rates rationalization specific; ad valorem many exemptions	25 specific rates 25 ad valorem rates	most abolished 1979/80	
1983	rate increases	rate increases		amended
1985		rate increases		payroll level
1986	rate increases c 50 rates, 0–750%	rate increases		reduced
1988	rationalization 6 rates; range 0–60% many exemptions ADMIN			range 15–75%
1989		rationalization to 6 rates range 0–60% many exemptions ADMIN	reintroduction 8 rates range 0–85% ADMIN	range 15–55% ADMIN
1991				range 7.5–40%
1992	4 rates range 0–40% fewer exemptions	4 rates range 0–30% fewer exemptions	single 20% rate a few spec. rates	range 5–30%

Notes: ADMIN indicates when a number of measures to improve tax administration and collection efficiency were introduced. Most specific rates were abolished by 1988 except for some excise duties.

Source: Various, including Lyakurwa (1992), Osoro (1992a, 1992b).

as reduced incentives to evade translated into increased efficiency of collection (defined by actual revenue as a percentage of potential revenue, the latter estimated by applying tax rates to the value of the tax base). Although tax revenue increased, this was at least partly attributable to the combined effects of devaluation and own-funds imports rather than the rationalization of the tax structure (Lyakurwa, 1992). As can be seen in Table 6.6, significant growth in tariff revenue occurred around 1986, at the time of devaluation but before rationalization.

Further tax reforms were instituted in the 1989 budget. First, sales tax was rationalized: the base was expanded to include more of the manufacturing and services sector, but the number and level of rates was reduced. Second, luxury consumption goods that had attracted high rates of sales tax became liable to reintroduced excise duties, which also applied to imports. Thus in 1987/8, 41

Table 6.6 Tax Revenue Trends, 1973/4–1989/90

Year (fiscal)	Tax Revenue TSh mill.	Duties C & E TSh mill.	Sales Tax TSh mill.	Income Tax TSh mill.	Tax % Total revenue	Duties C & E % Tax	Sales Tax % Tax	Income Tax % Tax
73/4	2 510.0	864.7	736.8	693.0	83.03	34.45	29.35	27.61
74/5	3 160.6	792.9	1 141.5	1 003.4	80.10	25.09	36.12	31.75
75/6	3 602.5	678.9	1 398.5	1 369.0	91.94	18.85	38.82	38.00
76/7	5 204.9	308.7	2 181.9	1 377.0	84.92	5.93	41.92	26.46
77/8	5 343.0	1 275.9	1 845.9	1 664.1	87.85	23.88	34.55	31.15
78/9	5 629.9	1 093.0	2 512.0	1 574.0	82.65	19.41	44.62	27.96
79/80	6 788.4	811.0	2 903.1	2 406.8	87.51	11.95	42.77	35.45
80/81	8 138.7	655.9	4 335.3	2 729.9	91.73	8.06	53.27	33.54
81/2	9 229.0	658.0	5 144.3	3 088.0	94.16	7.13	55.74	33.46
82/3	10 752.0	742.8	6 306.6	3 728.0	85.32	6.91	58.66	34.67
83/4	13 655.0	959.0	7 885.0	4 074.0	94.66	7.02	57.74	29.84
84/5	17 352.0	1 531.0	10 155.0	4 820.2	95.11	8.82	58.52	27.78
85/6	19 662.0	1 468.4	10 633.7	6 175.6	94.38	7.47	54.08	31.41
86/7	29 527.0	4 067.3	16 096.3	7 351.0	94.07	13.77	54.51	24.90
87/8	42 557.0	5 585.6	22 745.1	10 897.7	91.66	13.12	53.45	25.61
88/9	63 085.1	8 478.2	33 237.5	16 610.7	87.87	13.44	52.69	26.33
89/90	84 489.0	..	..	..	90.22	14.3*	36.1*	27.5*

Table 6.6 (contd...)

Fiscal year	Tax Revenue % GDP*	Duties C & E % GDP*	Sales Tax % GDP*	Income Tax % GDP*	Tax Revenue Index	Duties C & E Index	Sales Tax Index	Income Tax Index
73/4	..	..	..	..	27.20	131.41	14.32	22.44
74/5	..	..	..	..	34.25	120.50	22.19	32.49
75/6	..	..	..	..	39.03	103.18	27.19	44.33
76/7	..	..	..	..	56.40	46.91	42.41	44.59
77/8	..	..	..	..	57.89	193.91	35.88	53.89
78/9	..	..	..	..	61.00	166.11	48.83	50.97
79/80	..	..	..	..	73.56	123.25	56.43	77.94
80/1	19.2	1.6	10.3	6.5	88.19	99.68	84.27	88.40
81/2	18.8	1.4	10.4	6.6	100.00	100.00	100.00	100.00
82/3	19.1	1.2	10.4	6.5	116.50	112.89	122.59	120.73
83/4	20.0	1.4	11.6	6.0	147.96	145.74	153.28	131.93
84/5	20.4	1.8	11.9	5.6	188.02	232.67	197.40	156.09
85/6	17.9	1.4	9.5	5.9	213.05	223.16	206.71	199.99
86/7	19.8	2.7	10.8	4.9	319.94	618.13	312.90	238.05
87/8	21.7	2.8	11.4	5.9	461.12	848.88	442.14	352.90
88/9	23.5	2.9	11.2	8.4	683.55	1 288.48	646.10	537.91
89/90	23.4	3.3	8.4	6.4	915.47	..	..	..

Note: * Indicates source is Osoro (1992a), data only available from 1980/81; C & E = Customs & Excise.

Source: Lyakurwa (1992); 1989/90 tax revenue figures are revised budget estimates.

167

per cent of tax revenue was from sales tax on local goods, and 12 per cent from sales tax on imports. By 1989/90, the respective figures were 25 per cent and 11 per cent, whereas excise duties on local goods contributed 12 per cent of tax revenue and excises on imports 3 per cent (Osoro, 1992a). Furthermore, the scope for exemptions on tariffs and sales taxes was to be reduced with no exemptions allowed on commercial imports, and the position of aid-related imports to be reviewed (see discussion of 1992 reforms below).

Income taxes levied on employees, the self-employed and companies, contributed 34 per cent of tax revenue in 1980/81. The share of income tax fell to 28 per cent by 1984/5, largely attributable to a decline in company tax revenue. Although this overall level has been maintained in 1989/90, the tax contribution of individuals has fallen while the burden has shifted back towards companies, which contributed 19 per cent of total tax revenue in 1989/90 (Osoro, 1992a). The relative decline of income tax on individuals reflects equity considerations in the face of declining real earnings. Individual income tax bands are not indexed, therefore the tax rates were reduced each year in the late 1980s (Table 6.5).

Total tax revenue as a share of GDP remained fairly stable at just below twenty per cent over 1980/81 to 1986/7, but rose thereafter to about 23 per cent by the late 1980s (Table 6.6). Sales Tax as a share of GDP remained stable at between 10 and 11 per cent throughout (the low figure in 1989/90 excludes excise duties which accounted for 3.5 per cent of GDP); income taxes varied in some years, but tended to be about 6 per cent of GDP; import duties, however, were more volatile but more than doubled their contribution from about 1.5 per cent in the early to mid 1980s, to over 3 per cent by the late 1980s. The major jump was around 1986 and, as argued above, can be attributed to devaluation rather than changes in the tariff structure. These data also reinforce the earlier observation that tariffs were the most buoyant source of tax revenue. The same implications can be drawn by examining individual taxes' share of tax revenue, and the index of tax revenues which highlights when major changes occurred.

It is perhaps still too early to draw any conclusions regarding the impact of adjustment on tax revenues. The major reforms were to the tariff structure in 1988 and to sales tax (and excises) in 1989. However, we only have reliable consistent data up to 1990 which does not allow sufficient time to judge the effects. We can say that there appears to have been an increase in the tax/GDP ratio by the late 1980s, and this appears to be largely due to increased tariff revenue. We cannot claim that it was the rationalization of the tariff structure that yielded this increase, but the rationalization does not appear to have had any detrimental effect on revenue. We can suggest that devaluation and measures to ease restrictions on importing have allowed tariff revenue to rise with import value. To the extent that Tanzania avoided import compression as a part of adjustment, the increase in tariff revenue led to overall tax buoyancy.

4.3 Presidential Commission on Taxation and Expenditure

The Tax Commission, established in late 1989, was motivated by the concerns of the Ministry of Finance to increase domestic revenue. Consequently, the essential issue for the Commission was to recommend means of increasing the tax base and collection efficiency. The Commission, in its Report of December 1991, produced a number of recommendations, the most important (for our purposes) of which are detailed below.

Indirect taxes

The Commission recommended that customs duty should be further simplified to three rates: zero for capital and essential goods; 20 or 25 per cent for intermediate inputs; and 30 or 40 per cent for consumer goods (liable to either 40 or 60 per cent rates at the time). The 1992 Budget reduced the number of rates to five, going some way to meet these recommendations. The principal hope was that tax evasion would fall sufficiently, in response to lower tax rates, a more transparent system and better customs monitoring, so that revenue would at least be maintained, if not increased. Excises were to be confined to a narrow range of goods, notably beverages, petroleum, tobacco and luxury consumption goods. Hence, textiles, sugar and soap should be exempted, and were in 1992. The Commission opposed the re-introduction of export duties. Broadly speaking, the emphasis was on the simplification of tax structures and the efficiency of collection and administration.

Considerable emphasis was placed on the need to limit the scope of exemptions. Under the Tanzanian tax system many 'classes' of importers were exempted from tax (tariffs and sales tax) including, inter alia, government bodies, parastatals and aid agencies. In 1989 actual import tax revenue represented only 44 per cent of the potential yield had no importers been exempted (Tax Commission, 1992, p. 13). The Commission recommended that such exemptions be abolished. However, responding to pressures from manufacturing, it was proposed that imports of raw materials should be exempted from import duties in order to provide some assistance to producers, thereby being revenue neutral via increases in sales tax revenue.

Proposal to introduce VAT

Although many in the Commission were opposed to the introduction of a VAT, largely because it was seen as administratively difficult and not an obvious improvement on the existing system, the commission recommended that a VAT with three rates should be introduced by January 1994. The rate structure was to be: zero rate for basics (such as unprocessed food and farm inputs); a low rate of about 10 per cent on utilities and some essential items (e.g. baby foods); and a standard rate of no less than 20 per cent, but no more than 30 per cent, on all other goods.

The potential benefits were threefold. First, there was flexibility in setting the rate, and hence scope for generating increased revenue, while an integrated VAT avoided the tax cascading of the existing system. Second, it was anticipated that once a VAT was established, and traders became used to filling in the forms, evasion would decline owing to the self-policing nature of VAT. To distinguish between the value of purchased inputs and that of output, so that effectively VAT was only levied on value added, traders and manufacturers had to keep records of purchases and transactions. Thus, VAT would encourage proper record-keeping and encourage the purchasing and recording of inputs on which the tax has been paid, and would thus be self-policing (on the other hand, a VAT could encourage poor record-keeping insofar as this is a means of evasion, a possibility of which the Customs are well aware). Third, as the practice of keeping proper records spread, the tax base for VAT would grow and revenue would increase. In the same vein, VAT would have a wider coverage than the sales tax and would generate more revenue; it was favoured because it had a relatively high tax elasticity and buoyancy.

Many potential problems with the VAT were also recognized. First, even a simple VAT is likely to be a more complex system than the sales tax and would impose much higher collection and compliance costs. Second, given the limited existing system of keeping records, any VAT system would be difficult and costly, in both time and training, to introduce. Finally, the complexity of records required could encourage rather than discourage evasion, especially for traders whose turnover is near the exemption threshold.

Direct taxes
The essential problem with income tax is the low tax base, inherently because so many people are on low incomes but also because so little of income is actually taxed. To broaden the base, it was proposed to increase the definition of taxable income (to include cash bonuses, overtime, fringe benefits, special allowances, and so on) and to tackle evasion by levying 'standard assessments' on operators in the informal sector and requiring all taxpayers to provide annual income returns. The number of tax bands should be limited to about seven, the maximum marginal rate being 40 per cent with a minimum rate of 5 per cent applying to those earning above the minimum wage. Changes to company taxes were also recommended, notably to encourage payment of dividends and allow for high levels of inflation.

4.4   Prospects for the Tanzanian Tax System

It is widely appreciated that the overriding constraint on domestic revenue mobilization is administration. The tax collection agencies rarely have adequate records to monitor existing taxes, let alone the capacity to expand the tax base or introduce new taxes. In addition the working environment of tax collectors, especially those at the lower levels (such as customs points), is poor: resources are scarce; computerization is extremely limited; offices are congested; communications between central, regional and local offices are slow and irregular; training falls short of needs; and wages are very low which, at the least, undermines motivation and provides a potential incentive for corruption. An increase in pay levels would do much to improve the working environment and management training is required for those on higher levels.

The administrative limitations are most evident in respect of the proposal to introduce VAT by January 1994. Before the introduction of such a tax both collectors and payers require training, preparation and manuals. Its introduction, given the situation as of January 1993, would be very difficult: there is widespread unpreparedness; no or inadequate records; and the increased compliance costs will encourage evasion. The merit of the existing sales tax lies in its simplicity, at least relative to VAT.

An endemic problem in the tax system is evasion, which appears to be substantial and widespread. The greatest problem is undervaluation, which applies especially to own-funds imports, precisely because the importer has access to foreign exchange without going through the Bank of Tanzania. Central bank-funded imports (where the importer offers local currency) and government or parastatal imports are easier to value, but are probably exempt from tax. Administrative constraints and corruption at entry points increase the problem of undervaluation. Although customs maintains a schedule of major categories of imports from many countries, it is impossible to keep an up-dated valuation schedule for all categories of imports. A pre-inspection scheme was introduced in October 1992 as a further measure to cut down on undervaluation.

The tax reforms announced in the 1992 Budget (United Republic of Tanzania, 1992) attempted to tackle some of these problems and responded to the recommendations of the Commission. The reforms included: rationalization of the tariff schedule from five rates to four; reduction of income tax and sales tax rates (see Table 6.5); and reduction of corporate tax rates by 10 percentage points. There were some revisions to excises: while retaining specific rates, the ad valorem rate of 10 per cent was abolished and a standard rate of 20 per cent replaced six existing rates.

Some of the most important changes announced in the 1992 budget were the removal of exemptions (on tariffs, sales taxes and excises) on imports from all government bodies, parastatals, political parties and affiliates, non-government organizations (NGOs), charities and religious institutions, and commercial enterprises; some exemptions remained for donations that will not be sold. On the other hand, manufacturers were given exemptions for raw materials used in production but this measure proved very difficult to police and was opposed by tax collection bodies; it was rescinded in 1993.

5   THE IMPACT OF ADJUSTMENT ON PUBLIC EXPENDITURES IN THE 1980S

The adjustment measures of the 1980s, guided by the government's over-riding concern with minimizing budget deficits, involved restrictive fiscal policies. In the face of near stagnant revenues, coupled with a growing share of government expenditures allocated to the servicing of a rising domestic and external debt burden, many key sectors suffered from a severe resource crunch. This section analyses the impact of adjustment policies on public expenditure trends and patterns, paying particular attention to the impact of these policies on the social sectors (health and education).

5.1   The Impact of Early Reform Efforts on Public Expenditure Trends and Patterns: 1980/81–1985/6

An important objective of the early reform programmes in Tanzania (the NESP and the SAP) was to correct budgetary imbalances and the consequent monetary expansion that led to high inflation rates. It is evident from the analysis in Section 4 that neither programme was particularly effective as regards reforms to mobilize higher revenues. The reduction in budget deficits during the early reform period, from 14.2 per cent of GDP in 1980–82 to 8.5 per cent of GDP in 1982–6, was thus achieved largely through cuts in public spending, especially the development budget. While these cuts reflected to some extent the government's expenditure control programme, they were, in large part, forced upon the Government because of the loss in revenues from import tariffs as imports declined and reduced access to external finance.

As is evident from Table 6.7, total 'discretionary' government expenditures stood at around 30 per cent of GDP in 1980/81. By the end of the SAP in 1985/6 they had fallen to 23 per cent of GDP. This amounted to a fall of over 19 per cent in real terms. The bulk of this decline was borne by cuts in the development budget.

Development (capital) expenditures had exceeded 10 per cent of GDP in the 1970s owing to substantial expenditures on parastatal industrial projects (stemming from the basic industrialization strategy of the 1970s) and on social infrastructure. However by 1985/6, government capital expenditures had fallen to 3.9 per cent of GDP, largely owing to falling aid levels during that period.

Meanwhile, recurrent expenditures (including interest payments) fell by only 2 percentage points of GDP during the period 1980/81 to 1985/6. An examination of Table 6.7 also reveals that the decline in recurrent spending was mainly the result of cuts in spending on wages and salaries, and on 'other goods and services', while the share of transfer payments in the recurrent budget doubled between 1980/81 and 1985/6. An important component of transfer payments included transfers (and subsidies) to commercial and financial parastatals.[1] While explicit budgetary subsidies to public commercial enterprises were abolished in 1984/5, transfers to these enterprises continued to represent a drain on the Government budget (Table 6.8). From 1985/6, coverage of new overdrafts by crop authorities (involving payment to the National Bank of Commerce by the government to cover arrears of the marketing boards) and parastatal restructuring/rehabilitation (involving transfers to the Tanzania Investment Bank and direct government investment expenditures) increased.

An area which suffered severe financial cutbacks as a result of adjustment policies during the SAP was the provision of social services. After growing rapidly during the late 1960s and the first half of the 1970s (owing mainly to donor finance), government expenditure on the social sectors declined precipitously during the early 1980s. Real expenditure per capita (including central, regional and local government expenditures) on education declined from 30.2 TSh in 1980/81 to 16.5 TSh in 1985/6 while that on health fell from 13.9 to 7.3 TSh over the same period (see Table 6.10).[2] Insufficient funds were allocated for the purchase of basic supplies for schools and hospitals, and for adequate remuneration of teachers and health personnel. In addition, policies such as granting specific parastatals monopoly rights to the production and distribution of education and health supplies (a policy characterized as 'confinement') combined with management weaknesses throughout the system meant that even the funds that were available were frequently inefficiently used – textbooks, for example, piled up in storage while 30 or more pupils in a class would 'share' a single text.

This was reflected in the levels of social service provision presented in Table 6.9, as well as in the quality of services provided. Life expectancy at birth declined between 1979 and 1985, although the crude death rate remained constant over the period.

The health and education systems also experienced qualitative weaknesses and imbalances. Children in rural areas attended school, but standards of accommodation were poor, many of the teachers were poorly trained, and only 10 per cent of textbook requirements were available in the classroom. In the health sector, while the development of an extensive network of facilities during the 1970s had greatly improved the availability of health care, system performance suffered owing, once again, to the poor training of doctors, shortages of supplies, poor maintenance of infrastructure, and inadequate management of a dispersed rural health system.

5.2 The Impact of Reforms under the ERP on Public Expenditure Trends and Patterns

After the fall in expenditure experienced during the SAP, overall government expenditures recovered during the ERP period, particularly during the early

Table 6.7 Tanzania: Expenditure, 1976/7–1990/91

	77	78	79	80	81	85	86	87	88	89	90	91
1. Total expenditure: Net lending minus repayments (% of GDP)	27.9	29.9	37.3	30.8	29.8	24.4	22.9	24.0	23.4	29.0	24.7	27.6
2. Development expenditure (% of GDP)	8.2	10.7	15.3	12.5	10.7	4.4	3.9	6.0	5.5	6.8	..	..
3. Recurrent expenditures (% of GDP)	19.6	19.2	24.0	19.2	19.7	17.7	19.1	17.9	17.8	22.2	21.2	21.6
4. Recurrent expenditures on: (% of total recurrent spending)												
4.1 Wages and salaries	38.6	44.1	25.3	29.8	31.9	20.2	29.8	25.6	23.0	25.8	25.9	..
4.2 Interest payments	6.4	5.5	7.1	10.9	11.2	12.7	10.5	18.4	20.1	18.8	16.1	..
– domestic	..	..	..	..	..	..	7.5	11.8	10.6	8.3	7.3	..
– foreign	..	..	..	..	..	..	2.9	6.6	9.6	10.5	8.7	..
4.3 Other goods and services	42.2	39.0	62.2	53.1	50.9	39.6	47.3	42.9	40.0	38.9	34.6	..
4.4 Transfer payments	12.7	11.4	5.4	6.2	6.0	27.4	12.4	13.1	16.9	16.6	23.5	..
– transfers to parastatals	..	..	..	..	..	..	2.6	2.0	2.1	2.6	4.3	..

Source: IMF Government Finance Statistics Yearbook, various years.

174

Table 6.8 Direct Subsidies to the Parastatal Sector (TSh. million)

Fiscal years	80/81	82/3	84/5	85/6	88/9	89/90	Average 80/81–85/6	Average 86/7–89/90
Grants and subventions	350	845	889	1 886	5 137	8 170		
Subsidies and transfers	512	1 334	734	715	2 663	3 900		
Gross total	862	2 179	1 623	2 601	7 800	12 070		
Net total (see note below)	612	1 929	973	1 951	7 400	9 670		
Gross as % of total expenditures	6.0	11.8	6.2	8.0	7.6	8.8	8.5	8.2
Net as % of total expenditures	4.3	10.5	3.7	6.0	7.3	7.0	6.8	7.0
Memo:								
Parastatal income tax paid	1 185	1 690	2 959	8 066	8 349	..		
Parastatal dividends (excl. BOT)	48	92	161	350	863	..		
Net transfer to govt. (incl. inc. tax)	..	-341	159	519	616	-2 858	-5 024 (sum 81/2–89/90)	
Net transfer to govt.	..	-1 526	-1 531	-2 440	-7 450	-11 207	-37 089 (sum 81/2–89/90)	

Note: 1980/81 restructuring: NMC overdraft of TSh 2 000 million converted to 8 year loan. 1984/5 restructuring: Crop authorities' arrears of TSh 2 425 million to be repaid over 6-8 years. 1988/9 restructuring: Crop authorities' arrears of TSh 13 642 million to be repaid over 10 years at 8 per cent interest. Net total refers to gross to parastatals less required under NMC restructurings.

Table 6.9   Indicators of Service Position

Indicator	1979	1985	1989
Primary enrolment ratio (%)	70	87	66
Daily calorie supply	..	2 335	2 151
Infant mortality (per 1 000)	..	110	112
Crude death rate (per 1 000)	15	15	17
Life expectancy at birth	52	50	49

Source: World Bank, World Development Report, various years. In some cases data were unavailable and the primary rate does not always refer exactly to the year indicated.

Table 6.10   Education and Health Budget, 1970/71–1988/9[a]

Fiscal year	Share of Total Expenditure (%)		Real Expenditure Per Capita[b]		
	Education	Health	Total	Education	Health
70/71	13.7	6.2	186.6	25.6	11.5
74/5	12.2	6.9	277.1	33.9	19.1
78/9	12.4	5.9	311.3	38.6	18.4
79/80	12.3	5.6	296.3	36.4	16.5
80/1	13.5	6.2	228.4	30.2	13.9
81/2	13.6	5.9	213.0	29.0	12.6
82/3	14.4	5.7	172.9	24.0	9.8
83/4	13.4	6.3	142.2	19.0	8.9
84/5	12.8	8.0	129.5	16.6	10.3
85/6	14.6	6.5	113.5	16.5	7.3
86/7	13.2	5.9	124.6	16.4	7.3
87/8	12.5	6.6	138.8	17.3	9.2
88/9	10.0	6.0	164.7	16.4	9.9

Notes:
a. Includes central, regional and local government expenditures.
b. Absolute in Tanzanian Shillings.

Source: Derived from budget documents.

years of the ERP. Total expenditures increased from 23 per cent of GDP in 1985/6 to 29 per cent in 1988/9, before falling to an estimated 24.7 per cent in 1989/90. Recurrent expenditures rose from the 1985/6 levels of 19.1 per cent to 22.2 per cent in 1988/9, and fell to an estimated 21.2 per cent in 1989/90. Development expenditures also increased during the early years of the ERP, from 3.9 per cent in 1985/6 to 6.8 per cent of GDP in 1988/9, but appear to have declined to 3.5 per cent in 89/90.

A breakdown of the structure of recurrent expenditures as presented in Table 6.7 reveals that the increase recorded between 1985/6–1988/9 was attributable mainly to a rapid increase in interest payments, which rose significantly between 1985/6 and 1989/90: the share of interest payments in total recurrent expenditure rose from around 10.5 per cent in 1985/6 to just over 20 per cent in 1987/8, before declining to 16 per cent in 1989/90. This reflected the build-up of domestic and foreign-denominated debt contracted in the late 1970s and early 1980s, and the effects, on the domestic currency value of foreign debt servicing, of the depreciation of the TSh which has taken place since mid-1986. Interest payments on foreign debt which had amounted to under 3 per cent of the recurrent budget in 1985/6 accounted for as much as 10.5 per cent of total recurrent spending in 1988/9.

Transfer payments also increased during the ERP with their share in total recurrent spending rising from 12.4 per cent in 1985/6 to 23.5 per cent in 1989/90. This partly reflected an increase in crop authority debts taken over by the government and in transfers to cover foreign obligations, including those to international organizations.

On the other hand, the shares of both wages and salaries and 'other goods and services' in recurrent expenditures declined during the period 1985/6 to 1989/90. The former fell from 29.8 per cent to around 26 per cent (which in part reflected the hiring freeze in sectors other than health and education), the latter from 47.3 per cent to 34.6 per cent in 1989/90, reflecting continuing cuts in operations, maintenance and rehabilitation.

The policies falling under ERP conditionalities continued to place a greater emphasis on directly productive sectors, while social sector expenditures stagnated (Table 6.10). The share of education expenditures in the budget declined from 14.6 per cent in 1985/6 to 10 per cent in 1988/9, although real expenditures on education in per capita terms remained more or less stable during the second half of the 1980s at around TSh 16.5.

The government had introduced various measures to compensate for the drop in government expenditure allocated to the education sector in the first half of the 1980s which was noted above. It decided to shift most of the capital expenditure on education to villages, which were expected to assist in the construction of classrooms and housing for teachers. However, in 1986–7, only 1 517 classrooms out of the required 20 702, and only 1 208 houses out of the 61 405 needed to accommodate teachers were built (Mwajombe, 1988).

Reforms were introduced to increase reliance on private funds, especially in the form of user fees. The government also attempted to attract more funds from abroad; the share of external aid in the total education budget increased from around 9 per cent in 1981–2 to 15 per cent in 1986–7.

Nevertheless, the restrictions on resources associated with the adjustment package had a negative impact on the education sector, if measured by output indicators such as the primary school enrolment ratio (see Table 6.9). There are also indications that the quality of primary and higher level education suffered. With the decline in government resources available for education, the hiring of personnel gradually came to claim nearly all the resources earmarked for recurrent spending, leaving little for books and other educational material.

The health care sector also suffered as a result of policies linked to adjustment. The share of health in total expenditures declined from 6.5 per cent in 1985/6 to 6 per cent in 1988/9. While real absolute per capita expenditure on health care saw a slight increase during the period 1985/6 to 1988/9, over the entire adjustment period between 1978–9 and 1988–9 it fell by as much as 46 per cent. Local clinics and dispensaries were more adversely affected than hospitals.

More recently, motivated by a changing climate within the international financial institutions, the government appears to have opted for a strategy designed to correct the negative social consequences of policies under the SAP and the ERP, but with significant differences from the approaches adopted prior to adjustment. By decentralizing responsibility to district authorities and village communities, the government aims to minimize its role in the finance and provision of social services. Local authorities have been re-established and redesigned with a view to providing opportunities for raising revenue locally, and also to achieve greater community participation in the provision of services, thereby reducing their budgetary cost. The government has also continued efforts towards 'cost recovery' in the health and education sectors.[3] Much greater encouragement is being given to NGOs to support the social sectors. In education, the bulk of non-government resources are being provided by community groups. During the second half of the 1980s, more than 50 new secondary schools were established independently from the central government secondary system. Indeed, 200 of the 334 secondary schools in 1991 were run by NGOs. District associations, parents, private sources and local NGOs contributed to the costs of establishing and running new schools, often utilizing district-level trust schemes. There is also an expanding non-governmental involvement in health. While primary health (and education) care appears within local government budgets, about half of health care provision is privately funded, most of which involves NGOs providing primary health care in rural areas. Public health care is largely confined to urban areas; voluntary agencies in rural areas are either free or flexible as to how they are paid (e.g. through work or in kind).

5.3 Prospects for Public Expenditure Reforms

A conclusion emerging from the above review of public expenditure reforms is the need for improved management and planning of expenditures. This would involve a very careful assessment of expenditure priorities. In doing so, the government would need to (i) place a greater emphasis on the operations, maintenance and rehabilitation components of its current budget; (ii) increase the efficiency of development expenditures by improving project selection; and (iii) reflect in its budget structure the developmental priorities of the government, especially its commitment to rehabilitate infrastructure and to strengthen social services. The latter would require an increase in real per capita expenditures on health and education.

The reorientation of expenditure priorities would have to be accompanied by a strengthening of expenditure monitoring and control systems. Steps have already been taken in this direction, notably, the decision to establish sub-treasuries. These measures combined with continued improvements in accounting, flash reporting, and computerization focusing on the sub-treasury level, are likely to improve the government's ability to monitor budgetary expenditure throughout the fiscal year.

In addition, there is a need for institutional changes in budgetary planning and resource management, with a view to strengthening the links between the formulation of annual budgets and the selection and implementation of development projects, and also between central and local government budgets.

In the ultimate analysis, however, successful adjustment and the restructuring of public expenditure policies in Tanzania over the short to medium term will continue to depend very much on the availability of external finance. But the government will need to use donor funds more efficiently and also facilitate the better tracking of these disbursements so that they can be accurately reflected in government budgeting. One way of achieving this would be to improve the system through which donors can regularly report their recent and projected expenditures on specific programmes/projects/sectors, which could then be taken into account when preparing the annual budget and the multi-year financial framework for the development budget.

6 OUTCOMES OF THE ADJUSTMENT PROGRAMME

The economic reforms attempted by Tanzania in the 1980s fall within the remit of World Bank structural adjustment lending programmes (SALs). The experiences of the more than 50 countries that have undertaken SALs in the 1980s have been varied, but a number of lessons can be gleaned from these experiences, notably regarding the sequencing of reforms, that is, the order in which reforms in particular policy areas are attempted and implemented (for a review of the evidence on which the next few paragraphs are based, see Greenaway and Morrissey, 1993).

Political commitment and capability are central to the success of economic reform. There will be losers from reforms such as parastatals and those gaining from import protection; hence there will be political opposition. A committed government is necessary to overcome the opposition, and a capable bureaucracy is needed to implement the programme. The generally slow pace of reform in Tanzania suggests that either commitment or capacity was weak, and there is evidence that administrative capacity was weak (see the discussion of tax administration in Section 4.4 above). As we argue later, commitment to some reforms was greater than to others, and the former were more likely to be implemented.

The conventional view on sequencing of economic policy reforms suggests that attempts at macroeconomic stabilization, notably getting the exchange rate into a fairly stable equilibrium and reducing the fiscal deficit, should come first. Tanzania made progress on the exchange rate, with rapid and considerable devaluations from 1986, although it had less success with the current account and budget deficits. Trade liberalization, including tax reform by way of tariff rationalization, should be undertaken early in the reform process, as indeed it was for Tanzania. The initial reforms made it easier to import, devaluation made exporting more profitable, and tariff reductions featured early in the ERP phase. The hoped-for export response was not forthcoming largely because of structural weaknesses in agricultural marketing, hence the balance of payments remained a problem. Other tax reforms followed, notably of the sales tax. Overall, tax revenue was not buoyant; tariff revenue increased in line with an increasing domestic currency value of imports, but other taxes had a relatively low tax elasticity. Tanzania was following many of the appropriate measures, in the appropriate sequence, although the results were not highly positive.

Policy makers may have been aware that reforms which were unsustained and/or rescinded would lead to a loss of public confidence. The experience of the early 1980s may have led policy makers to appreciate the importance of credible reforms (which agents believe the government will implement and sustain), which was reflected in a 'gradualist' approach. Examining the reforms listed in Tables 6.3 and 6.4 above suggests that the overall approach was rather gradual. Under the ERP from 1986, exchange rate, fiscal and trade reforms were largely complied with, but there was minimal progress on other fronts. Although economic growth was restored, the fiscal and trade deficits deteriorated (Table 6.11). The ESAP continued these reform processes, but again there was little progress on other fronts, and it is too early to evaluate the impact. Tanzania appears to have tried to implement many of the 'right' reforms, in more or less the 'right' order, but without significant success. This is cause for concern.

6.1   Comparison of Indicators in the Adjustment Periods

Table 6.11 provides some comparative data on macroeconomic indicators for each of four sub-periods over 1977–90 identified in Section 2 above. As revealed in Table 6.11, there were a number of important differences in performance during each sub-period.

Table 6.11   Comparative Data for Sub-Periods[a]

Variable	Pre-Crisis 1977–80	Crisis/ NESP 1980–82	SAP 1982–86	ERP 1986–90
Real GDP growth:				
Total	2.5	0.0	1.7	4.0
Agriculture	1.0	1.2	4.7	5.0
Manufacturing	0.6	–7.3	–3.5	4.2
Urban RPI	16.7	28.2	31.6	29.8
Trade balances (real):				
Import growth	8.9	–24.0	17.6	35.1
Export growth	–9.4	–21.9	9.0	30.8
CA/GDP	–8.9	–8.2	–6.5	–15.5
Fiscal balance (% GDP):				
Tax revenues	17.1	17.5	15.6	16.1
Recurrent spending	22.6	23.4	19.7	23.4
Development exp.	12.7	10.1	5.5	5.8
Overall deficit[b]	–14.9	–14.2	–8.5	–11.7
External financing:				
% Total exp.	18.7	14.3	12.2	26.0
% GDP	6.6	4.8	3.3	7.6

Notes:

a.   Growth rates are simple annual averages based on non-overlapping sub-periods: 1977–80 (3 years; 1977–8, 1978–9, 1979–80); 1980–82 (2 years); 1982–6 (4 years) and 1986–90 (4 years). Percentage shares and RPI are based on overlapping sub-periods: 1977–80 (average of share in each of the five years); 1980–82 (3 years); 1982–6 (5 years); and 1986–90 (5 years).

b.   Includes non-tax recurrent revenue.

Sources: Real GDP growth at 1976 prices from Bureau of Statistics (1992, pp. 33–4); real trade figures derived from Table 6.1; Urban RPI from Statistical Abstracts 1990 (1992, p. 190). Fiscal and External Financing data derived from Lyakurwa (1992), current domestic currency values in fiscal years. Sub-periods are: 1977/8 to 1979/80 (3 years); 1980/81 to 1981/2; 1982/3 to 1985/6 and 1986/7 to 1988/9 (3 years; 1989/90 data incomplete).

Economic performance in the pre-crisis years (1977–80) was, to say the least, lacklustre, with negative growth in per capita GDP. The current account deficit of 9 per cent of GDP on average disguises the increasing deficit as imports grew while exports fell in real terms. Tax revenues of 17 per cent of GDP were insufficient to cover even recurrent expenditure. It is clear that external financing amounting to 7 per cent of GDP supported a large portion of expenditure, and contributed significantly to maintaining development spending.

There were not many significant differences in average annual performance between the pre-crisis and crisis years (1980–82) but four trends deserve mention. First, the virtual stagnation of GDP growth can be attributed to the large decline in real manufacturing output; agricultural output did grow in real terms over 1980–82. Second, there was a dramatic increase in the level of inflation, growth in the urban RPI reaching an annual average of 28 per cent over 1980–82. Third, tax revenues and recurrent spending rose roughly in unison, but the budget deficit fell slightly because of a cutback in development spending. It is perhaps more than coincidental that the decline in external financing is almost matched by the decline in development spending over 1980–82. Fourth, the current account deficit fell slightly, relative to GDP, largely owing to import contraction exceeding the decline in export revenues.

There were many encouraging signs of recovery during the SAP period (1982–6). The rate of decline of real manufacturing was almost halved while agriculture grew at a fairly rapid rate, leading to real GDP growth of almost 2 per cent per annum (although this was insufficient to avert the decline in per capita GDP). On the other hand, the rate of inflation increased to over 30 per cent per annum. The current account deficit fell to 6.5 per cent of GDP on average. The overall budget deficit was significantly reduced to 8.5 per cent of GDP on average. Although both tax revenues and recurrent spending were reduced as shares of GDP, the brunt of the reduced deficit was borne by development spending which almost halved to 5.5 per cent of GDP on average. As in the crisis period, the contribution of external financing as a share of GDP fell, to 3.3 per cent per annum, and this appears to have adversely affected development spending.

The ERP period (1986–90) was one of mixed performance. Adjustment appeared to be having some effect in restoring growth, and inflation began to fall, but the trade and fiscal deficits widened. Continued real agricultural sector growth of 5 per cent per annum with manufacturing growth of 4 per cent per annum ensured real GDP per capita growth. However, import growth outpaced export growth, and from a larger base, and the current account deficit escalated to over 15 per cent of GDP on average. While tax revenues and development spending only rose slightly relative to GDP, recurrent spending rose quickly and the overall deficit was 12 per cent of GDP on average. The relative importance of external financing more than doubled, accounting for 26 per cent of total government spending on average.

6.2   Fiscal Outcomes in the Reform Periods

Table 6.12 summarizes a number of aspects of the fiscal impact of Tanzanian reforms, distinguishing the four sub-periods identified earlier and in Table 6.11. The reader's attention is drawn to the fact that the magnitude and trend of the tax/GDP ratio in Table 6.12 (derived from Osoro, 1992a) is quite different from that in Table 6.11 (derived from Lyakurwa, 1992). Unfortunately we are not in a position to reconcile the discrepancy as both use local, although not the same, primary sources. The ultimate fiscal objective was to mobilize domestic resources and data in Table 6.12 suggest that the reforms appear to have been moderately successful.

Our particular interest is to compare the crisis period 1980–82 with the latest sub-period, the ERP of 1986–90. Tax revenue increased from just under 20 per cent of GDP, when economic growth was stagnant, to about 22 per cent of GDP, attributable largely to a virtual doubling of tariff revenues in the later period when economic growth was relatively high. Much of the increase in tariff revenue, as previously argued, is due to devaluation but there is a clear implication that rationalization of the tariff and sales tax structures has not been revenue depleting. Furthermore, as the revenue loss through exemptions and collection inefficiencies is still quite substantial, there is significant scope for further increasing tax revenue. Income tax revenue tended to decline in the 1980s, reflecting continual reductions in tax rates as a means of compensating for declining real earnings. Future growth in the economy will render the income tax system more buoyant. Thus, in respect of mobilizing domestic resources, the reforms of the 1980s have been broadly successful.

The evidence on public spending is far less encouraging. Real government expenditure fell by about one-third between the crisis and ERP periods. Referring to Table 6.11, it appears that the greatest reductions were in development spending, which does not augur well for the future, while the budget deficit was only reduced slightly. The evidence of Section 5 suggested that the level of service provision, and the standards of human development, deteriorated throughout the 1980s. Furthermore, external financing assumed much greater importance in terms of financing government spending and imports. Thus, the success in mobilizing domestic resources has not been nearly adequate for the needs of the country, and reliance on external financing is likely to continue for the foreseeable future.

Table 6.12   Comparative Fiscal Data for Sub-Periods

Variable	Pre-Crisis 1977–80	Crisis/ NESP 1980–82	SAP 1982–6	ERP 1986–90
Tax/Total revenue (%)	86.0	92.9	92.4	91.0
Tax/GDP (%):				
Total tax	..	19.0	19.4	22.1
Duties	..	1.5	1.5	2.9
Sales	..	10.3	10.9	10.5
Income	..	6.6	6.0	6.4
Tax composition (% Total):				
Duties	15.3	7.6	7.6	13.7
Sales	41.0	54.5	57.3	49.2
Income	30.3	33.5	30.9	26.1
Govt. expenditure:*		1980–83	1984–6	1987–9
Real (incl. interest)		100.0	64.8	69.8
Real (net of interest)		100.0	63.4	64.3
Wages (real)		100.0	74.4	58.3
Wages (% net)		20.8	24.2	18.7

Notes: * From Sahn (1992, p. 676–81): real total government expenditure, including and net of interest (Index, 1980 = 100); wages and salaries, real (Index, 1980–83 = 100; includes 1977–9 value) and as a percentage of net expenditure.

Source: Derived from Table 6.7. Sub-periods are: 1977/8 to 1979/80 (3 years); 1980/81 to 1981/2; 1982/3 to 1985/6 and 1986/7 to 1988/9 (3 years; 1989/90 data incomplete).

6.3   Overall Outcomes of Tanzanian Reforms

Table 6.13 summarizes the outcomes of the most important of Tanzania's reforms. The general objectives of the successive reform packages were to increase the rate of economic growth, which had been achieved by the late 1980s, and, in doing so, to reduce the dependence of Tanzania on external financing; in fact, such dependence rose considerably. The major areas of reform were in respect of fiscal policy, trade policy and, to a lesser extent, monetary policy. Overall, the fiscal policy reforms achieved some success: while the data are ambiguous, it appears that the reforms to tariffs and sales taxes have increased the buoyancy and revenue of the tax system. Although much remains to be done, the simplifications to the tax structure should have increased collection efficiency. Public expenditure has been controlled and, accepting concerns about the level of education and health care provision, the budget deficit has been reduced. Insofar as we can determine, the fiscal impact of the reforms has been beneficial in terms of mobilizing domestic resources, an objective to which the government was committed.

The objectives of trade liberalization encompassed expanding exports (especially in agriculture by offering higher prices and improved marketing) and improving access to foreign exchange for imports, with the hope that the current

Table 6.13   Objectives, Instruments and Outcomes of Reforms

Objectives	Instruments	Outcomes
1. Fiscal policy		
increase tax revenue	rationalize taxes	revenue rose
	collection efficiency	improved
reduce budget deficit	budget planning	deficit fell
	control spending	spending fell
2. Trade policy		
reduce payments deficit	devaluation	deficit rose
expand exports	decontrol prices	exports rose
	marketing efficiency	
ease access to imports	rationalize tariffs/QRs	imports rose
ease access to forex	liberalize forex markets	easier access
3. Monetary policy		
reduce inflation	fiscal policy	inflation rose
	counterpart funds	
positive real interest rate	financial liberalization	achieved
4. General objectives		
increase economic growth		real GDP growth
reduce dependence on		dependence rose
external finance		

Notes: There is not necessarily a one-to-one correspondence between the objectives, instruments and outcomes listed; most are in fact inter-related. No instruments are allocated to 'general objectives' as these were the objectives of the overall reform programme. Forex refers to foreign exchange.

account deficit would be reduced. The introduction of own-funds imports from 1984 and the open general licence (OGL) scheme that was in place by the end of the decade, the easing of the foreign exchange market, and the provision of external financing allowed Tanzania to maintain its imports. Although devaluation should have improved prices to exporters, the inefficiency of agricultural marketing boards and adverse movements in world prices meant that although exports were substantially increased, it was insufficient to avert a widening trade gap. It would be unfair to blame this failure entirely on endogenous policy: virtually all prices were decontrolled and reform of marketing boards commenced in line with devaluation, but conditions in the world market were not favourable to rapid growth in export revenues based on primary products. It should also be noted that as the external financing associated with the reform programmes was specifically to pay for imports, the value of imports would rise directly in line with the external financing so that in the short run, the trade deficit is likely to widen.

Monetary policy did not receive much emphasis in either the ERP or ESAP programmes. The ERP set a target of a positive real interest rate by July 1988, which was not achieved until 1989. The growth of the money supply was to be constrained in particular by setting targets for the repayment by government of domestic bank debt, which the government started to do in 1988; reducing the budget deficit was consistent with this. Nevertheless, there was little success in reducing the rate of inflation, until the 1990s.

7   CONCLUSIONS: PROSPECTS FOR TANZANIA

The observation that the reforms of the 1980s have had mixed results in terms of the impact on economic performance can be attributed to a number of factors. First, the external environment was unfavourable in the late 1980s and early 1990s: the barter terms of trade seem to have deteriorated somewhat; the debt burden increased and the cost of debt-servicing increased, owing both to higher interest rates and devaluation. Second, internal adjustment remained sluggish: the agricultural sector grew but was subject to many structural constraints; manufacturing grew very slowly; and development investment was probably insufficient to maintain the physical and social infrastructure (development spending fell significantly with the decline in external financing after 1983, but was never fully restored once external financing increased again after 1986). Third, the government does not appear to have been fully committed to all of the reforms. The tax reforms, to which it was committed, were the most 'successful' in terms of attaining objectives. Commitment to the reform of parastatals has remained weak. Non-payment of counterpart funds (the domestic currency equivalent of the external finance provided for balance of payments support) has been a method to subsidize parastatals which undermines monetary policy, and the low productivity of the economy, at least in part attributable to parastatals, has constrained supply response.

The early 1990s were not a particularly good time for Tanzania. On the positive side, real GNP grew by just over 3 per cent in 1989 and 1990; while this just exceeded the estimated population growth, it was below the 4.5 per cent target growth rate set in ERP II. Inflation, as revealed by the urban CPI, fell from 28 per cent in 1988 to 24 per cent in 1989 and 19 per cent in 1990, attributable to improved availability of consumer goods and a stable exchange rate. The labour force was growing at some 3 per cent per annum, while formal sector employment grew at only 2 per cent per annum; agriculture and the informal sector were expected to absorb the difference (United Republic of Tanzania, 1991a). The negative events were more ominous. The Gulf crisis led to a significant increase in the cost of oil imports in 1990 and 1991, whereas a fall in world coffee prices and a decline in export volumes of cotton and sisal eroded the value of exports. Consequently, the balance of payments situation continued to deteriorate. Domestically, the combination of floods in some areas, droughts in others, and pests, resulted in the likelihood of food shortages in 1991/2: paddy, wheat and maize production all fell between 1989/90 and 1991/ 2. Among cash crops, output of cotton fell by about a third and cashew nut production declined slightly, although coffee, sisal, tea and pyrethrum all increased (United Republic of Tanzania, 1991a). Do the experiences with reforms to date give any guidance for future prospects?

A major objective of the tax reforms was to increase revenue, both by expanding the tax base and by increasing collection efficiency. Tariffs and sales tax were considerably simplified; while it is not obvious that collection rates have risen, the relative incentives for evasion have been reduced and investment in the tax administration could yield potentially high returns in terms of collection efficiency. The reforms have not done much to expand the tax base, but have probably increased the elasticity of the major taxes. As a result of the tax reforms after 1988 Tanzania is well placed to mobilize domestic resources, especially if there is any economic recovery.

Tanzania has followed a reform programme with at least a sensible sequence: stabilization and devaluation were attempted first, followed by trade liberalization and tax reform. There has been substantial liberalization of agriculture with price decontrol and reform or abolition of marketing boards. The country has also benefited from a high degree of political stability. The experience of the 1980s suggests that where the government is committed to reforms, they can be implemented with a high degree of credibility and, thus, can be effective. Three major limitations should be recognized. First, Tanzania is institutionally weak: the tax administration is willing but under-resourced and under-trained; the marketing boards have collapsed; the financial and investment sectors are undeveloped. Further successful reform requires institutional support. Second, supply response is very weak, reflecting inefficient parastatals and a history of inefficiency in agriculture, and should be the direct focus of new reforms (which is consistent with Sectoral Adjustment Loans (SECALs)). Third, and finally,

---

— see below —

Tanzania is likely to remain dependent on external funding and extremely vulnerable to terms of trade shocks for quite some time. Effective reforms, and donors, should recognize this vulnerability.

NOTES

1. The parastatal sector comprises around 400 separate entities representing 24 per cent of non-agricultural wage employment and generating about 13 per cent of the economy's total value added. The largest concentration of these enterprises are in the industrial, agricultural, mining, and energy sectors.
2. Primary education (which accounts for about half of total educational expenditure) was transferred to local government in 1984.
3. The Tax Commission (1991) accepted the principal of increasing the use of user charges, and this has become more widespread.

REFERENCES

Afshar, Haleh and Carolyne Dennis (eds) (1992), *Women and Adjustment Policies in the Third World* (London: Macmillan).

Bureau of Statistics (1991), *Foreign Trade Statistics 1989* (Dar-es-Salaam: Bureau of Statistics, Planning Commission, October 1991).

Bureau of Statistics (1992), *National Accounts of Tanzania 1976–1991* (Dar-es-Salaam: Bureau of Statistics, Planning Commission, August 1992).

Collier, P. (1991), 'Aid and Economic Performance in Tanzania', in U. Lele and I. Nabi (eds), *Transitions in Development: The Role of Aid and Commercial Flows* (San Francisco: ICS Press), pp. 151–71.

Ellis, F. (1988), 'Tanzania', in C. Harvey (ed.), *Agricultural Pricing Policy in Africa: Four Country Case Studies* (London: Macmillan), pp. 66–103.

Greenaway, D. and O. Morrissey (1993), 'Structural Adjustment and Liberalisation in Developing Countries: What Lessons Have We Learned?', *Kyklos*, 46, 241–61.

Lele, U. (1991), 'The MADIA Countries: Aid Inflows, Endowments, Policies and Performance', in U. Lele (ed.), *Aid to African Agriculture: Lessons from Two Decades of Donors' Experience* (Baltimore: Johns Hopkins University Press), pp. 14–106.

Lele, U. and R. Jain (1991), 'The World Bank's Experience in the MADIA Countries: Agricultural Development and Foreign Assistance', in U. Lele (ed.), *Aid to African Agriculture: Lessons from Two Decades of Donors' Experience* (Baltimore: Johns Hopkins University Press), pp. 107–67.

Lyakurwa, W. (1992), 'Fiscal Implications of Trade Policy Reforms in Tanzania', paper presented at the CREDIT–CSAE Workshop on Trade and Fiscal Reforms in sub-Saharan Africa, St Anthony's College, Oxford, 6–8 January 1992.

Mwajombe, R. (1988) 'Education for Self-Reliance in Practice: Elementary Education since 1967', paper presented at the National Symposium on 20 years of Education for Sel-Reliance in Tanzania, Arusha, 1988.

OECD (1992), *Geographical Distribution of Financial Flows to Developing Countries* (Paris: Organisation for Economic Development and Cooperation).

Osoro, N. (1992a), 'Tax Reform in Tanzania', paper presented at the CREDIT–CSAE Workshop on Trade and Fiscal Reforms in sub-Saharan Africa, St Anthony's College, Oxford, 6–8 January 1992.

Osoro, N. (1992b), 'Revenue Productivity of the Tax System in Tanzania, 1979-89', *Journal of African Economies*, 1:3, 395–415.

Sahn, D.E. (1992), 'Public Expenditures in Sub-Saharan Africa During a Period of Economic Reforms', *World Development*, 20:5, 673–94.

Tax Commission (1991), *Presidential Commission of Enquiry into Public Revenues, Taxation and Expenditure: Final Report* (Dar-es-Salaam: Government Printers).

UNCTAD (1991), *The Least Developed Countries 1991 Report* (Geneva: UNCTAD).

UNDP (1992a), *Human Development Report 1992* (New York and Oxford: Oxford University Press for the United Nations Development Programme).

UNDP (1992b), *Development Cooperation Tanzania: 1992 Report* (Dar-es-Salaam: United Nations Development Programme).

UNICEF (1990), *Women and Children in Tanzania: A Situation Analysis* (Dar-es-Salaam: UNICEF).

United Republic of Tanzania (1991a), *Speech by the Vice-Chairman of the Planning Commission and Minister of State (President's Office)*, Professor K.A. Malima (MP), when presenting to the National Assembly the Economic Survey for 1990 and the Annual Development Plan for 1991/2, June 1991 (Dar-es-Salaam: Government Press).

United Republic of Tanzania (1991b), *Speech by the Minister for Finance*, Hon. Steven A. Kibona (MP), introducing to the National Assembly the Estimate of Government Revenue and Expenditure for the financial year 1991/2, June 1991 (Dar-es-Salaam: Government Press).

United Republic of Tanzania (1992), *Speech by the Minister for Finance*, Prof. K. A. Malima (MP), introducing to the National Assembly the Estimate of Public Revenue and Expenditure for the financial year 1992/3, June 1992 (Dar-es-Salaam: Government Press).

Wagao, Jumanne H. (1990), 'Adjustment Policies in Tanzania, 1981–89: The Impact on Growth, Structure and Human Welfare', *Innocenti Occasional Paper* no. 9, UNICEF/ICDC.

Wagao, Jumanne H. (1992), in G. Cornia, R. van der Hoeven and T. Mkandawire (eds), *Africa's Recovery in the 1980s: From Stagnation to Human Development* (UNICEF/Macmillan, 1992).

White, H. and M. Wuyts (1993), 'Import Support Aid to Tanzania: Evaluation for SIDA', Draft Interim Report (The Hague: ISS/ISSAS) (processed).

World Bank (1992), *World Development Report 1992* (Washington, DC: Oxford University Press for the World Bank).

Index

Abbott, J.C. 34
Addison, T. 43
administrative constraints 12–13
Agricultural Sector Adjustment Credit
(Malawi) 80, 81, 82, 84, 94
agriculture, importance of 27–8
Ahmad, S.E. 28, 32, 37, 41
Alano, B.P. Jr 38
Amin, I. 151
Annual Development Programme 61,
67, 70, 71
Arusha Declaration 1967 151
Ascher, W. 39
Asian Development Bank 57
Askari, H. 28
Atkinson, A.B. 24

balance of payments 32, 36, 45, 158
Balassa, B. 23, 32, 36
Bangladesh 1, 3, 9–10, 51–77
    Annual Development Programme 61
    Board of Investment 58
    budget balance, overall 70
    donor agencies and conditionality
        59–60
    exchange rate policy 53, 59
    expenditure 53, 57–8, 67–70
    Export Coordination Unit 55
    export processing zone 55, 58
    financing arrangements 82
    future policy action, scope and
        directions for 15
    gross domestic product 9, 51, 52,
        61–4, 65, 67, 70
    International Monetary Fund 51, 52,
        54, 59
    investment policy 53, 58
    medium term consequences and
        prospects for sustainability 72–6
    initial conditions, credibility and
        political economy 72–4

sequencing and timing 74–5
supply side response 75–6
monetary policy 59
National Revenue Board 74
performance relative to objectives and
    medium-term concerns 70–72
revenue 53, 56–7, 65–7
Road Corporation 57
Statutory Restrictive Orders 55
structural adjustment programme 54
Supplementary Direct Duty 55
sustainability of fiscal reform 13, 14
taxes, major 63
taxes, structure of 67
trade and industrial policy 53, 54–5
World Bank 51, 52, 54, 55, 59, 60
Banking Act 81
Basu, P. 51–77, 78–108, 110–48,
150–88
Bates, R.H. 39
Bhagwati, J.N. 23
Binswanger, H. 28
Bird, R.M. 39
Boiteux, M. 22
Bolivia 44
Botswana 34
Bourguignon, F. 43
Brennan, G. 21
Britain 151
Brownbridge, M. 1–17
Buchanan, J.M. 20, 21
Buiter, W.H. 39
Burgess, R.S.L. 33, 35, 41

Chamley, C. 86, 88
Chenery, H.B. 23
Chile 43
China 58
Cnossen, S. 36
Coady, D.P. 5, 18–45
Collier, P. 73, 156, 157